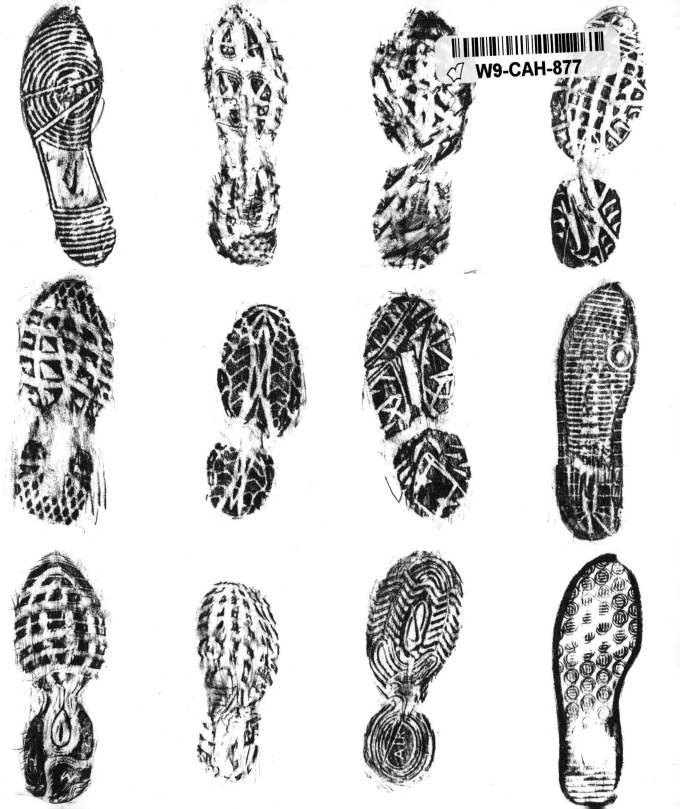

SPECK

SPECK

No. 1

Peter Buchanan-Smith

[WITH THE INVALUABLE ASSISTANCE OF MEAGHAN KOMBOL]

Contributions from:

Ron Barrett, Shannon Fagan, Jesse Gordon, Stacy Greene, Steven Guarnaccia, Cyrus Habib,
Grant Heaps, David Horowitz, Maira Kalman, Knickerbocker, Robert Lemons,
Phil Milstein, Ian Phillips, Lauren Redniss, Angela Reichers, Wade
Shuman, Eddie Simon, Dan Taylor, Richard Torchia,
Mark Ulriksen, Amy Unikewicz,
John Willis, Adam Yates.

PRINCETON ARCHITECTURAL PRESS, NEW YORK

*from the index of *The Joy of Cooking*

If you will cling to Nature, to the simple in Nature, to the little things that hardly anyone sees, and that can so unexpectedly become big and beyond measuring; if you have this love of inconsiderable things and seek quite simply, as one who serves, to win the confidence of what seems poor: then everything will become easier, more coherent and somehow more conciliatory for you, not in your intellect, perhaps, which lags marveling behind, but in your inmost consciousness, waking and cognizance.

— RAINER MARIA RILKE

This book is for the man who goes by "H.O.T."

(a great man indeed)

1

THE RED BALLOON

NOTES: On the dusk of August 14, 2000 one red helium balloon was released into the hazy Brooklyn sky. Attached was a tag that read: "If you find this red balloon, please write to *Speck* at the below address..."

PHOTOGRAPHY: Dan Taylor

THE FOUND ALPHABET

AUTHOR: Amy Unikewicz

NOTES: All of us have our guilty pleasures. My indulgence happens to be poking around trash cans and dumpsters gathering objects for my alphabet. Since becoming a rubbish fancier, I have amassed nearly two hundred broken, decayed, and rusted objects which straddle that fine line between trash and typography. To the untrained eye, however, this precious collection of one-of-a-kind letterforms amounts to no more than a pile of junk. Alas, that is the beauty of it.

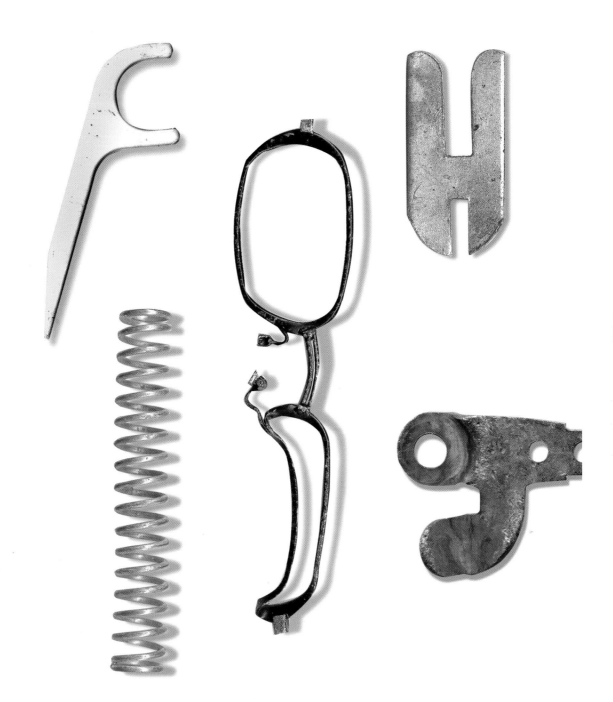

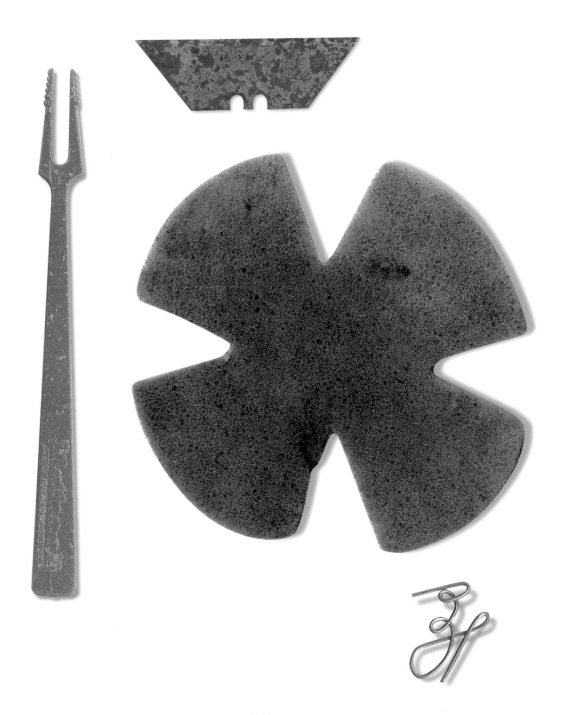

THE LAST DRY SHINE

AUTHOR: Robert Lemons

NOTES: This project began as an effort to learn what distinguishes a good shoeshine from a bad shoeshine. A friend who had heard about the project was surprised that I had not yet interviewed Harry Kitt. Apparently, I had a legendary shoeshiner in the subway station (Lexington Avenue and Fifty-third Street) below my office building. My friend introduced me to Harry and by the time I left his stand, I had a pair of rejuvenated shoes and a new focus for the project: Harry.

The following is Harry's take on a good shine, good customers, and how to make ends meet...

PHOTOGRAPHY: Angus McWilton

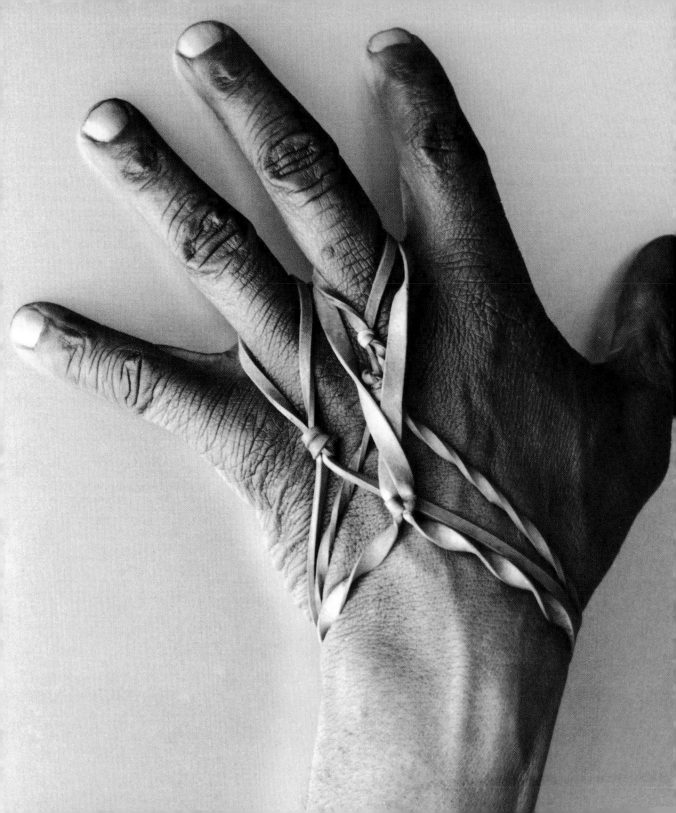

HARRY KITT

KNOWS HOW

TO SHINE.

Q: So, how long have you been shining shoes?
A: Well, it's been now about forty-five years. I started when I was nine. You know, like most kids had paper routes. And where I was from in Philadelphia...too many kids, you didn't have customers. So I just started me a little shoeshine route. This way you only had to get up early on the weekends and still you made more money than the guys did selling the papers. It was just one of those things that I picked up early in life and I liked doing it because it's a challenge.
Q: Who taught you how to shine shoes?
A: Well, I frankly taught myself. Because I had an older brother who was two years older than me. He worked in a barber shop and I would go over with him and watch the things that he did and I just took it up behind him...followed in his footsteps. He was one of the greatest.
Q: Is he still shining shoes?
A: No, no. He's retired. You see he had two jobs, just like I've always had two jobs. You see I worked at the Port Authority as a dispatcher. I was there twenty-three years. But not anymore because I was with Trailways and they went out of business. So I just had

to fall into this. But I love doing it. That's the main thing about a job. You got to love what you do.
Q: So what's your favorite part of shining shoes?
A: It's making something that's old and destroyed come back to life. That's my most enjoyable thing. I feel satisfied, so I know the customer's satisfied. Each pair of shoes that comes in is a challenge. And if you are a professional you know what to do with those shoes because all this is nothing but a routine thing—different colors you clean differently, but the way the style go today, you see the guys, they just throw a little water on the shoe and a little polish and boom they're finished. But that's not the correct way to do it and I can't work like that.
Q: I understand that you do what's called a dry shine.
A: Yeah, it's a dry shine. You stay away from as much water as you can because first you want the shoe to have oil in it. If you put water on top of the shoe, for a lot of managers it's going to look good because it's real fast. You know, it dries into the leather and the shoe is shined. But it's not good because then you're going to lose customers. You see, after they go into the air when the shoe's been sprayed with water, the

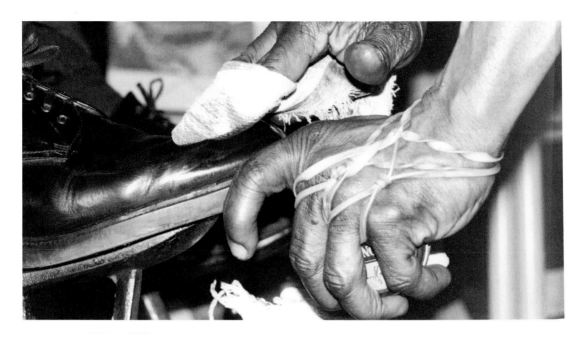

air hit the bubbles and the shine is gone.

Q: Then when you're shining a pair of shoes the right way, what's the process?

A: Well, the first thing is to clean the shoe. Clean all the residue, all the old polish, everything right off.

Q: That's with a rag with nothing on it?

A: No, you got a rag with something on it: cleaning fluid. That's what I use on every pair. I clean the shoe. I just don't throw polish on it. Because first of all, the shoe's leather has pores where the leather's supposed to be able to breathe, and if you take it and just pack polish on top of that, you cover up all the holes. So the leather can't breathe and the peoples' feet gives off a bad odor from the inside of their shoes. That's why that happens. Yep. That's what makes it sweat and give off that odor. Because the leather can't breathe. Years ago they had a thing called Carfoyne, which was a type of a leather. It's like a patent leather, but they had to take it off the market. Why? Because it couldn't breathe. No air holes in it or nothing. So they took it right off the market.

Q: What do you do after you clean the shoes?

A: Let it get a little dry. Now you put your base on it. Which is your polish. Your first coat of polish is your base. Where you're loosening up all the dirt you done took off there, now you're putting your oil base into the leather. That causes the leather to stretch back out. The leather can breathe again. Go to the next shoe, you do the same thing, you come back and you brush it, you don't rag it.

Q: Why do you brush it instead of ragging it?

A: You brush it because then you pull off all the loose stuff that's on it. You see that's part of cleaning it. You brush all the residue everything back off it. Now you put on another coat of polish, you ready to go to work. You brush and you rag and that's it. It's simple but you gotta put yourself in and you gotta care about it. Everything ain't just the dollar. If you're a professional, you care about your work. In the long run you make more money and you get more justification out of it. You know, understand, you like what you did. I don't like it where you do a person and they go out and then they come back in, "Oh, you know what happened?" You know. Because you got speed demons. You got some guys who care about nothing but the dollar. And that's not a professional.

Q: Do managers pressure you guys to go faster and . . .

A: Most managers they like to see them do that because it's making them look good on their register. But then when you start losing customers, they want to know what happened.

Q: What's the worst part of the job?

A: The worst part of the job is when you take the time and do the right thing and then the people don't do the right thing. You know, it hurts you, but you take all that in part because there ain't nothing you can do about it.

Q: Are most people pretty decent tippers?

A: Oh yeah. I have quite a few customers. That's the only way that you can make a living. That means that you're doing the right thing.

Q: Do people ask you to shine other things besides shoes?

A: Yeah, we get boots, gloves, briefcases, anything that is normally . . .

Q: What's the weirdest thing that anyone's has ever asked you to shine?

A: A cap.

Q: A cat?!?

A: No, a cap. Leather caps.

Q: Oh. How about a bald guy's head?

A: No. No.

Q: And can you usually tell ahead of time if someone's going to be a good tipper or a bad tipper?

A: No, you can't, except for the Europeans. I'm gonna tell you, I had come into this shop about three years ago an older fellow who looked like he didn't have a dime. And all the guys they were in a rush and nobody wanted to get to him. I told him to sit down. The man gets down after he gets his shine and he go up and pays and he goes up to me and gives me a folded up bill. It was a hundred dollar bill. Nobody else wanted to catch him because they looked at his shoes and they made that judgment. I haven't seen him since then. He wasn't even from this country. He was tired and he was traveling.

Q: Did you ever shine any celebrities' shoes?

A: Oh yeah. Mark Gastineau. I did Walt Frazier. They had very big shoes. Very big shoes. Lot of profession-

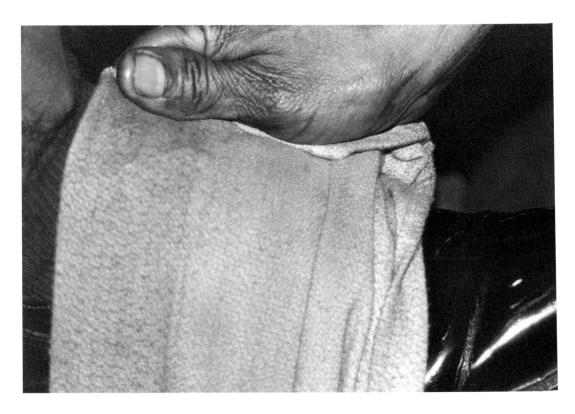

al athletes. You see I had my own place of business. At South Street Seaport. That's all I used to get in there was celebrities. Most of the Jets. Giants. All those guys they come down there with their ladies, they come up to the bar and sit around, you know. I've met some very interesting people. Yes, I have.

Q: Do the celebrities usually tip well?

A: Well, some of them. Just like normal people. Some ain't goin' to give up nothin' and then you got some that's pretty good.

Q: So why did you stop working at your place?

A: What, down there? They closed up that whole part of the Seaport. They closed that building out you know when they took that fish market out. You know they had a fish market down there where the people would come in and eat lunch. It used to stay packed. And you was open from ten 'til ten. The only day you closed was Christmas. From ten 'til ten, seven days a week. I was working nights, too, because then I had two guys working for me. Two fellows were working for me.

Q: Do you ever get stock tips from your customers?

A: Well I had a guy come in four or five years ago and he gave a good tip on the stocks, but I wasn't available to put no money into it. But the owner, I think that he made a little investment.

Q: Where do all the other guys at the stand come from?

A: Well, mostly they're Brazilian. The owner's from Canada. At some places you get a lot of illegals. You see that's what really hurts our business. These guys go into the office buildings, you understand? Where normally people have to come down to get their shoes shined, now you got guys up there on the floors shining the shoes and that hurts you, too, but what can you do about it. That's just all part of it, you know.

Q: And how long have you been here at Sole Brothers?

A: I've been here now twelve years and never missed a day. Rain, shine, sleet, snow. I can't afford to miss.

Q: You work every day of the week?

A: Only five days. Monday to Friday. I have to have the weekend off because my wife has multiple sclerosis. I have to get out of here in time to be with her for a while. I take care of her. I had an interview with a newspaper, it must have been now, it's been about seven or eight years ago, they carried it for about three weeks straight. It was called, "One Man, One Family, Three Jobs." That's what I was doin'. I was doin' three jobs. One of them was my main job and then I had two part-time jobs. You know, because to make ends meet. Don't forget I had five kids. One of my sons played for the Cleveland Browns for four years. Number thirty-seven. He got his knee torn up. Then my older son, Junior, he went to the University of North Carolina, but he didn't want to play no ball, so now he's working in Washington. One of my daughters now she's going to the University of Maryland. She went on a full scholarship. And now I've just got the two at home. My whole gratification is to see my kids make it.

Q: So are you going to be able to rest soon when the last two kids go to college?

A: Well, I guess in another ten years. Yeah about another ten years. I'll be alright. See, I'm fifty-four now. I'm goin' to be alright.

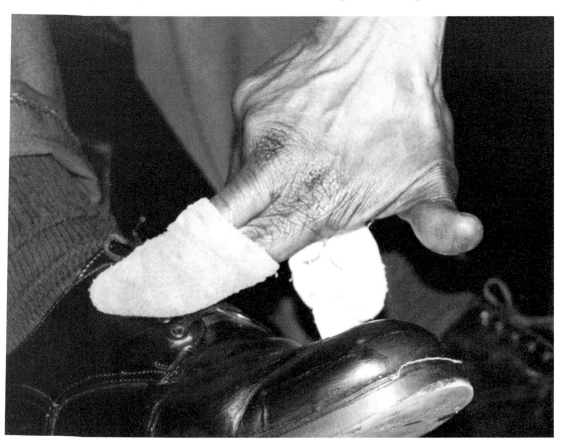

AFTERWORD: The vast majority of the law firms and investment banks in Manhattan now allow their employees to wear casual clothing to the office year round. People are not wearing as many "shineable" shoes as they used to. It has been over a year since I interviewed Harry, and his business continues to slow.

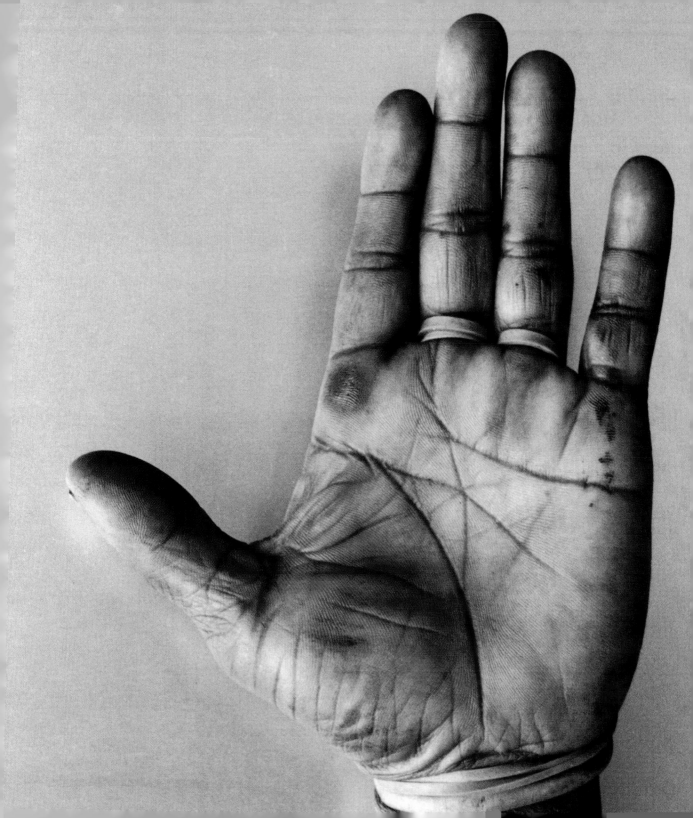

URBAN FOSSILS

AUTHOR: David Horowitz

NOTES: I grew up in an urban environment: beams, steel, stone, glass, empty lots of debris to play around in. As a young adult I trained myself in a number of arts, skills, and techniques. For me, the most satisfying of these is mold-making and ornamental plasterwork.

The original manhole designs were not done by artists. These designs were the expressions of skilled craftsmen. When I went back to the streets of the city to take molds of manholes, I did not clean them. I allowed the dirt or whatever it was to remain. In this way it became a timepiece, a moment frozen in time, an "urban fossil."

"4 Jane Street"

"120,000 sec./$250.00"

"Waverly Street"

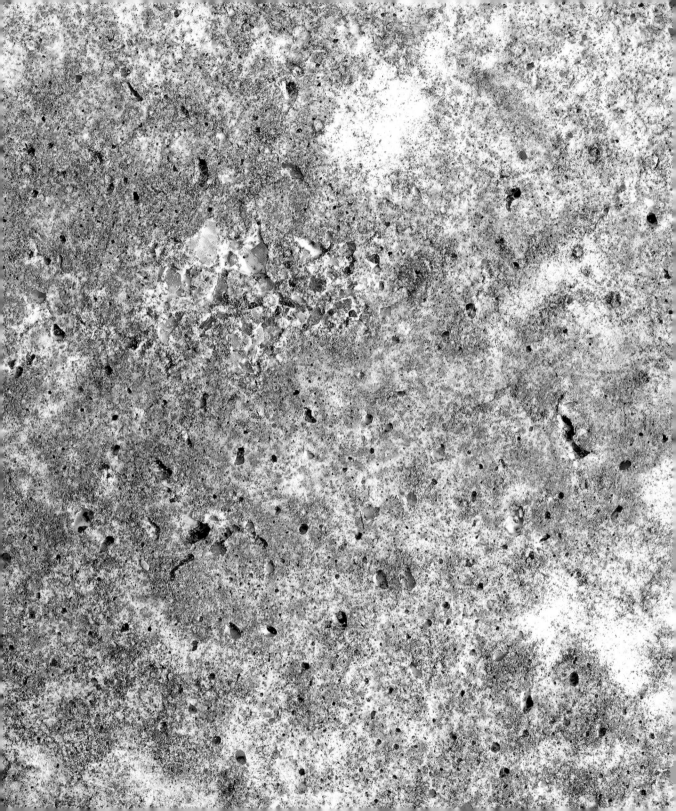

"Christopher Street, between Hudson and Ganesvroot"

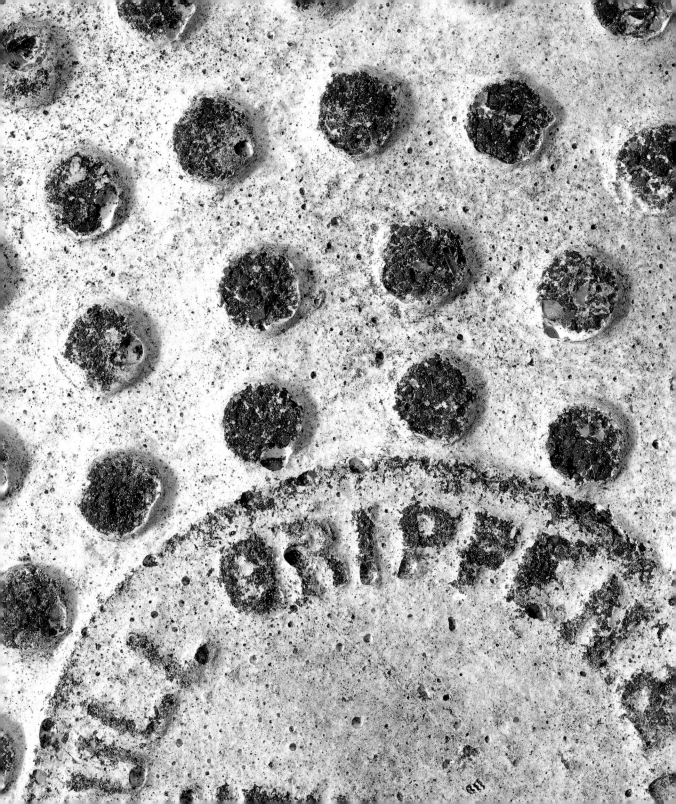

5

THE SUBWAY LINES

AUTHOR: Meaghan Kombol

NOTES: This is about the motion, within the locomotion, of the New York City subway system. To document this, I attempted to draw a straight line, on a piece of paper, mid-journey, while riding each of the twenty-three New York City subway lines.

The Constant*

* drawn while sitting on the Newkirk platform waiting for the Q train.

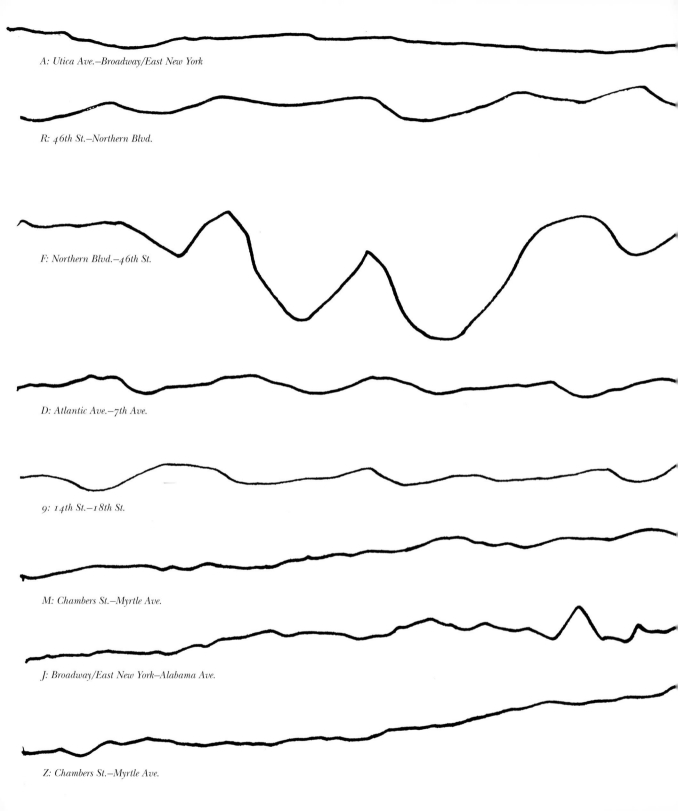

A: Utica Ave.–Broadway/East New York

R: 46th St.–Northern Blvd.

F: Northern Blvd.–46th St.

D: Atlantic Ave.–7th Ave.

9: 14th St.–18th St.

M: Chambers St.–Myrtle Ave.

J: Broadway/East New York–Alabama Ave.

Z: Chambers St.–Myrtle Ave.

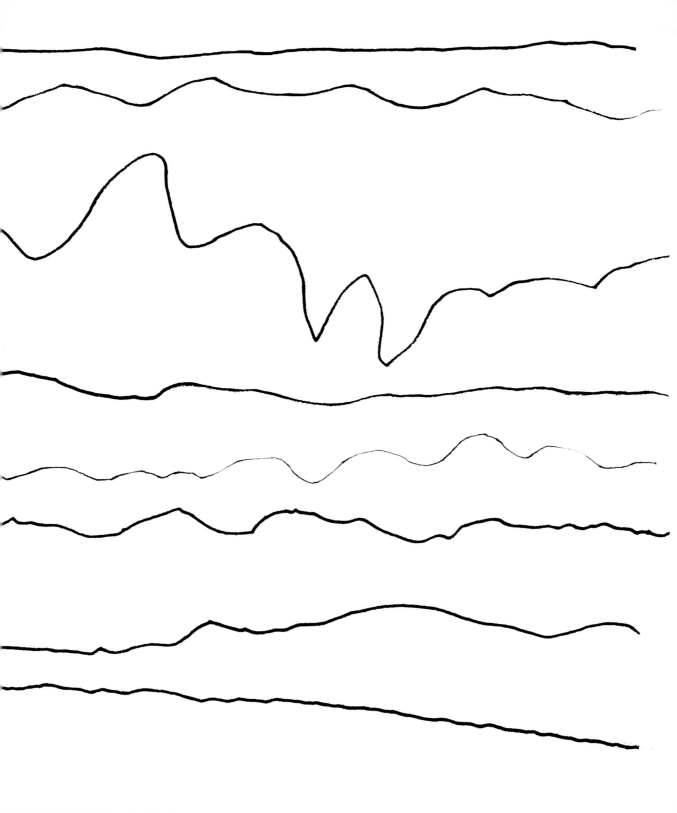

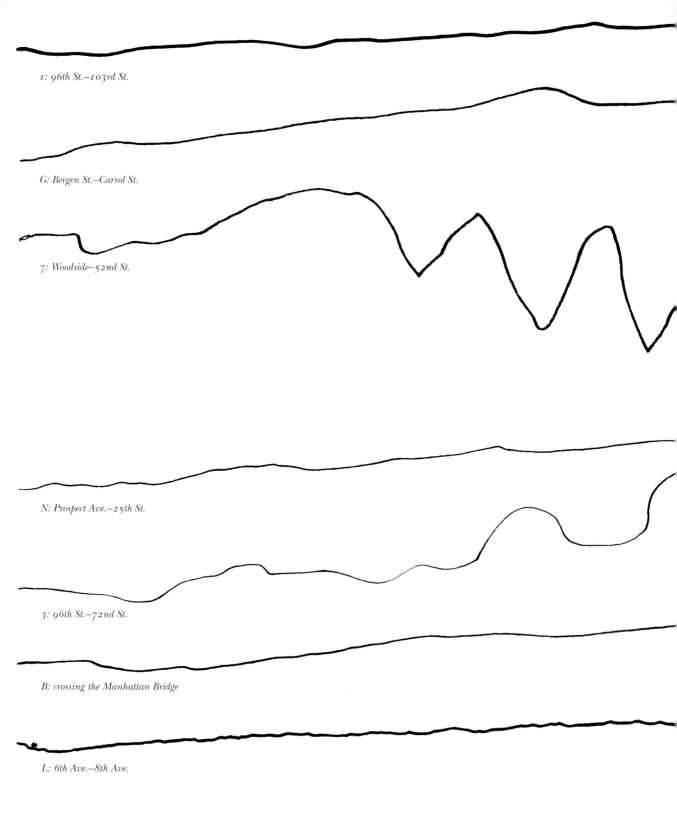

1: 96th St.–103rd St.

G: Bergen St.–Carrol St.

7: Woodside–52nd St.

N: Prospect Ave.–25th St.

3: 96th St.–72nd St.

B: crossing the Manhattan Bridge

L: 6th Ave.–8th Ave.

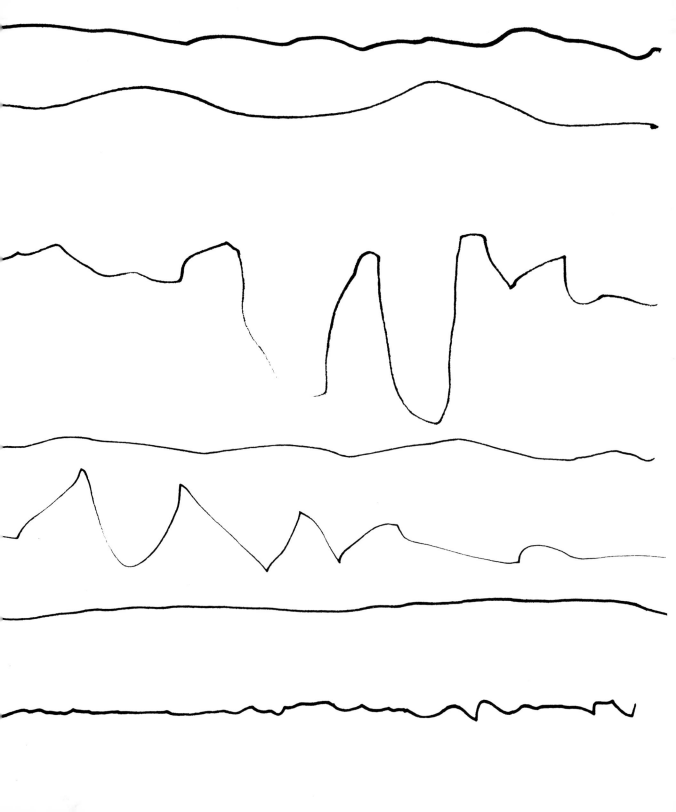

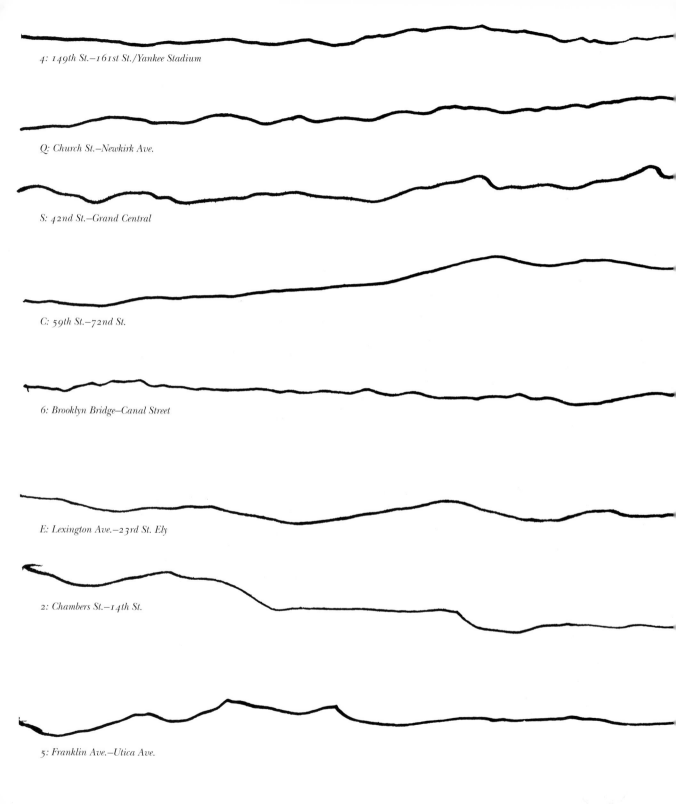

4: 149th St.–161st St./Yankee Stadium

Q: Church St.–Newkirk Ave.

S: 42nd St.–Grand Central

C: 59th St.–72nd St.

6: Brooklyn Bridge–Canal Street

E: Lexington Ave.–23rd St. Ely

2: Chambers St.–14th St.

5: Franklin Ave.–Utica Ave.

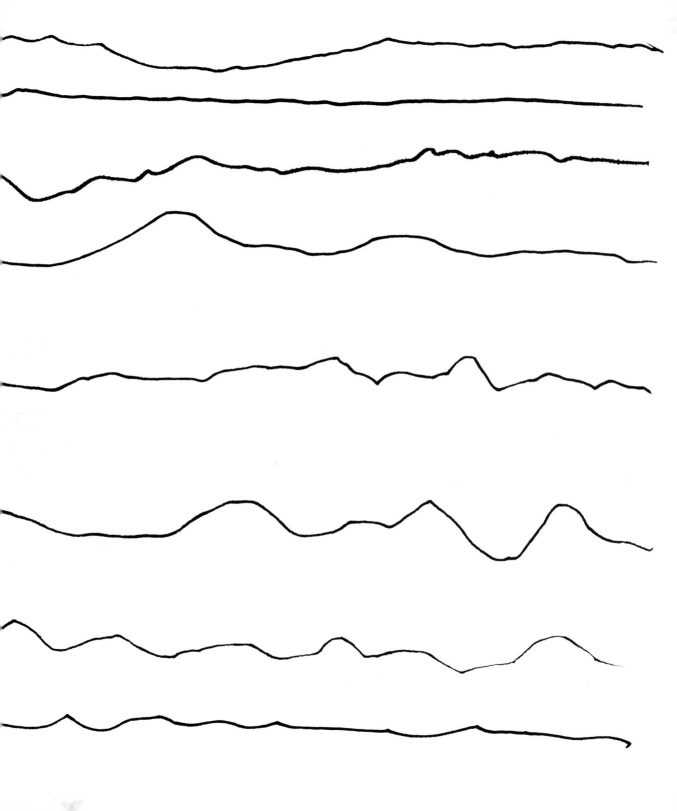

6

THE BLACKBOARDS

AUTHOR: Shannon Fagan

NOTES: One evening several years ago, after classes had
ended and before custodians made their rounds, I began
to photograph the blackboards that I saw everyday in
class. Using a 35-mm camera and the overhead fluores-
cent lighting in the classrooms, I exposed fine-grain black-
and-white film to the chalk smears and text messages.

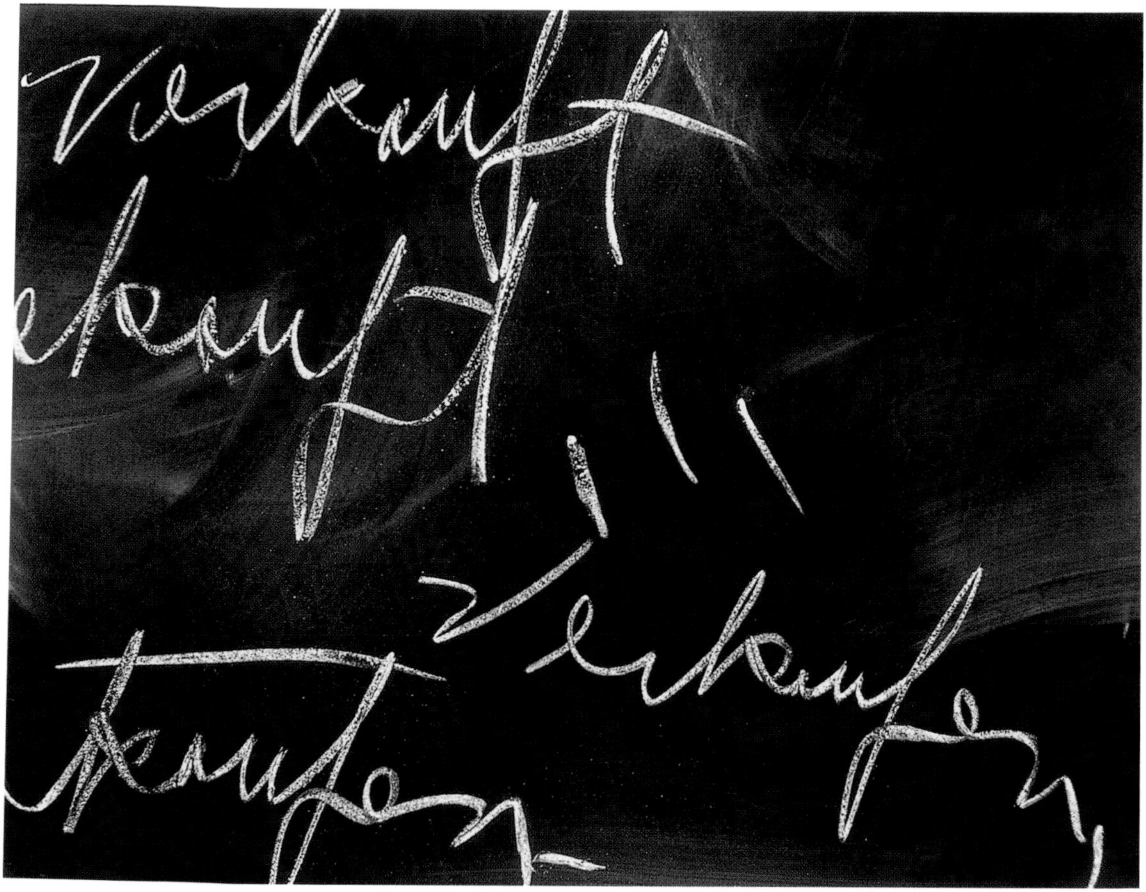
verkauft
ekauft
verkaufen
kaufen

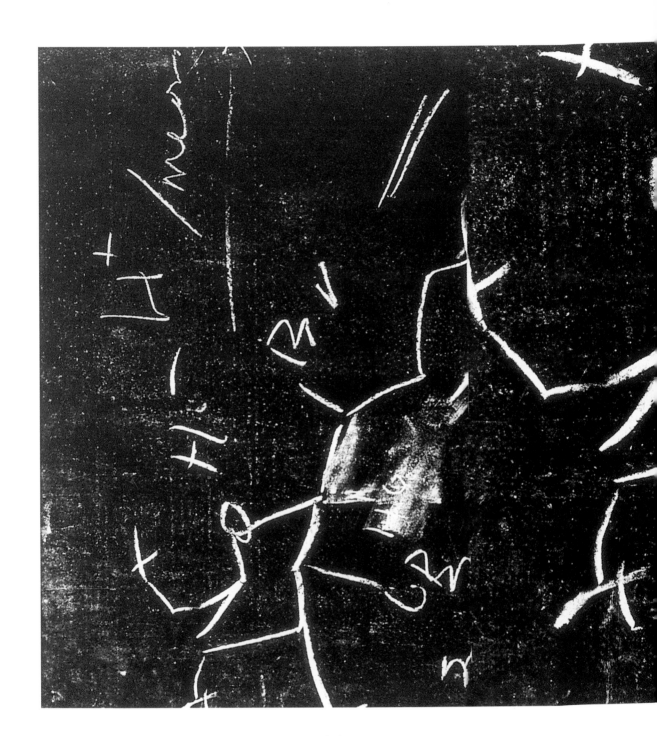

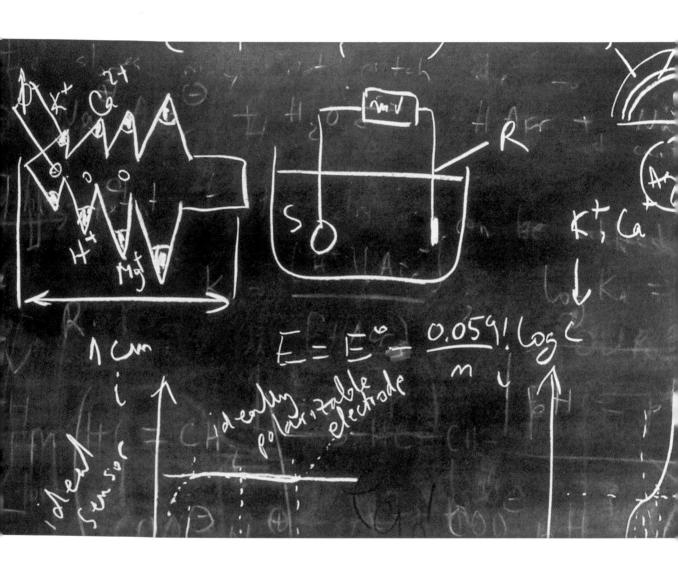

$$E = E^\circ - \frac{0.059!}{n} \log c$$

ideally polarizable electrode

ideal sensor

THE WONDER BREAD TESTS

AUTHOR: Robert Lemons

NOTES: In the Brothers Grimm fairytale, Hänsel laid a trail of bread crumbs to guide Gretel and himself back home. The trail of bread helped Hänsel and Gretel successfully navigate their return. But would a bread trail work in the modern world?

On a dreary day in March 2001, I undertook an experiment to test the utility of pieces of bread as trail markers. Racing against an impending nor'easter, I cut a gentle arc across lower Manhattan from my home to my girlfriend's apartment. To mark my trail, I left slices of an entire loaf of fresh Wonder bread.

Unlike Hänsel, I left home voluntarily, and thus had the luxury of recording the precise location in which I left each piece of bread, and the condition in which I found each piece (if I was able to find the piece) upon my return trip. Additionally, I collected the slices with tongs and deposited them in Glad Zipper Storage Bags to preserve them for further analysis. The following pages contain the stories and photographic records of each slice of Wonder bread.

The Loaf

To make finding the pieces easier upon my
return trip and to give the bread a better chance
of survival in the harsh streets of New York City, I
used whole slices of bread instead of crumbs.

No. 1

West side of Gold St. between John St. and Fulton St. **DEPOSIT:** 12:12 P.M. **ATTEMPTED RETRIEVAL:** 3:02 P.M. I left the first heel, a.k.a. No. 1, crust-side up on a low ledge in a rarely traveled side street. I found No. 1 untouched upon my return; fittingly, the plastic cup next to No. 1 and half-filled with beer/urine also appeared undisturbed.

No. 2

City Hall Park, northeast corner of dry fountain basin. **DEPOSIT:** 12:19 P.M. **ATTEMPTED RETRIEVAL:** 2:50 P.M. I record the location and time of deposit of No. 2. Painstaking notation was wise, as No. 2 was nowhere in sight upon my return. A sinister man with a broom and a large plastic bag was present.

No. 3

West side of Lafayette St. between Federal Plaza and Worth St. **DEPOSIT:** 12:28 P.M. **ATTEMPTED RETRIEVAL:** 2:46 P.M. No. 3 was missing upon my return. Is Congress hiring too many janitors with the budget surplus?

No. 4

Southeast corner of Lafayette St. and Franklin St. **DEPOSIT:** 12:32 P.M. **ATTEMPTED RETRIEVAL:** 2:41 P.M. I left No. 4 in a puddle of oily water. Surprisingly, the spongy interior of the slice survived while the harder crust completely disappeared.

No. 5

Southeast corner of Lafayette St. and Canal St.
DEPOSIT: 12:35 P.M. **ATTEMPTED RETRIEVAL:** 2:37
P.M. The first of two Chinatown stops on my route,
No. 5 was not to be found upon my return trip.

No. 6

Southeast corner of Canal St. and Broadway.
DEPOSIT: 12:38 P.M. **ATTEMPTED RETRIEVAL:** 2:35
P.M. No. 6 was in neither of the depicted trash
receptacles. It seems likely, however, that the thief
of No. 6 was a fastidious resident or merchant of
Chinatown.

No. 7

Mercer St. between Canal St. and Grand St.
DEPOSIT: 12:42 P.M. **ATTEMPTED RETRIEVAL:** 2:30
P.M. No. 7 did not survive its abandonment in the
middle of the cobblestone street.

No. 8

West side of Mercer St. between Spring St. and
Broome St. in phone booth on metal ledge under
phone. **DEPOSIT:** 12:47 P.M. **ATTEMPTED
RETRIEVAL:** 2:26 P.M. I found No. 8 underneath a
white napkin with strange stains and an imprint,
all from unknown sources. Another question
raised by No. 8: Does trash attract trash?

No. 9

North side of Spring St. between Wooster St. and Greene St. on step in front of Chanel store. **DEPOSIT:** 12:51 P.M. **ATTEMPTED RETRIEVAL:** 2:23 P.M. No. 9 migrated ten feet to a trash can and weathered the journey intact, merely collecting a fine layer of dark soil.

No. 10

East side of West Broadway between Prince St. and Spring St. on a ledge next to John Dellaria Salon. **DEPOSIT:** 12:55 P.M. **ATTEMPTED RETRIEVAL:** 2:20 P.M. As I recorded the deposit of No. 10, Mr. H. D––, the street artist depicted above, stole No. 10 and stalked away with a scowl on his face. Upon my return, I was unable to locate No. 10.

No. 11

South side of Prince St. between West Broadway and Thompson St. on doorstep of Vesuvio Bakery. **DEPOSIT:** 12:58 P.M. **ATTEMPTED RETRIEVAL:** 2:17 P.M.. No. 11 was unmarred, but it left its mark on the bakery's doorstep.

No. 12

Southeast corner of Thompson St. and Bleecker St. on step of entrance to La Margarita Mexican restaurant. **DEPOSIT:** 1:02 P.M. **ATTEMPTED RETRIEVAL:** 2:14 P.M. I retrieved No. 12 from an open garbage bag near the step. Apparently, the garbage bag was very clean, as No. 12 absorbed only a small spot of dirt.

No. 13

Washington Square Park, in front of entrance sign of George's Dog Run. **DEPOSIT:** 1:07 P.M. **ATTEMPTED RETRIEVAL:** 2:09 P.M. No. 13 was lightly soiled around the edges and small portions of the crust were missing. Small brown field mice observed near No. 13 are the primary suspects.

No. 14

North side of West 4th St. between 6th Ave. and 7th Ave. **DEPOSIT:** 1:14 P.M. **ATTEMPTED RETRIEVAL:** 2:03 P.M. No. 14 still appeared untouched upon its retrieval. Apparently, the customers of the Pink Pussycat Boutique have more interesting things than Wonder bread on their minds.

No. 15

South side of West 4th St. at Sheraton Sq. **DEPOSIT:** 1:18 P.M. **ATTEMPTED RETRIEVAL:** 2:01 P.M. No. 15 never stood a chance: it was devoured by nine pigeons moments after its deposit as I watched in dismay. Additionally, a rottweiler lunged for the remnants of No. 15, but its owner managed to restrain it. The depicted hot dog morsel occupied No. 15's place upon my return.

No. 16

Intersection of Perry St. and West 4th St. **DEPOSIT:** 1:22 P.M. **ATTEMPTED RETRIEVAL:** 1:55 P.M. No. 16 fared no better on asphalt than No. 7 fared on cobblestone. As foreshadowed by the photograph, No. 16 was likely rolled away on a tire tread.

No. 17

South side of West 12th St. between West 4th St. and 8th Ave. **DEPOSIT:** 1:26 P.M. **ATTEMPTED RETRIEVAL:** 1:51 P.M. No. 17 remained in the bicycle basket with the only damage being a thumb-indentation left by me.

No. 18

Southwest corner of West 12th St. and Greenwich St. **DEPOSIT:** 1:29 P.M. **ATTEMPTED RETRIEVAL:** 1:45 P.M. Because my girlfriend was not home, I did not leave the second heel exposed to the elements for long. Although I left No. 18 crust-side down on top of a Village Voice dispenser, No. 18 was still pristine upon my return.

Conclusions:

Despite New York City's reputation of litter-filled streets, the Wonder bread test demonstrates that New Yorkers, particularly those in shopping districts such as Chinatown and SoHo, aggressively patrol for litter. The bread pieces that I actually found upon my return trip were surprisingly durable. Knowing this, my trail of bread might have survived more intact had I used mere crumbs as Hänsel did. This observation reveals the great futility of using breadcrumbs as a navigation system: if a piece of bread is conspicuous enough to be findable by the maker of the trail, the piece is too visible to predators such as shopkeepers and pigeons.

8

SIGHT SEEING

AUTHOR: Cyrus Habib

NOTES: If our sensory input acts as the impetus for almost all of our decisions and actions, then you might understand why the imposition of a condition such as blindness can so affect even one's most mundane perceptions. People often ask what it is that I see. "Is it totally dark?" they ask. What they fail to consider is that blindness is an essentially desensitized state: it is the absence of sight, not the dull, unremarkable expanse experienced when you close your eyes. But the Swiss-cheesification of my sensory plain is mitigated by those other windows onto the world upon which we all rely.

As you use your eyes to enter my neighborhood, understand and appreciate, that for me, this is a journey who's landmarks are defined only by sounds, smells, and auras. It is my experience: welcome to it.

THE SPECK REPOSITORY

ITEMS NO. 1

Earth, Air, and Water

I always kidded around with my customers at the barbershop. I told them when they went down south they should wave their hands and push the warm air up. So one of my customers decided to bring some sand back. After that, I decided that this was a good idea. So, when my customers or I went anywhere, we would bring back some souvenirs: usually dirt, sand, water, air, and sometimes fog or even smog! I put them all up in my barbershop. The customers got a big kick out of seeing the samples they brought back on the racks in the shop.

There was that fella who went to Amsterdam and he brought me back some water from the canal that flowed past the house where Rembrandt lived. Someone brought back a piece from an Inca Temple. I have a sample from the Island of Crete: the students from the Tyler School of Art were doing some excavations there and they picked up a piece of the temple for me. There was a friend who brought back water from the Baja peninsula. I did not realize it, but sea water is living. When it was bottled, it was all right. I poured it into a small bottle, but oh my God! Trying to scrub that stuff off my hands. It was potent.

One of my customers went to Israel and picked up stones from the wailing wall. Afterwards, I had a number of rabbis who were customers, and when they had to bury somebody, they would ask me for a couple stones from the wailing wall to put in the coffin.

My wife and I have been to Africa, Italy, Spain, England, Israel, Egypt, Canada, Mexico, Haiti, South America: all of which I have gathered samples from. Now that I have retired from the barbershop, I still get some stuff but not as much as before. We are hoping to go to Portugal soon. I don't have anything from there. There is a whole lot of places that I still want pieces from. In the beginning I used to say that my ambition was that when I retire I would like to return each piece to the place of its origin. I never did it.

Occasionally I will go down to the basement, to the wall where I keep all the samples, and pick one up. Sometimes I can visualize the person who gave it to me. A lot of that stuff has interesting stories with it. I have enjoyed it. Send me anything unusual, something small.

—EDDIE SIMON, PHILADELPHIA

LOCH LOMAND 6/73

GREAT WALL OF CHINA

AUSTRALIAN SAND

ELBA

CLARK AIR BASE TAICHUNG, TIAWAN

QUE NATIONAL LCA POAS, HAWAII

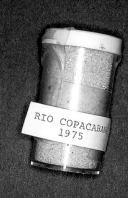

RIO COPACABANA 1975

CANAL WATER IN FRONT OF HOUSE OF REMBRANTS AMSTERDAM. HOLLAND

GUAIM

CALIF.

FOOLS GOLD (IRON PYRITE)

COPPER KINK MINES

SWITZERLAND
CHAR-

LAVA, VESUV

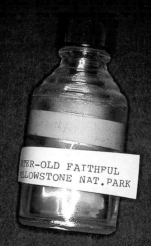

ATER-OLD FAITHFUL
LLOWSTONE NAT. PARK

ALASKA, GL
FLOUR

PLACE PIGALLE
PARIS, FRANCE

CHURCH OF
NATIVITY

MIAMIA AIR
2/29/63

TORTOIA, BVI

AIR BAXTER CAVE
VA

COLUMBIAN ICE
CANADIAN ROCKI
ALBERTA, CANAD
GROUND GLACIER

WATER FROM
CREATER LAKE
OREGON

BRAZIL, RECIF

BERMURADA
,JOHN
KEY

ONTEGO BAY,JAM
Sand
Montego Bay

YANGTZE RIVER
RIVER

D CARRABIA

STONE FROM
GREEK TEMPLE
HURKLEN,CRET?

RHODES, GREECE
FROM OCEAN BOTT

WYOMING VALLEY AIR
(O2, N,)etc.

MALDYSIA,MAL

COPENHAGON,DE
USEUM OF RES
OVEMENT

San
SAN JUAN
Pu
PU

WATER FROM
BUDAPAST, HUN

BALA INDON
VOLCANIC RO

WATER MAZATLAN

the
LA E
SALT-SALT L
1968

OLYMPIC SIT

VEH ISRAEL
AGOGUE W.T.
ACUS.NETHERLANDS

AIR.MEXICO
CITY

LAKE ERIE
SAND

SAND SOUTH
CHINA SEAS

BLE BEACH
SSAU.BURMADA

OPERATION
DESERT STORM
SAUDI ARABIA

ST.LAWREN
/63.
CAN.

Morrocco

TAIWAN

MOSEL RIVER AT
TRIER-FRENCH &
GERMANY BOARDER

SALT FROM DEVILS
GOLF COURSE, DEATH
VALLEY, CAL.

ALASKAN WATER

DIRT FROM
SUBWAY AT THE
SPECTRUM

DIRT-DONTARRY CASTLE
LIMERICK ISLAND, SCOTLAND

TORREMOLINIS

& BOG TURF
Y GALAWAY
AND

LUXOR, VALLEY
OF THE KINGS

LUXENBUR

LMERAL
TLE
LAND

BALMORAL
CASTLE, SCOTLA

POMPII, ITALY

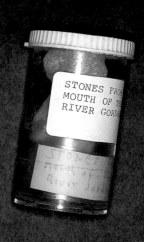
STONES FROM
MOUTH OF TH
RIVER GORDA

Stone
Porto Cristo
Mallorca, Spain

STONE FROM CAVE
AT PORTA CRISTO
MALLORCA

WESTERN UKRAINZ
GALICIA PROVENCE
(OBIAST) 14KM-N
OF CITY OF LVIV

GREEK TEMPLE
500-1000 B.C.
HERAKLEAN, CRETE

WATER-OLD FAITHFUL
YELLOWSTONE NAT. PARK

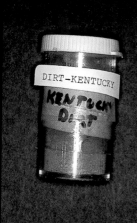

DIRT-KENTUCKY

KENTUCKY
DIRT

Hope Town Harbour
Little Abaco
Bahamas

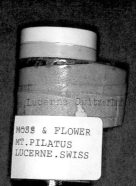

Lucerne Switzerland

MOSS & FLOWER
MT. PILATUS
LUCERNE. SWISS

MANILTA
PHILIPPINE

Smog
Hollywood & Vine
Hollywood

SMOG HOLLYWOOD & VINE
HOLLYWOOD (1)

PRICKLY
ANGUILLA

ROMAN FORUM

DANANGE 2/68
VIETNAM

SAND FROM WH[I]
SANDS-NEAR L[AS]
CROCES & ALA[M]
NEW MEXICO

MONUME[N]T
[AL]AMOGOR[DO]
[NEW MEX]ICO

TIANANMEN SQUA[RE]
BEIJINE, CHINA

COLLISIUM, [ROME]

DEAD SEA

SAHARA DESERT
(EGYPT)

AMIN, JORDAN

[FOR]BIDDEN CITY
[B]EIJING, CHINA

FoRBIDD[EN]
CiTY
BEIJING

ILIKAS
HAWAII

[0]0 Year Old Volca[no]
[S]unset Crater, A[Z]

NAHA, OKINAWI
5/20/94

EQUADOR

GALAPAGOS
APRIL 19[

GA[L]APA[GOS]
ISLAND
APRIL
ECUAD[OR]

DEAD[ ]
HAR[B]ER

HOLY WATER
FATIMA

MANILA

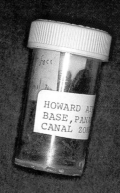

HOWARD AI
BASE, PANA
CANAL ZO

ROSARIO. ARGANTINE

OKINAWIA

SILVER ORE
MEXICO, OXUAM

NORWAY, ARTIC
CIRCLE 6/86

SAND-HELSINKI
FINLAND

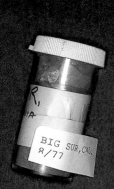

R,
HA

BIG SUR, CAL.
8/77

JAPAN

OLD SAND
OME ALASKA

COPAN RUINS
MAYAS, Hond

OKLA. AIR

BASLE, SWITZE...

TRINADAD

NEIZI TEMPLE
TOKYO, JAPAN

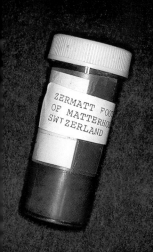
ZERMATT FOO...
OF MATTERHO...
SWITZERLAND

RONZI BEACH
HAWAII

SAND FROM
EGG ISLAND
BAHAMAS

Pigeon Point
Tobago
Sand + Coral

ORTH WALES

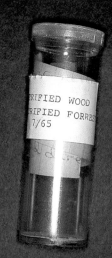
...RIFIED WOOD
...RIFIED FORRES...
7/65

Bay of Pigs
CUBA
2-1-78

PRINCE EDWARDS
Edward...
Island

EVILLE SALT
S BOB REID
9/75

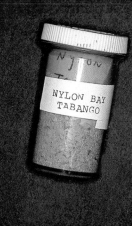

DIRT FROM
TRINIDAD

NYLON BAY
TABANGO

ARIZONIA

Chanute AIR
FORCE BASE
RANTOUL, ILL

KANYA

CHINA-RED
BORDER

YOKOHAMA
JAPAN-4

water   egypt

ND & WATER
CIFIC COAST
FROM
LAG
Ma

Catatono's Italy

CASA BLANCA

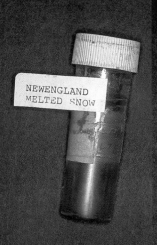

NEWENGLAND MELTED SNOW

BRUTE 66 NEW

PHILMOUNT SCOUT CAMP

TIJUANA MEXICO

FOG LONDON

AMALFI. ITALY

SNOW

ISLE DUTCH SAINT MAARTIN

WATER SAN JUAN PURETO RI WEST INDI

LAS VAGES, NEV

WAILING WALL JERUSAULM

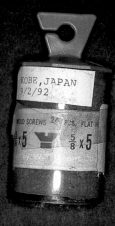

KOBE, JAPAN 9/2/92

WOOD SCREWS

CAIRO. EGYPT

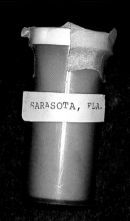
PENTOPANUS
COSTA RICA

SARASOTA, FLA.

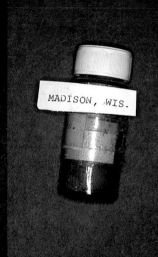
MADISON, WIS.

PUSAN, KOREA
24-92

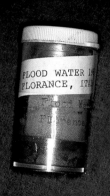
FLOOD WATER 1
FLORANCE, ITA

18th HOLE
PEBBLE BEACH
CALIF.

ELSINORE
Denmark
NORE, DENMARK

KOPENHAGE
DENMARK
Foot of Sea
HAGEN, DENMARK

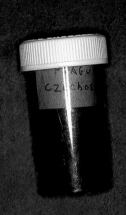
PRAGUE
CZECHOS

T.BELGIUM

BANGKOK

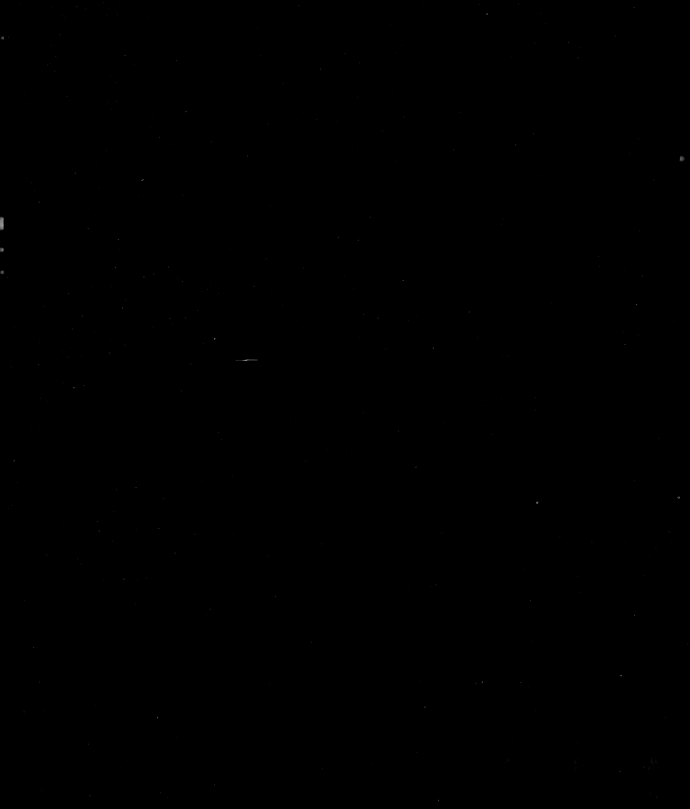

Lint

This stack of approximately 300+ (I still need to count them) discs of laundry lint is the tidiest, most organized part of a larger collection of lint Betty Ruth Curtiss gathered from her dryer in the basement of her home in Princeton, New Jersey, from the late 1970s to the early 1980s. A student of chemistry at Vassar, Betty Ruth came to be regarded as a maker of jewelry and a found object sculptor. Her enthusiasm for the immediacy of instant printmaking techniques, such as rubber stamps and photocopy processes, was also well-known. In addition to, and as part of, her practice she also collected a variety of everyday objects and materials (spent light bulbs, chewed gum, egg cartons, plastic combs, plastic bread ties). These occupied a sort of "on deck" status for her jewelry, sculpture, photocopy prints, and rubber stamps. They were materials and objects gathered and waiting to be used in her work but while being gathered and waiting, they almost achieved the status of works by default.

On the front porch of the house there was a large wood card rack (painted a pale pink) displaying individual gloves found by herself and anyone else who might wish to place one there—not only for possible retrieval but for any other reverie they might afford. At one time, there might be twenty or so waiting, some still holding the gesture of the hand that lost them.

The Curtiss household dryer was equipped with a circular lint screen that shaped the laundered material into delicate, crepe-like samples, each with a hole in its center like a token or Chinese coin. As a printmaker interested in all kinds of paper and the nuances of how it was made, it is tempting to consider that Betty Ruth thought of doing the laundry as a ready-made variation of paper making.

I am pretty sure I remember her saying that on occasion she experimented with ways of controlling the color and texture of the discs, cultivating strategies for mixing particular colors and types of laundry items. An orange towel, for example, might be combined with a red polyester sweater and some blue socks to generate the most interesting combination of surface and hue. In the end, despite her expectations and calculated guesses, the results probably always surprised her.

—RICHARD TORCHIA (WITH LISA CURTISS), PHILADELPHIA

Bottom

ITEMS NO.3

Misspelled Names

My Norwegian surname "Ulriksen" ties most everyone it encounters in knots. It is also easily mis-spelled. When I was working as a magazine art director in the late 1980s and early 90s I would receive buckets of mail every week, mostly work samples from photographers, illustrators, and artist's agents. Right off the bat I was intrigued by the creativity with which I was addressed. Ironically, my last name is phonetically simple Ul-rik-sen. Fascinated, I decided to collect all the typographic inventions.

—MARK ULRIKSEN, SAN FRANCISCO

Rod Dresser
Photography

MARK ULLRICKSON

Mark Ullrichson
San Francisco Focus
680 Eighth Street
San Francisco, CA 94103

FAUZIA OSMAN

REPRESENTS

San Francisco Focus Magazine
2601 Mariposa
San Francisco CA 94110

Mark Ullriksin
San Francisco Focus Magazine
2601 Mariposa
San Francisco CA 94110

San Francisco Focus
Mr. Mark Euboriksen
680 8th Street
San Francisco CA
94103

MARK ULRIKSNE
680   EIGHTH ST
SAN FREANCISCO
SAN FRANCISCO, CA 9410
DELIVERED 03/20/90 08:25
SIGNED: S. MAYNARD

MARK ULRICKSON — ART DIRECTOR

Mr. Marc Uckickson

Mark Olrickson
Focus Magazine
2601 Mariposa Street
San Francisco, CA 94110

Mark Ulriksin
Art. Director
San Francisco Focus
680 Eighth Street
San Francisco, CA 94103

Att. Mark Viriksen, Associate

Mark Ullrichson
Art Director
SAN FRANCISCO
680 Eighth Street
San Francisco, CA 94103

Att. Mark Viriksen

S.F. Focus
Mark Uliksen

Attn: Mark Yliksen

Mark Arlickson
San Francisco Focus/KQED, Inc.
680 Eighth Street
San Francisco, CA 94103

C

San Francisco Focus
Attn: Mark Ulrichson
2601 Mariposa
San Francisco, CA 94111

San Francisco Focus Magazine
688 Eight Street
SAn Francisco, CA 94103

Attn: Mark Olicson

k Ullerson
us Magazine
8th St.
Francisco, Ca. 94103

ATT: MARK OrickSON

k Mark Olrickson
t Director
n Francisco Magazine
0 Eighth Street
n Francisco, CA 94103

n Francisco Focus

ark Ulrickson

Mark Urlickson
Art Director
San Francisco Focus/KQED, Inc.
680 Eighth Street
San Francisco CA 94103

Focus Magazine
Mark Uhlrickson
2601 Mariposa
San Francisco, CA 94110

ark Orkson?

Mr. Mark Olikson
Focus
680 8th St.
San Francisco, CA 94103

Mark Ulricksen
SAN FRANCISCO FOCUS
680 Eighth Street
San Francisco, CA 94103

TO:
MARK OSHRICKSON
S.F. FOCUS

Mr. Mark Olickson
Focus Magazine

Mark Ulricksen
San Francisco Focus/KQED, Inc.
680 8th Street
San Francisco CA 94103

MARY KVLRISKCEN
C/O SANF RAN FOLKS
680 8TH ST
SAN FRANCISCO,
DELIVERED 11/02/89 CA 94103 AA
SIGNED: K. MACDONALD 12:18
RECIPIENT SUBTOTAL

Mark Ullrichson
San Francisco Focus
680 Eighth Street
San Francisco, CA 94103

Mark Ullrichson
San Francisco Focus
680 Eighth Street
San Francisco, CA 94103

Mark Ulkiksen
SAN FRANCISCO FOCUS
680 Eighth Street
San Francisco, CA 94103

Mark Olrickson

Mark Ulrilsen
Associate Art Director
San Francisco Focus
500 8th St.
San Francisco, CA 94103

Mark Urliksen

ARK VLRIKSEEN
AN GRAN-FOCUS MAG
30 8TH ST 2ND FL
N FRANCISCO CA 94
LIVERED 09/29/89 08:4
GNED: S.MEDRANO

ATTN: Marc Ulrichsen)

Mr. Marc Verliksen
Photo Editor
SAN FRANCISCO FOCUS

MARK OLDRICKSEN
841 SCHRADER
SF CA 94117

FOCUS
ATT: MARK Urliksen
680 8th Street
2nd Fl.
S.F. CA

MARK ULIRKSEN

ZINE/KQED
ATTN: Marc Ulrich

MARK
SAN
089
SAN

To
MARK URICKENSEN/SAN FRANCISCO FOCUS

Mark Oldriksen
San Francisco Focus
2001 Mariposa Street
San Francisco, CA 94110

Mark Ulrickson
San Francisco Focus/KQED, Inc.
680 8th Street
San Francisco CA 94103

Art Ulriekson

MARK UIRLICKSON
SAN FRANCISCO FOCUS/KQED INC
680 8TH ST
SAN FRANCISCO CA 94103-4942

Dear Mr. Ulrickson,

San Francisco Focus
Attn: Mark Ulrichson
2601 Mariposa
San Francisco, CA 94111

Mark Eriksen
Focus
680 8th Street
San Francisco,CA 94103

San Francisco Focus
Attn: Mark Ulrichson
2601 Mariposa
San Francisco, CA 94111

Mark Arlicksoa
San Francisco Focus Magazine
680 Eighth Street
San francisco, CA 94103

San Francisco, CA 94103

Mark Rikson

Dear Mr. Arbrekson:

Mr. Mark Urlickson
FOCUS
2601 Mariposa St.
San Francisco, CA 94110

Mark Ulriickson
San Francisco Focus/KQED, Inc.
680 8th Street
San Francisco, CA 94103

Mark Uiriksen

Name: George Lange
Address:
Phone:

Call: MARK ORRICKSON
553 2860

S. F. Focus Magazine
680 - 8th Street
San Francisco, CA 94103
Attn: Mark Worksen

Mark Eriksen, Art Dir.
San Fran. Focus, KQED Inc.
2601 Mariposa St.
San Frabcisco, CA 94103-4942

Mark Oueriesd
SAN Fraalcisco Focus
680 Eight St.
SAN FraalJcisco, CA 94103

AMO: MARK UIKRICKSON

MARK ULUICICH

Mark Uirlickson
San Francisco Focus/KQED, Inc.
680 8th Street
in Francisco CA 94103

Mr. Marc Veriksen
Photo Editor

Mark Olrickson

Mr. Marc Veriksen
Photo Editor
SAN FRANCISCO FOCUS
680 Eight Street
San Francisco, CA 94103

MARK ULIKSEN
c/o SAN FRANCISCO Focus
500 EIGHTH ST.
SAN FRANCISCO, CA 94103

Mark Orlram

Mark Arlickson
San Francisco Focus/KQED, Inc.
680 Eighth Street
San Francisco, CA 94103

C

Mark Olrickson

503 - 234 - 4757
PORTE...

Mark Vrikson

San Francisco Focus
680 Eigth Street
San Francisco, California 94103
Attention- Mark Olrickson

---

*San Francisco Focus
Mark Olrickson
Mathew Drive
680 8th St
San Francisco, Ca*

S.F. Focus
680 Eighth Street
San Francisco, CA 94103

ATT: Mark Irlickson

Mark Ubriksen
S.F.Focus
2601 Mariposa St.;
San Francisco, Ca. 94110

Merk Ulikler
841 Schrder St.
S.F.,Ca. 94117

July 17, 1991

Mark Alrichson
San Francisco Focus Magazine
San Francisco CA 94103

Mark Olrickson
Focus Magazine
2601 Mariposa Street
San Francisco, CA 94107

Mathew Ulrikson
SAN FRANCISCO FOCUS
680 EIGHTH ST.
SAN FRANCISCO, CA 94103

Mr. Marc Veriksen

Mr. Marle Urlickson

San Francisco Focus
Mr. Mark Euboriksen
680 8th Street
San Francisco CA 94103

Mark Ullichson in ?

SAN FRANCISCO FOCUS Magazine

To Mark Ulichson

San Francisco Focus
Mr. Mark Euboriksen
680 8th Street
San Francisco CA 94103

Mark Ulriksen
SF Focus (KQED)
2601 Mariposa Street
San Francisco, CA 94110

ATTN: MARK ULMKSON
...CISCO, CA 94110

---

531 Howard Street
San Francisco
California 94105

March 26, 1991

Mr. Mark Olrickson
Art Director
San Francisco Focus

*MR. MARK ULRICKSIN
ART DIRECTOR
SAN FRANCISCO FOCUS
K Q E D CORP.*

% TOM URLICKSON

MARC ULRIKSEN
S.F.FOCUS
2001 Mariposa
San Francisco, CA 94110

Mark Olrikson

Mark Ulrickson
San Francisco Focus/KQED, Inc.
680 8th Street
San Francisco, CA 94103

Mr. Marc Veriksen
Photo Editor
SAN FRANCISCO FOCUS
680 Eight Street
San Francisco, CA 94103

Dear Mr. Veriksen:

TO

Mark Urlickson

ITEMS NO.4

Cat Whiskers

In 1989 I rented a loft in Philadelphia. It was a hundred and seventy-eight feet long, and I thought with a space that big I could have a cat, a cat and a piano being my prerequisites for home. Soon after I moved in I acquired Norman, a large tuxedo cat of nebulous origin. Norman had a very easygoing personality, yellow-green eyes, and the most impressive whiskers I had ever seen on a cat.

As it turns out, cats shed their whiskers now and then, and I took to collecting them. It became quite a thrill to come across a new whisker left behind at the food bowl, or on a favorite chair. I have an eye for finding whiskers actually, people were shocked that I so readily came across them in that huge space. My girlfriend shared the space with me and could never find one. But they leapt out at me all the time. To me they were a precious commodity, a remarkable, beautiful thing, and each whisker was different in texture, shape, and coloring.

When Kate moved in, she brought her cat Amos (a female cat unfortunately named after an old family dog), and I added Amos's whiskers to my assortment, though not without some hesitation, since I was mixing the genetic makeup of the collection.

Eventually, Norman died and I moved to New York and acquired a new cat named Sophie. Sophie has also contributed to the collection, though I will maintain that Norman still had the best whiskers. I must confess that, when visiting a house that contains a cat, I am not above making off with a whisker if I find one laying about, so that I am sure my collection contains the whiskers of more then these three particular felines.

One must be careful that foreign matter is not inadvertently added to the collection, as some dog hair, broom bristles, or other like articles can easily be mistaken for the real thing. I keep the collection in an antique bottle that I dug up as a child. I do not know how many whiskers I have but there are certainly a great many. Cat whiskers have integrity. And the truth is, no one knows with certainty what a cat does with them.

—WADE SHUMAN, NEW YORK CITY

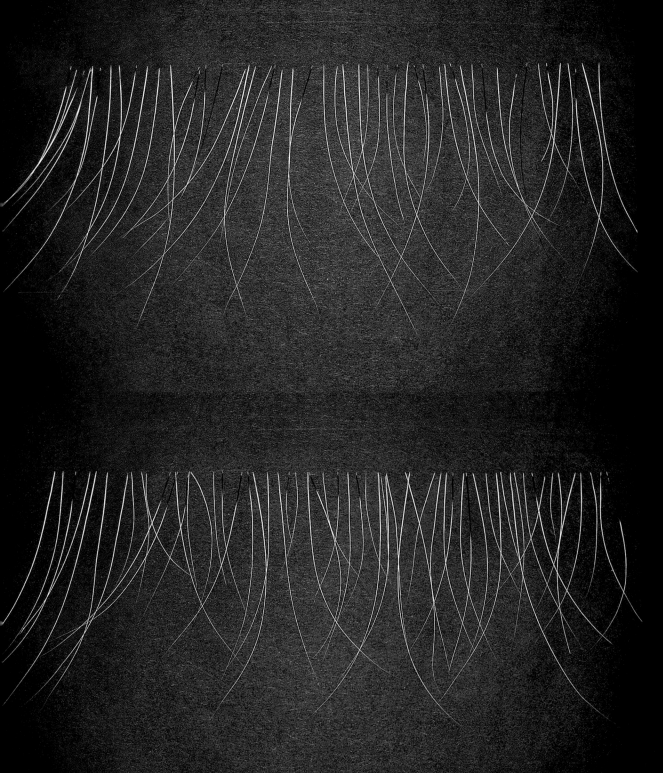

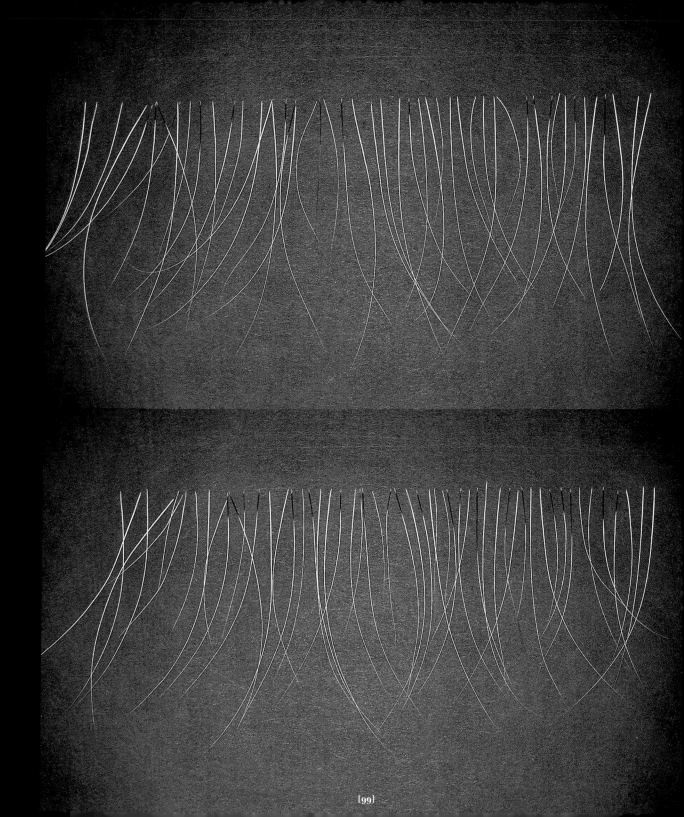

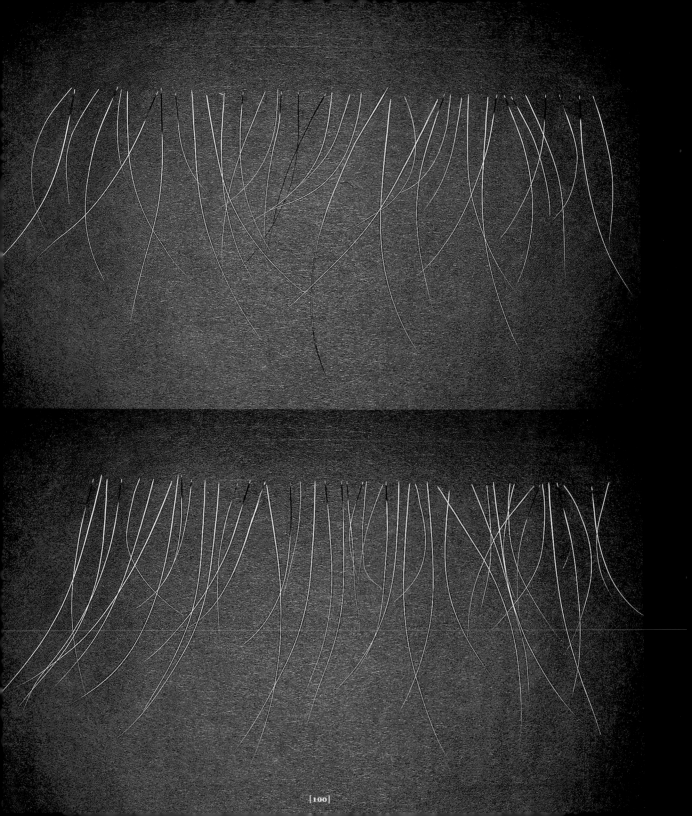

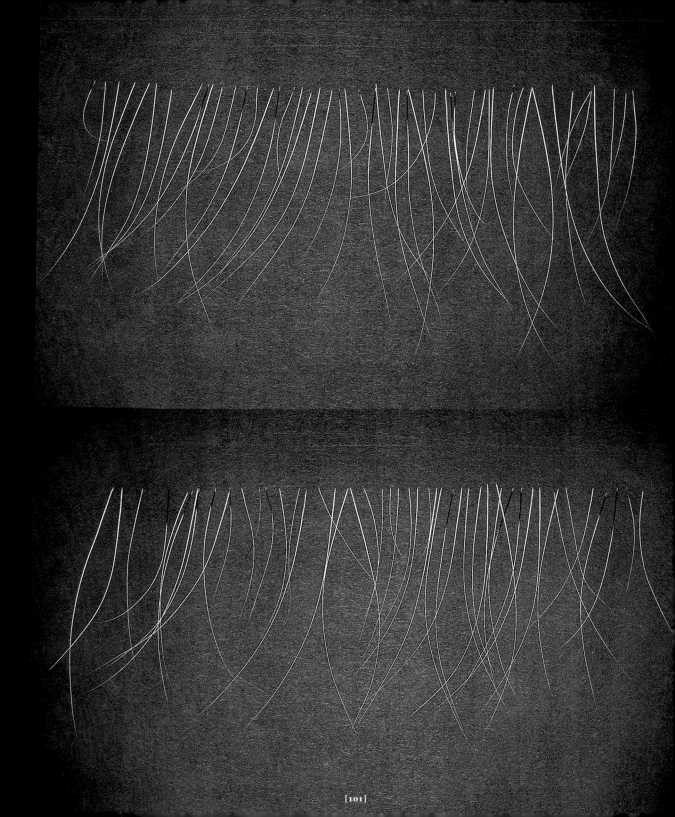

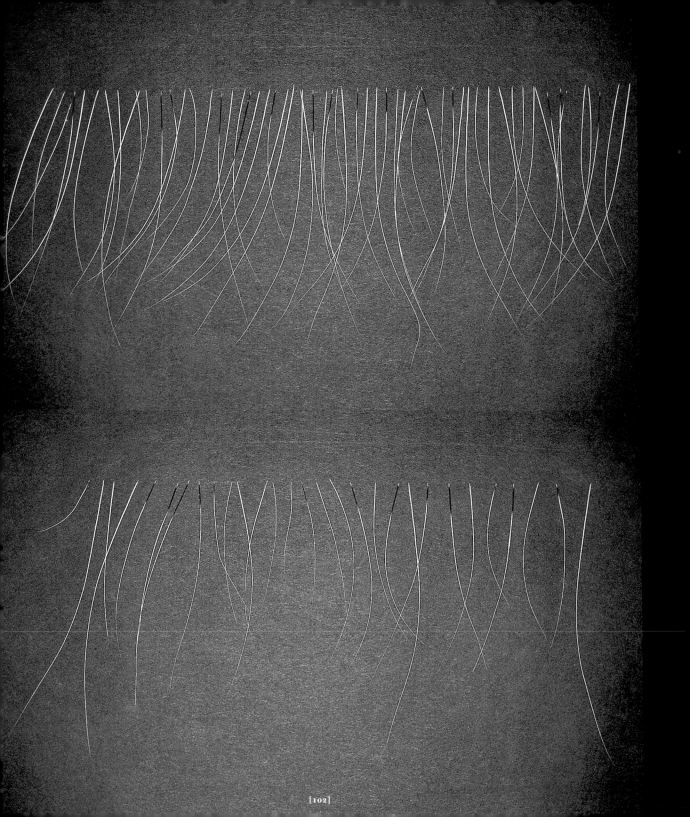

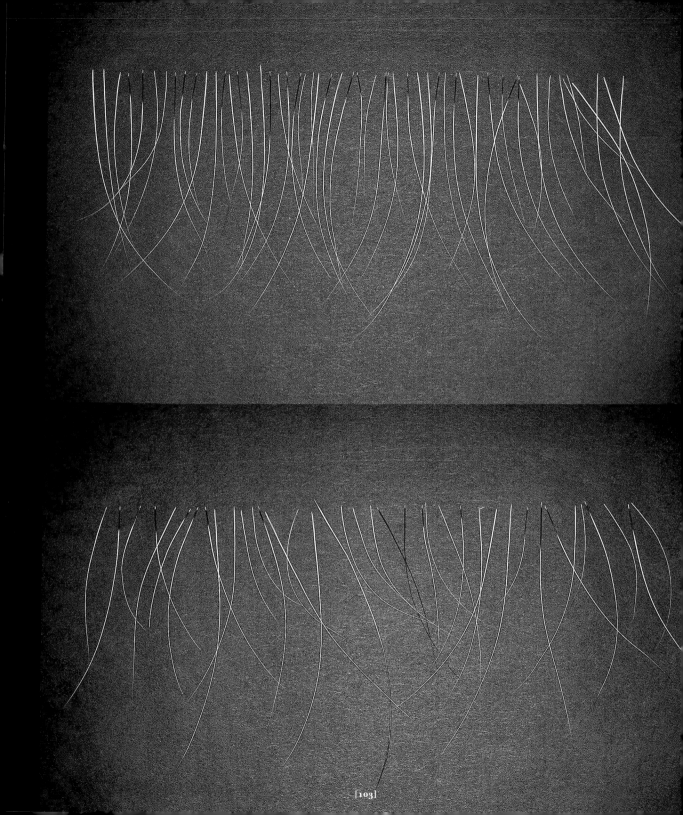

ITEMS NO.5

Scribbles

You want art? Grab it—it's yours for the taking. If you don't, they're only going to throw it away. If, though, you're in the market for free art, you could do worse than hang around your local art supply store. There you will find those fastened-down notepads on which customers can try out pens and markers prior to purchase. I think they're cool—dashing, colorful, funny, and, if you get lucky, a little smutty. The most important thing is that each is a unique piece of art, and they're all for free. So go grab yourself a handful of art and don't be shy: it's doubtful that a store would prosecute you should they catch you in the act (in fact, a recent Nebraska State Supreme Court decision found art supply store test sheets to be in the public domain).

— PHIL MILSTEIN, BOSTON

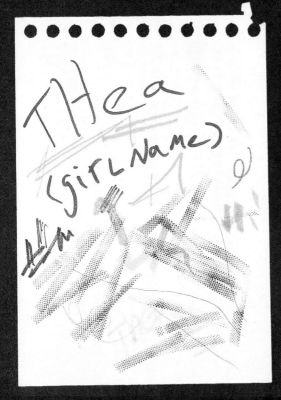

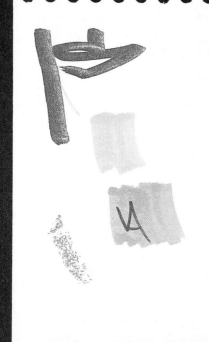

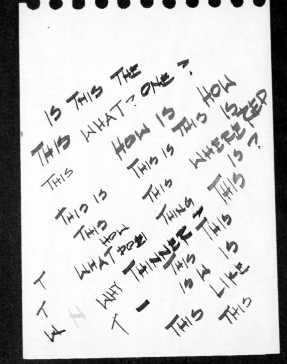

Inspected by Tags

I often visited Brooks Brothers on my lunch hour. In 1962 Brooks Brothers was a creaky old store: fox hunt prints on the walls, grandfathers behind the counters, and suits and trousers stacked on long tables. Every pair of trousers was folded so the right rear pocket faced up. As I fondled the gabardine, quite by chance my hand found its way into a rear right pocket. A slip of paper met my fingertips. I withdrew it. It read "INSPECTED BY #3." "Nice typography," I thought. "Two centered lines, some kind of crude gothic." I checked another pair of trousers and found INSPECTED BY #12. Another pair, and another pair. More slips of paper. More numbers: 44, 28, 52.

I began to look for INSPECTED BY tags in other stores. In Bloomingdale's someone stepped on my hand as I reached for a CHECKED BY #14 on the floor.

I was fascinated by the diversity of style within such small limitations. Fascinated? No, obsessed. I stole an inspector's certificate from an elevator. I ripped a huge bond-like tag from a Japanese car. In combat, I found a large, waxy inspection tag packed with the base plate for my mortar. I found tags with names from the heartland: INSPECTED BY TOM TROUTMAN, CHECKED BY MINNIE LARK. I found some in the form of endearing notes:

> Thank you for buying these shoes. I have examined them carefully and have found them to be free of defects in workmanship and material. I pass them on to you with pride.—Janice

I found tags of many lands KONTROLLIERT V15, CONTROLE No 2, REVISADORA #12.

Friends gave me gifts of tags. Each received a Certificate of Thanks from The Institute for the Collection and Preservation of Inspected by Tags.

—RON BARRETT, NEW YORK CITY

Examined & Packed
By Operator No.
2
In referring to irregularities in contents
of this box please mention Operator No.

This garment has been
inspected by No. 2C
I-3

This garment has been
inspected by No. 2C
I-3

En cas de réclamation
prière de nous retourner cette fiche

CONTROLE N° 2

INSPECTED BY
EXAMINER
No. 2

INSPECTED
BY
2

Button Sewer
No. 2

CONTROLE
2

Controllo
qualità
∗
Collaudatore
N. **2**

INSPECTOR
No. 2

INSPECTOR No. 2

N° 45727

PACKED BY
No. 2

THIS GARMENT
PASSES FINAL
INSPECTION

No. 2

Inspected By
No. 2

INSPECTED
BY
2

REVISADORA
N.° 2

Inspector 3

INSPECTED
BY NO. 3

3

Inspected by
No. 3

Inspection Slip

SHRINK WRAPPING provides a skin-tight transparent package which allows immediate identification and protects against soiling, dog-earring and atmospheric changes.

This order has been inspected as part of our quality control program.

INSPECTED AND PACKAGED BY __#3__

If there are any problems with this order, for immediate action
Call . . . In New York City — (212) MU 9-5100 Ext. 269
In Westchester — (914) 949-9340 Ext. 24

INDEPENDENT PRINTING CO., INC.

IN NEW YORK CITY (Main Office).
215 E 42nd STREET, N.Y.C., N.Y. (212) MU 9-5100
IN WESTCHESTER (Main Office).
5 NEW STREET, WHITE PLAINS, N.Y. (914) 949-9340

PACKER'S IDENTIFICATION SLIP

In case the contents of this package do not check with invoice or label, return this slip with package as received.

3

Inspected by

3

EXAMINER

3

INSPECTED
BY

3
SS

THIS COAT
INSPECTED BY

NO. 3

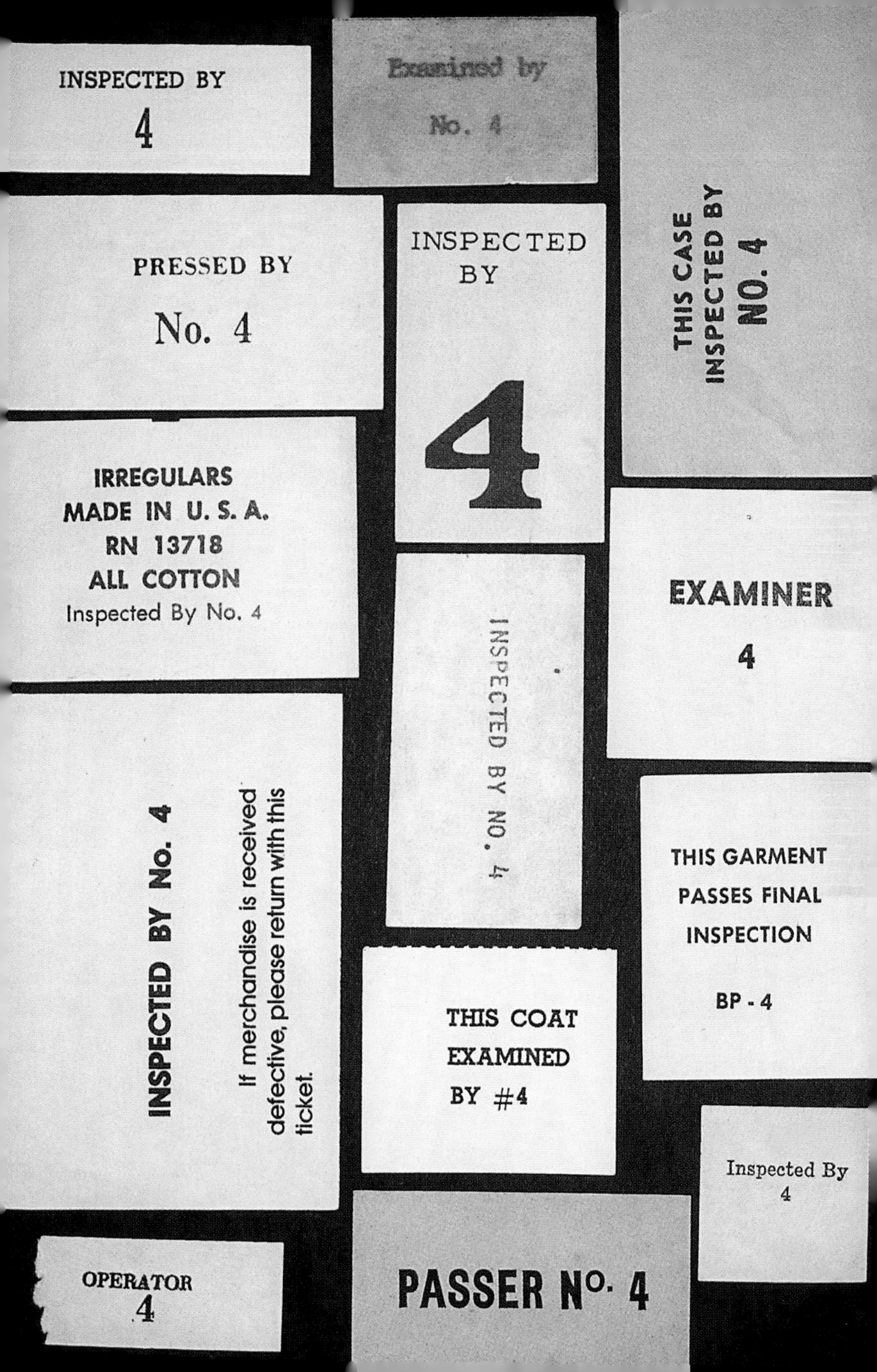

INSPECTED BY

4

Examined by

No. 4

PRESSED BY

No. 4

INSPECTED
BY

4

THIS CASE
INSPECTED BY
NO. 4

IRREGULARS
MADE IN U. S. A.
RN 13718
ALL COTTON
Inspected By No. 4

INSPECTED BY NO. 4

EXAMINER

4

INSPECTED BY No. 4

If merchandise is received defective, please return with this ticket.

THIS GARMENT
PASSES FINAL
INSPECTION

BP - 4

THIS COAT
EXAMINED
BY #4

Inspected By
4

OPERATOR
4

PASSER NO. 4

INSPECTOR 5

EXAMINER

5

How To Care For Your Never-Iron Shirt

WASHING: On machines, use warm water setting and run for full cycle. By hand, use, warm (not hot) water. Rinse thoroughly but don't wring or twist.

DO NOT BLEACH.

AUTOMATIC DRYING: USE MEDIUM HEAT SETTING. Remove from dryer immediately after garment is completely dry.

DRIP-DRYING: REMOVE GARMENT from washer before spin cycle, or from tub after shaking out loose water. Hang and smooth out wrinkles. When dry, fold or hang neatly.

Examiner No. 5

controllo

EXAMINED BY No. 5

THIS SLIP MUST ACCOMPANY ALL CLAIMS

INSPECTED BY 5

Inspected By No. 5

INSPECTED BY INSPECTOR # 5

5

Examiner No. 5

This garment has been carefully examined. If defective, please return it with this slip.

Inspected by No. 5

Z-5

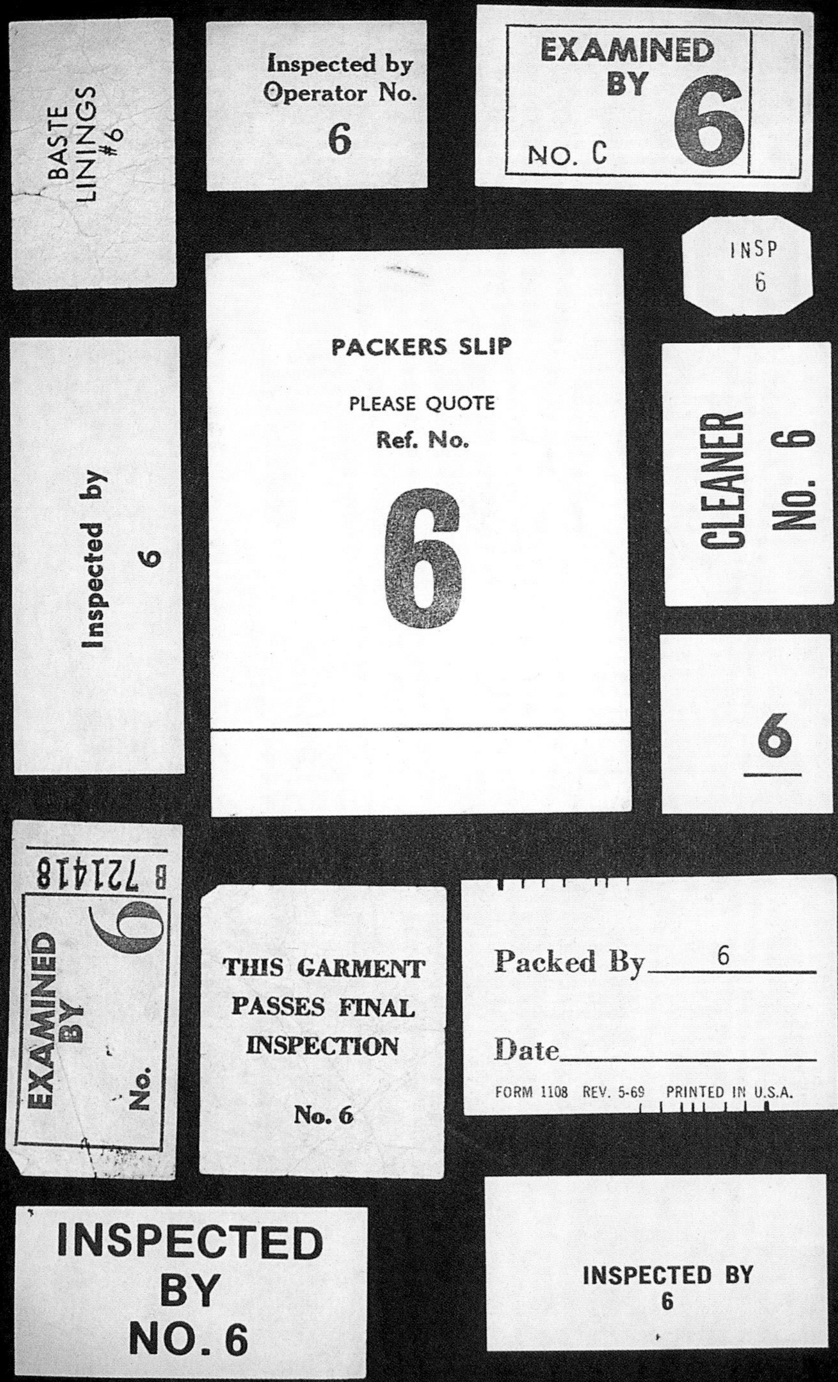

BASTE
LININGS
#6

Inspected by
Operator No.

6

EXAMINED
BY
NO. C **6**

INSP
6

PACKERS SLIP

PLEASE QUOTE
Ref. No.

6

CLEANER
No. 6

Inspected by

6

6

B 721418

EXAMINED
BY
6
No.

THIS GARMENT
PASSES FINAL
INSPECTION

No. 6

Packed By _____ 6 _____

Date _____

FORM 1108   REV. 5-69   PRINTED IN U.S.A.

INSPECTED
BY
NO. 6

INSPECTED BY
6

INSPECTED BY
7
LITTLE TOPSY'S, INC.

INSPECTED BY
7

INSPECTION
7

INSPECTED BY
7

INSPECTOR

No.7

INSPECTED BY 7

EXAMINER
7

This Shirt
Inspected
by
No. 7

THIS COAT
EXAMINED
BY #7

INSPECTED
BY
7

INSPECTOR
7

Inspected by
7

FORM XX
INSPECTED BY
No. 7
If any defect should be discovered
Return this ticket with garment.

THIS CASE
INSPECTED BY
NO. 8

This Box Packed By

No. 8

Examined by #8

INSPECTED
BY

8

*Controllo
qualità*
✻
Collaudatore
N. 8

INSPECTED BY

8

THIS GARMENT
PASSES FINAL
INSPECTION

No. 8

EXAMINED BY

#8

Packed by No. 8

8

PACKED
BY
No. 8

CONTROLE

8

Contrôle

Nº 8

INSPECTED BY

8

Inspected By No. 9

Inspector   9

Inspected by

9

INSPECTOR
No. 9-F

IRREGULARS
MADE IN U.S.A.
RN 13718
100% Cotton (Coton)
Inspected By No. 9

WASH COLORS SEPARATELY·
NO BLEACH

THIS CASE
INSPECTED BY
NO. 9   3

INSPECTED BY

9 - 10

2 6 NOV 1977
Date: ....

Inspected by:

9

A. Pizzi - S.p.A.

- Quality Material
  - Good Workmanship
    - Careful Inspection
All combined in an effort to
give you a Perfect Garment
Inspected By 9-4

Controllo

9

INSPECTED
BY

9

9

In caso di reclamo per
ammanco merce unire il
presente talloncino.

Capi N. ....

FINAL INSPECTION
By Number
10
EXAMINER

FINAL
INSPECTION
BY
No. 10

Exd by
10

Examined By No. 10
M - 65

- Quality Material
  - Good Workmanship
    - Careful Inspection
All combined in an effort to
give you a Perfect Garment
Inspected By 10-11

**PACKED
BY
No. 10**

Inspected by
No. 10
In case of defect
kindly return this ticket.

nspector
No.
10

INSPECTED BY
No. 10

Packed By_____10_____

Date_____

FORM 1108 REV. 5-69   PRINTED IN U.S.A.

M
Exam.
No. 10

INSPECTED BY
10

PACKED BY NO. 10

IN CASE OF SHORTAGE OR DEFECTIVE
PARTS, PLEASE RETURN THIS SLIP TO
YOUR DEALER OR DIRECT TO THE FAC—
TORY.

Shortage claims not allowed unless
accompanied by this slip.

INSPECTED BY
10

ITEMS NO.7

Missing Animal Signs

We both started collecting lost and found pet posters in the late 1980s. It started as an interest in the drawings people did of the animals but developed into a fascination with the willingness of panicked pet owners to expose themselves through their public cries for help.

To collect a wider range of posters we launched a mail-art project (an international postal exchange)—people sent us missing pet posters from their neighborhoods in exchange for a compilation of others from around the world. It proved to be a wildly successful project—for a few years we received new posters almost daily—from every continent except Antarctica. Besides posters, we have received flea collars, dog tags, paintings of chickens, and letters declaring "You will not get a missing pet poster from Iceland because pets do not go missing there." We have also heard many heart-wrenching stories, some with happy endings like the one about the blind dog lost in a New England snowstorm, and we have been told at length that the Dutch do not put up posters when their pets disappear, they just run out and get new ones.

It was very difficult to narrow down the collection for this book—there are posters of every conceivable pet, as well as posters for dead animals found along the roadside, missing animal parts, stuffed animals, and dolls. It is something that people in every city have seen, but I think most overlook.

—IAN PHILLIPS & GRANT HEAPS, TORONTO

MISSING PET RAT

BIG BLACK RAT
ESCAPED. REWARD
TO FINDER. RATS
NAME IS POISON.
PLEASE HEIP! CALL
YAEL @ 6591137.

MISSING PET RAT

Wir Vermissen
unser Kätzchen
Seit dem 21. 4. 96.
Sie ist ganz Schwarz
mit einem weissen
fleck auf der Brust.
Ihr Name ist Puspus. Evtl.
Ist sie in einem estrich, da sie
übers Dach der Klybeckstr. 78
weg gegangen ist. Bitte
Schaut überall nach. Danke.
Fam. Kaiser. Tel. 691 35 02
691 35 02

LOST FEMALE

DOG

CHILDREN CRYING
(MINIATURE
(SCHNAUZER)

DOES NOT HAVE
SCHNAUZER CUT. HAS
LONG TAIL. PLEASE CALL

784-9329

MISSING

GRILLED CHEESE!

IF YOU KNOW WHO STOLE THIS SANDWICH:

last seen:
Kosmo Deli
in Kerry town
on Fifth Ave.

very friendly, loves kids.

PLEASE CONTACT
741 - 9152

REWARD

DESPERATELY SEEKING
SANDWICH. PLEASE HELP

DESPERATELY SEEKING SUSAN

$10,000

REWARD

OR $250.00
FOR INFO LEADING
TO HER RETURN.

BLACK FEMALE POODLE
(aprox. 6 lbs. • 2 yrs. old)
MiSSiNG SiNCE DEC. 23
FROM MELROSE & LAUREL AVE. AREA
(213) 653 - 2295

SALLY SCHERMERHORN
DOES NOT TRY TO FIND
HOMES FOR YOUR PET.
SALLY IS A LIAR. DO NOT
TRUST HER. SALLY WILL
EUTHANIZE PERFECTLY
ADOPTABLE CATS.

LOST BLACK LAB

No Collar, No Legs,

NEEDS Medicine!!!

Call 334-5015

Ask for Unca Tom Jennings

RIND ENTLAUFEN

Am Abend vom Sonntag, 16. Februar
auf den Montag, 17. Februar
ist uns ein Rind entlaufen.

Es hört auf den Namen Lucien und hält sich mit
Vorliebe in Restaurationsbetrieben auf.
Wenn Sie das Rind finden, bitte sofort Tel. 274'04'74
anrufen. Der Viehtransporter kommt unverzüglich.

VORSICHT BSE-GEFAHR

Si vous trouve
un lapin comme ça
avec les tache
brun   appelez

4745 7380
        S.V.P.

(vivant ou mort)

LOST. Ferret

COLOR: BLACK
AND WHITE

NAME
"LiL"

"CALL... 781-0321

ジョンです

鼻の右側に
2.3cmの 黒い部分が
あります。

捜しています

7月22日土曜日午後3時頃に,
家から出たまま戻って来ません!

　種類トイ・プードル
　性別オス 2才
　色 ベージュ 耳の所が茶系

　　お心当りの方は,お電話下さい

3367-0478 杉山方
千葉

HAVE YOU SEEN MY SNAIL?

Sammy the snail was stolen from his Fern
Ave. front garden home just before Easter.
He was a Wedding Gift and is sadly missed.

Sammy is approx. 1 ft. high and 2 ft. wide
and is made from Mexican pottery stone.

If you took Sammy, *PLEASE RETURN HIM*
to his home, no questions asked. If you
know of Sammy's whereabouts, *please call
539-0102* and leave a message.

LOST
WOLF
CALL
331-8211
REWARD

REWARD

Missing —
Four head
stock cows.

Call
(913) 964-3447

Lost Cat

It is a half Persian cat and half tabby. It has a fluffy tail. It has no coller. If you find this cat Please return it to 10 minoque units. Thank you. Please find my home.

HELP, I'M LOST! 11/27

← 3½ FT →

My name is "BO" & I am a king snake. My owner surely misses me as much as I miss him. I swear I didn't mean to get lost, it just sorta happened. If you see me around campus, please call my owner Vick Itonel at: (213) 256-8759 & tell him where I'm located. I am sure my owner will gladly provide a reward. Thanks, Bo.

LOST DOG DUE TO CARJACKING IN S.F. 6/13/94

Man, woman sought in carjacking

SAN FRANCISCO Police are looking for a man and a woman who stole a Pontiac Transam from its owner at gunpoint, making off with the car and the owner's 10-year-old dog, Cleo.

The carjacking occurred Monday afternoon at 16th Street and Potrero Avenue, Sgt. Barbara Davis said. The owner told police he had been in his parked car when a man opened the unlocked passenger door, slid in and told him at gunpoint to get out.

As the owner climbed out of the 1982 black Transam, a woman climbed in the passenger side, and the couple sped off, with Cleo the Sharpei sitting in the back seat.

The car has a California license plate of 2MXW233. Cleo is fawn-colored, with a dark brown circle on her left hind quarter.

Compiled from Examiner staff and wire reports

NAME: CLEO
BREED: SHAR PEI
AGE: 10 YRS OLD
DESCRIPTION: Brown with small
dark-brown circle on left side.
Animal friendly/people shy

ANY INFORMATION
PLEASE CALL: (445) 826-4869

Have YOU SeEN
my CAT?

I lost my CAT sunday.
She is white and is
also deaf. Someone pease
catch her and call 843-7066

CAT
843-7066

CAT
843-7066

CAT
843-7066

CAT
843-7c

CAT FOUND
Siamese

11-26-94

In order to safeguard the welfare of the cat and ensure that it is returned to it's rightful owner, the person claiming ownership of the cat will be required to provide: five (5) forms of identification and references including but not limited to, verifiable telephone number and place of occupation. Also, a very specific physical description and photo must be given before return. I will personally check up on the cat at a later date.

Andrew (213) 934 7502

BACKS OF PAINTINGS

AUTHOR: Adam Yates

NOTES: Adam Yates' photographic series, "The Back Side of Paintings" (2001) was discovered by accident. Yates' work signals a dramatic departure from the frontal approach to two-dimensional art.

The following paintings are from the collection of Mr. and Mrs. Wade F. B. Thompson, New York City.

Pablo Picasso, *Nature Morte au Citron et au Verre*, 1944

Alexander Calder, *Untitled*, 1968

Philip Guston, *No. 10*, 1952

Franz Kline, *Green, Red and Brown*, 1955

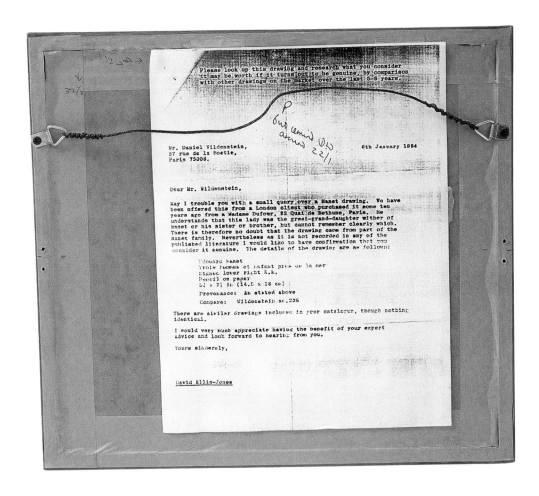

Edouard Manet, *Trois Femmes et Enfant Près de la Mer*, 1862

Camille Pissarro, *Près D'Angieres*, 1864

10

THE OLDEST PIECE OF DUST

AUTHORS: Knickerbocker & Jesse Gordon

NOTES: Active since the time of the dinosaurs, this rarely glimpsed piece of filth remains at large to this day. Last sighted in a tenement basement on the Lower East Side (where this photograph was taken), it is rumored to have been blown across the Hudson River on the stormy night of March 27, 2001. A motion has been filed in the General Assembly of the United Nations to have this ancient dust-ball declared a planetary treasure. If seen, please report its whereabouts immediately. Do not clean up.

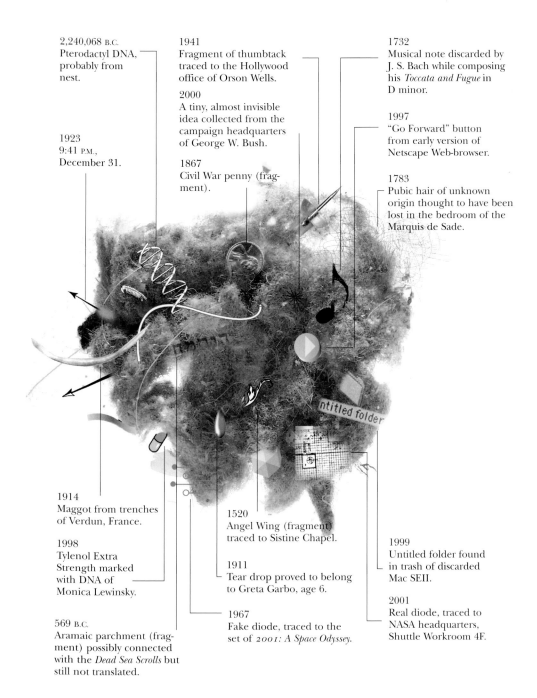

2,240,068 B.C.
Pterodactyl DNA, probably from nest.

1923
9:41 P.M., December 31.

1941
Fragment of thumbtack traced to the Hollywood office of Orson Wells.

2000
A tiny, almost invisible idea collected from the campaign headquarters of George W. Bush.

1867
Civil War penny (fragment).

1732
Musical note discarded by J. S. Bach while composing his *Toccata and Fugue* in D minor.

1997
"Go Forward" button from early version of Netscape Web-browser.

1783
Pubic hair of unknown origin thought to have been lost in the bedroom of the Marquis de Sade.

1914
Maggot from trenches of Verdun, France.

1998
Tylenol Extra Strength marked with DNA of Monica Lewinsky.

569 B.C.
Aramaic parchment (fragment) possibly connected with the *Dead Sea Scrolls* but still not translated.

1520
Angel Wing (fragment) traced to Sistine Chapel.

1911
Tear drop proved to belong to Greta Garbo, age 6.

1967
Fake diode, traced to the set of *2001: A Space Odyssey*.

1999
Untitled folder found in trash of discarded Mac SEII.

2001
Real diode, traced to NASA headquarters, Shuttle Workroom 4F.

SCALE:
Above is the specimen magnified to 10^3.
The actual specimen is 10^{-3}, the size of the period at the end of this sentence.

11

THE LIFE OF YOUNG D.

AUTHOR: Angus McWilton

NOTES: In a small used bookstore in Southwest Texas, I found a yearbook. It was published in 1966 and once belonged to D., a junior at La Grange High School in Lake Charles, Louisiana. D. was a valued member of the La Grange "Mighty Gators" football and baseball teams, was voted Mr. Beau (for good looks and neat appearance), and was dating D. D., Miss Junior. The handwritten messages of his classmates in the back and front of the book show a gleaming and wonderful D., going places.

* With a call to 411 the author was given D.'s number in Lake Charles, Louisiana. When he called the number a woman answered. He asked for D. She said "Just a minute please," and returned asking who he was. The author stated his name and intentions and she said "No D. lives here." The author persisted with his inquiries but she continued to tell him that there was no D. there. He then called La Grange High School. They gave him D.'s address and phone number as of his graduation in 1967. The author tried this number and not surprisingly, no one there knew of D.

Autographs

I can't put down my feelings (in words) for La Grange. It has been such a wonderful year. The people are so wonderful too. I wish you all the luck in the world. You've b a great friend and I hope we c become better friends. Keep you great personality and Good Luck with

TO A GREAT guy AND Athlete.
RemeMBea At's Oue
GOOP Times Together.
GOOD LucK Wit It

To a real and cute guy great pers Remember E

[157]

D.,

I'm sort of at a loss for words right now, believe it or not! But I guess April 1, 1966, is the best place to begin. Remember that night? I'll never forget it and all of the fun we had. This last month has really been great! It seems like we've been dating ("going together") for more than a month, doesn't it? I assure you, I have enjoyed every day, every hour, every minute, and every second of it!

Congratulations on getting "Mr. Beau" again this year (you'll get it next year too!). That's a really wonderful honor, and you're a naturally wonderful person! You're really the easiest person in the world to get along with! You are kind, sweet, considerate, good-looking, thoughtful, understanding, sincere, loveable and mine (I hope!) Remember that!! (Please?)

D., you've got a lot of ability and very good potentials. You're a real athlete and an outstanding individual, both of which promote your being a great asset to La Grange Sr. High.

I sincerely hope that we continue dating for a very, very, very long time (even forever)! Even though you haven't taken me fishing or climbing trees, I still love ya! I guess we'll go one of these days, huh?

You know what? For two people who "fight" and "agree" all of the time, well—at least 3/4 of the time, we're really happy (at least, I am!!)! I've never enjoyed myself more!

Well—I can't find anymore words which express my feelings fully. It's hard to write down how you feel about someone, isn't it? But, I think you've gathered from what I've said that I do care a bunch, even more than I can say!!!

Best of luck to you next year + always, especially in football + baseball. God bless you and keep you! Love you! D. D.

P.S. Remember our fishing trip that we have to go one! Okay? You bet!!
P.S. This much [proceeded by a female stick figure with arms outstretched over entire page]

D.,

Well another year has past + it was pretty great. It wasn't as successful as our soph. yr. and our Sr. year is going to be the best ever. Both you + I know that for a fact.

It has really hard to express what your friendship has mean't to me these past 2 years. I know that our friendship will last forever. Although it is hard to point out some of our great memories; I can point out a few, such as, summer practice when we were sophs, (remember Vinton) those talks we had on all of the trips + that night we got to play against New Iberia. (you liked to have gotten killed because of me).

I remember when we came to this school, how big it was, + how everyone thought we were brothers because we acted so much alike. I suppose we really do because we both seem to understand each other better than anyone else can. Over the last 2 yrs. we have always remained friends. Sometimes we were real close ones. When I think of those times, I don't think of you as a close friend, but a brother.

We have one more year left at L.G. + we must make it the best ever. We have both felt the thrill of victory + the agony of defeat. We both know what we like the best. Lets really work hard this summer + become stronger, faster quicker, + more dedicated. This yr. we are the leaders, so lets be the best ever. I know all of this will come true because of you great competitive spirit.

I know we'll have great times this summer with baseball, fishing + maybe going to Houston. Good luck with D. D. (regardless of what you think, she does like you.)

Your friend always, W. B., #88

P.S. Remember next yr: say "Ball in middle rotate left on drop back Pass." Have a good "relationship" + don't do anything "turrible"

To a good athlete and fellow student: I hope we will remain friends for a long time.
R. L.

D.
To a real nice friend and buddy when I was one of the manager on the football. May you always be happy playing football. Best of Luck from a nutty professor
A. L.

To a cool friend of mine who good times I've had with,
R. M.

To one of the cutest and sweetest guys I know. Good luck,
J. B.

D.
Well D. I can't say how glad I am to have made you a good friend this year. I sorry + could not have known you sooner. I also might say I am very proud for you because you and D. D. make a swell pair. She's a swell (girl), so good luck.
Your friend M. W., cheerleader 67

D.,
I know I have a bad habit of getting on your nerves but I'll try in the future to be better. Good luck in everything D. and never change (exception-temper)
Love B. H.

Well, it's been a great year and I have enjoyed having class and playing ball with you. Good luck next year in football. I know ya'll go places
Friends always,
B. G., Sr. 66

D.
You really have a great personality (a funny one). If you use your abilities—I know you'll go far.
L. C.

To a real nice guy and great football player. Keep pitching those perfect games. Got to win state in baseball. Good luck in football next year. Oh yea, I wish I was as good looking as you are, Mr. Beau!!! Good luck with D. D.!
A friend
J. J.- You must get a chance with Lupo!

To a real sweet and cute guy with a great personality. Remember English III.
J. O.

D.

It really has been great knowing you (although I don't know you too awfully well). You are a wonderful boy and your friendship means more to me than I could ever express to you. Good luck throughout your remaining years.
J. C.

D.,

Lots of luck to a sweet guy. Remember the good ole days in English. Sr '66
Best wishes
C. L. B.

Dear D. —

We have had a lot of good times together and I know there are many more to come—don't drink too much water and good luck in football—
J. D.

D.,

I can't put down (in words) my feelings for La Grange. It has been such a wonderful year. The people are so wonderful too. I wish you all the best in the world. You've been a great friend and I hope we can become better friends. Keep your great personality and Good Luck with D. D. —
Love, L. M.

D.,

To a great guy and football player. Keep intercepting them passes.
T. C.

Congratulations D.,
I agree with the year book. Lots of luck. I wish we
were better friends.
P. M.

To a real good friend that has some faults like big
nose and lips but he makes up for it in many way
and I hope we will always be friends.
W. J.

D.
We may of had our differences but we will always
be friends. You are a hell of a F player and yall
will win state next yr. Good Luck in the future
and hope we will always be friends
Lots of Luck, Give Sulphur Hell
D. C. Sr. 66

To one of the greatest guys I have known!
Your friend
Always!
V. M.

To a great guy and athlete. Remember all our
good times together. Good luck with D. D. You've
got a good thing, which is understandable, MR.
BEAU
Your friend
J. H. (the virgin)

12

LIPSTICK

AUTHOR: Stacy Greene

NOTES: I was walking out of the 1991 Whitney Biennial opening, when my friend Rosie dropped her lipstick. I picked it up and unscrewed it for her. Rosie's lipstick excited me more than anything I had seen at the Whitney. Rosie's lipstick sparked my photographic career.

The most time consuming part of this series was finding the lipsticks. Most women embraced the idea, readily handing over their lipsticks; others could not part with them; others would unscrew their sticks, knowing they had incredible shapes and tease me by not giving them up. One woman proudly unscrewed her lipstick, which had a beautiful orange breast-like shape with a nipple in the middle. She refused to hand it over. It killed me. It was also a curious thing when women were embarrassed and apologetic because they thought their lipsticks too simple and boring.

Lisa

Ellen

Gwen

Victoria

Beth

Lisa

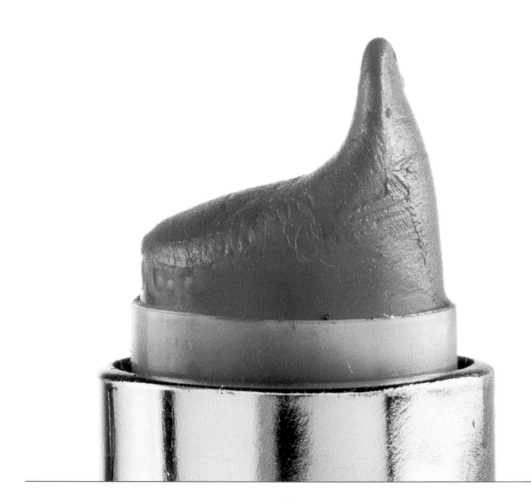

Simona

Roberta

Wendy

Jerelyn

13

CONTENTS OF POCKETBOOKS

AUTHOR: Maira Kalman

NOTES: In the eighteenth century the Countess Palavicini-Wenckheim carried on her person a simple small green silk purse. In it was the heart of her beloved husband Cosimo who had died of typhus while on their honeymoon. Suffice it to say, there is a great deal of mystery and romance in what one carries about. Possessions reveal some small and large truths about the owner. What, I do not know.

Ecuadorean finger puppet
Altoid mints
8 keys
Swiss Army knife with Babar face
pill container with:
2 Fiorinal for headaches, 3 Advil for pain, 1 Valium for
dentist visit
packet of pills from dentist (Nembutol)
cell phone
address book with 80 entries
3 yellow Post-it notes with names and numbers of downtown bars
4 pairs of reading glasses
1 pegboard hook
1 fountain pen
8 other pens
1 hair clip
1 book of Elephant Walk matches
4 bits of paper with phone numbers
2 notepads
driver's license
credit cards: Visa, American Express, Barneys
museum membership cards to:
the Whitney, P.S.1, the Guggenheim,
the Smithsonian, the Metropolitan
library card
medical insurance card
checkbook
baby pictures
Mac lipstick in Plastique
lip liner
Tampax
airline ticket stub
$47.00

1 *Fazzoletto* (hankie)
1 set of keys (use unknown)
1 packet of Bendix Bittermints

Sandra's Father
(wallet)

---

crumpled photo of wife
courtesy card from the Tropicana Hotel, Las Vegas

1 checkbook
photographs: a room, a house, a beach
datebook
Swiss Army knife
Minox camera
automatic pencil
red pen
regular pen
asthma spray
manicure set
broken clock
battery for broken clock
medical insurance card
Armani Exchange savings card
MetroCard
driver's license
Citibank card
American Express Gold card
$380.00
79¢
1 dried pomegranate

27 pencils
1 notebook
$40 (stolen)

Fidel Castro
(small leather shoulder bag)

---

2 combs
1 lucky monkey foot presented to
Fidel by Ernest Hemingway in 1960
absolutely no money
copy of *Lolita* by Vladimir Nabokov

4 eggs
1 bitterroot
1 pair of socks that need to be mended
1 single lilac glove
absolutely no money

Japanese Band-Aid
movie listings (*Times*) for *In The Mood For Love*
nail file
2 Lactate Tablets
9 twenty dollar bills
3 five dollar bills
2 singles
a poem:

I thought there could be
No more love left anywhere.
Whence then is come this love,
That has caught me now
And holds me in its grasp?

14

THE SKETCH ARTIST

AUTHOR: Lauren Redniss

NOTES: "I've seen it from the bottom to the top....
We've recovered secret service documents that some
agent was transporting, $10,000 cash, show dogs, you
name it. We've had items that a plastic surgeon was using
and left in a box of dry ice—earlobes and an eyebrow. You
don't forget that....We used to get a lot of false teeth but
we don't get too many any more. I guess the glue must be
getting better."

So Fred Chidester told me about life running the lost-
and-found at Grand Central Station. Not all of us have
$10,000 to lose—or even an extra earlobe for that matter
—nonetheless, loss is universal. The following is a record
of objects lost, but not forgotten.

CHARLES AARON GOLUB
VETERAN, CO-OWNER GREEN STREET MARKET
AGE: 86
LOST: US ARMY OVERSEAS CAP
WHEN: 1944
LAST SEEN: SALERNO, ITALY ON HEAD OF
           COMMANDING OFFICER

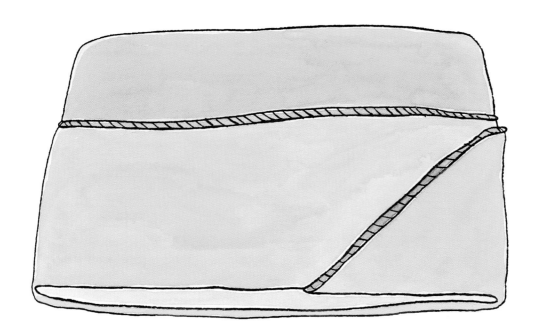

BORROWED BY SERGEANT WHO REPORTED:
"IT HAPPENED THIS WAY, CHARLIE. WE WERE
RIDING IN THE TRUCK, AND AS WE PASSED
A TREE WITH A LOW BRANCH, YOUR CAP
FLEW OFF."

LULU LOLO
PERFORMANCE ARTIST
AGE ?
LOST: SEWING SCISSORS FROM PARIS
WHEN: 1971
LAST SEEN: IN SUITCASE ON CAR ROOF HEADED
                  TO DETROIT

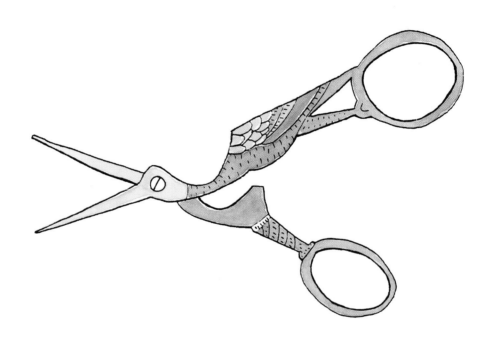

"OVER TIME I HAVE ALWAYS THOUGHT OF THOSE
SCISSORS. I HAVE SEEN OTHERS, BUT THEY
WERE NEVER THE SAME. I THINK WHAT I
LOST WAS MY TANGIBLE OBJECT OF THE
ROMANCE + EXCITEMENT I FELT IN PARIS"

JIMMY SUAREZ
EIGHTH GRADER
AGE 13
LOST: RING
WHEN: SUMMER VACATION 2000
LAST SEEN: BEACH IN THE DOMINICAN REBUPLIC

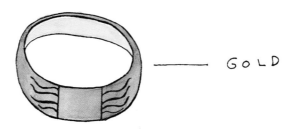 GOLD

"MY MOTHER SAID TO BE MORE CAREFUL NEXT TIME, BUT I THINK IT WASN'T MY FAULT."

YOUNG JOO NOH
ILLUSTRATOR
AGE: 27
LOST: HOME MADE DOLLHOUSE
WHEN: 1986
LAST SEEN: INCHON, KOREA

BOXES
MY MOTHER
THREW
AWAY →

"THINGS CHANGED WHEN I WENT TO JUNIOR HIGH SCHOOL. I HAD TO THINK ABOUT STUDY AND OLDER, REALISTIC STUFF. SO I GAVE IT TO MY COUSIN. BUT SHE DIDNT CARE SO MUCH."

MARTINE CORBIÈRE
DIRECTOR, FOREIGN EXCHANGE PROGRAMS
AGE: 53
LOST: MAN'S WRISTWATCH
WHEN: 1971
LAST SEEN: FALLING INTO THE OCEAN

"YOU KNOW, MY FATHER DIED WHEN I WAS EIGHT YEARS OLD. HE WAS AN ADORABLE MAN, BUT I KNEW HIM TOO LITTLE. HIS WATCH HAD BEEN LEFT IN THE CORNER OF AN ARMOIRE, LIKE A RELIC. ONE DAY, I POCKETED IT. IT WASN'T A FANCY WATCH, A LITTLE WORN, THE GLASS ALL STRATCHED, THE BAND MUCH TOO BIG FOR ME. BUT IT WAS MY FATHER'S WATCH, A SORT OF TALISMAN."

ALFRED "PATCHES" HAFFENDEN
VENDOR OF INCENSE, ESSENTIAL OILS + PARAPHENALIA
AGE : 52
LOST : WALLET
WHEN : SEPTEMBER 2000
LAST SEEN : AROUND THE HOUSE

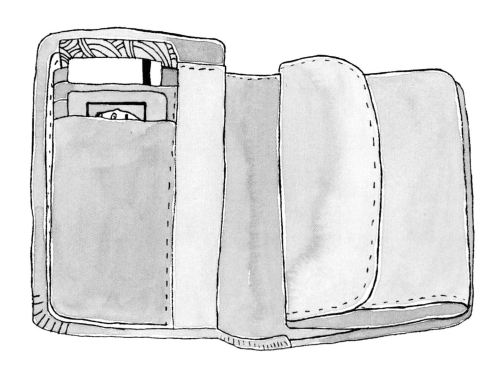

"IF ITS AROUND THE HOUSE, MAYBE
IT WILL TURN UP."

MEGAN STEWART THORNDIKE
PHOTOGRAPHER
AGE 29
LOST: GOLD LOCKET
WHEN: 1976
LAST SEEN: GRANDMOTHER'S HOUSE

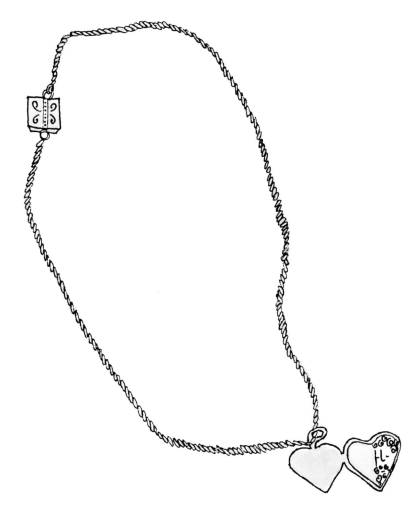

"MY FATHER IS A SCIENTIST AND USED TO LIVE IN
THE ARCTIC. IN THE PICTURE HE HAD A FROZEN-UP
BEARD."

COLIN McGRATH

MUSICIAN
AGE: 28
LOST: COMPUTER CIRCA 1984
WHEN: SPRING 1993
LAST SEEN: COLLEGE DORM ROOM

— AN UNLIKELY ITEM TO LOSE

" IT WAS AN OLD MAC MY FRIEND WILL HAD GIVEN ME, SLOW AS COLD HONEY. HE HAD GOTTEN A BETTER ONE AND IT STILL HAD SOME OF HIS OLD JOURNAL ENTRIES ON IT, WHICH I HAD TO DO MY BEST NOT TO READ. "

FRED CHIDESTER

DIRECTOR, LOST + FOUND, CUSTOMER SERVICE DEPARTMENT
    GRAND CENTRAL STATION
LOST: BRAND NEW BOOTS
WHEN: FIRST DAY OF NEW JOB, 1964
LAST SEEN: METRO NORTH TRAIN, NEW HAVEN LINE

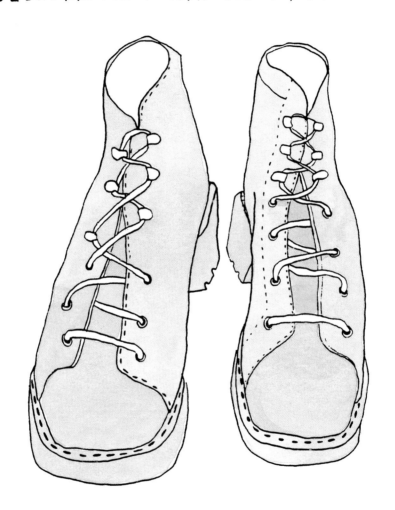

"THEY WERE STILL IN THE BOX. NEVER WORE 'EM.
IT WASN'T SO PAINFUL TO LOSE THE BOOTS, IT
WAS PAINFUL TO TELL MY WIFE. SHE HAD
SACRIFICED TO GET THEM."

15

MARCH 24, 2000

AUTHOR: Angela Reichers

NOTES: "The hardest thing to see is what is in front of your eyes."—Goethe

PANTONE®
131 C

toast
7:15am

PANTONE®
511 C

blackberry jam
7:18am

PANTONE®
465 C

café au lait
7:20am

PANTONE®
109 C

mango
7:30am

PANTONE®
216 C

del rio lipstick
8:18am

PANTONE®
5743 C

coat
8:22am

PANTONE®
293 C

B 67 bus
8:26am

PANTONE®
151 C

son's classroom
9:10am

PANTONE®
354 C

#6 train
9:28am

PANTONE®
160 C

tea
9:47am

PANTONE®
128 C

banana
9:55am

PANTONE®
327 C

computer
10:05am

PANTONE®
Warm Gray 3 C

phone
10:08am

PANTONE®
1795 C

tomato soup
1:18pm

PANTONE®
390 C

avocado salad
1:42pm

PANTONE®
279 C

friend's shirt
2:20pm

PANTONE®
4625 C

espresso
4:33pm

PANTONE®
116 C

taxi
6:55pm

PANTONE®
2655 C

crocuses
7:18pm

PANTONE®
5635 C

husband's eyes
10:08pm

16

RECYCLED PAPER

AUTHOR: John Willis

NOTES: Not too far from my home in the mountains of New England there is a paper mill nestled down by the river, in an otherwise pristine vista of forested mountains. The steam rises from the stacks day and night.

There is a platform just outside the mill that spans over two acres of land. It is covered with bales of bound paper scraps delivered for recycling, which the mill will turn into reams of tissue paper. As the winds kick up, sending shreds of paper whirling in the air, the mill workers pick through the bales finding the appropriate ones to add to the paper mix, while continually replacing them with newly arrived bales.

The variety of images one can find in these bales by searching through the random placement of paper scraps continues to amaze me.

The following photographs were originally taken in a 7 x 7" format. Due to the dimensions of *Speck*, approximately 1" was cropped from each image.

17

THE RED BALLOON (PART II)

NOTES: We patiently waited for a response from our dispatched red balloon (see Part 1). Four months and twenty-two days later, this letter arrived from Miranda and Thea Lewis, Atlanta, Georgia.

Dear Speck,
On the night of the equinox,
we left out food for the fairies.

We carefully prepared a
delicous feast consisting of
apples with cinnamon, a special
herb drink and dried fruits. When
we wokeup imagine our
suprise when we saw your balloon
in its place! The night before
↓
Love,
igotmorning
Miranda and Thea Lewis

THE CONTRIBUTORS

Ron Barrett is an illustrator of the children's classic *Cloudy With a Chance of Meatballs* and looks for "Inspected By…" tags in New York City.

Shannon Fagan is a photographer in New York City.

Jesse Gordon is a filmmaker who lives in Brooklyn, NY.

Stacy Greene is a photographer, painter, and filmmaker who lives in Brooklyn, NY.

Steven Guarnaccia is an illustrator and designer who, never mind the forest, can't even see the trees, because he's too busy looking at the leaves.

Cyrus Habib currently attends Columbia University. After college, Cyrus' plans include law school, travel abroad, and pianistic explorations.

Grant Heaps lives in Toronto in a self-created museum of junk.

David Horowitz studied sociology at Florida State, has travelled and lived in the Middle East, and now lives in New York City with his wife and two children.

Maira Kalman is a children's book author and illustrator.

Knickerbocker, a.k.a. Nicholas Blechman, is principal of Knickerbocker Design in New York City. With Christoph Niemann, he co-publishes *One Hundred Percent*, a drawing project.

Meaghan Kombol received her degree from Washington State University. In 1998 she drove from Seattle to New York City and in eight hours got a job at M&Co. where she still works (to her heart's content).

Robert Lemons lives in New York City and practices law in his spare time.

Angus McWilton is alive and well.

Phil Milstein is compiling a book based on excerpts of anti-masturbation literature throughout the ages. He is the founder and curator of the American Song-Poem Music Archives.

Ian Phillips is a Toronto-based illustrator.

Lauren Redniss is blind in one eye.

Angela Richers is the Art Director of *Harper's Magazine*. She lives in Brooklyn, NY.

Wade Shuman is a painter, musician, and teacher, who lives in New York City. At the moment he has one cat (Sophie) with better than average whiskers.

Eddie Simon is a retired barber who lives in Philadelphia.

Dan Taylor is usually looking for something to do and takes pictures along the way.

Richard Torchia is an artist and director of the Beaver College Art Gallery, Glenside, Pennsylvania.

Mark Ulriksen is an illustrator and artist living in San Francisco. He is a frequent contributor to the *New Yorker* magazine.

Amy Unikewicz is a typophile and trash fancier with a penchant for experimental alphabets and rusting ice machines.

John Willis teaches photography at Marlboro College in Vermont.

Adam Yates is an artist based in New York City.

NAME: Chan Man Choi
AGE: 21

NAME: Tse Kwok Fun
AGE: 29

NAME: Tsui Hong Por
AGE: 25

NAME: Wu Man
AGE: 38

Speck was printed in Shen Zhen Shi, China, at the Prosperous Printing Company. Before it went to press, disposable cameras were sent to the printing plant where those who would eventually be involved in the printing of this book kindly volunteered their portraits to be documented. We would like to thank the workers at the Prosperous Printing Company and all those involved in the actual production of this book.

ACKNOWLEDGMENTS

To all the *Speck* contributors: for their willingness to volunteer their time and brilliant work.

Hats off to Maira Kalman who pushed things to a place that never seemed possible. Without Maira, *Speck* would never, ever, (ever^9) have made it.

Without Steve Heller, *Speck* would be gathering dust in the pages of a portfolio. He started it all.

To Meaghan Kombol and her devotion and patience for—what was so often—such a dubious cause. This would have been a disaster without her.

Steven Guarnaccia was the catalyst. He was the one who unveiled the infinite beauty of small things.

To everyone who helped along the way and to those who have stood closely by: Michael Beirut, Nicholas Blechman, Clare Jacobson, Robert Lemons, Kevin Lippert, Dan Nadel, Lita Talarico, and Dan Taylor.

To my sister and to supportive parents everywhere (especially mine).

— *PBS, Brooklyn*

THE SCRIBBLES

COVER
MANUFACTURER: Bic, U.S.A.
MODEL: Cristal Grip
ORIGIN: Staples, 34th St. and 6th Ave.

PP. 10
MANUFACTURER: Paper Mate, U.S.A.
MODEL: Eraser Mate
ORIGIN: Borrowed from man selling hot
dogs on the Staten Island ferry
sometime ago

PP. 60
MANUFACTURER: Bic, France
MODEL: 4 Color ballpoint
ORIGIN: found in bottom of pen drawer

PP. 160
MANUFACTURER: Stick Tite, Taiwan
MODEL: Replacement Security
ORIGIN: Citibank, 7th Ave., Brooklyn

PP. 175
MANUFACTURER: Paper Mate, U.S.A.
MODEL: Dynagrip (chewed)
ORIGIN: found in jacket after night out

PP. 208
MANUFACTURER: Itoya, Korea
MODEL: Gripper
ORIGIN: gift from blind man on D train

Princeton Architectural Press
37 East Seventh Street
New York, NY 10003

For a free catalog of books, call
800.722.6657
Visit our website at www.papress.com

Editor: Jennifer N. Thompson

Special thanks to Nettie Aljian, Ann
Alter, Amanda Atkins, Nicola Bednarek,
Janet Behning, Megan Carey, Penny
Chu, Jan Cigliano, Tom Hutten, Jane
Garvie, Clare Jacobson, Mark Lamster,
Nancy Eklund Later, Linda Lee, Anne
Nitschke, Lottchen Shivers, and Deb
Wood of Princeton Architectural Press
—Kevin C. Lippert, publisher

Printed and bound in China

Library of Congress
Cataloging-in-Publication Data

Buchanan-Smith, Peter Gordon.
    Speck : a curious collection of uncom-
mon things / Peter Gordon
Buchanan-Smith.– 1st ed.
      p. cm.
    ISBN 1-56898-297-6 (alk. paper)
    1. Design–United States–History–20th
century.   I. Title.
    NK1404 .B83 2001
    745.4–dc21
                                    2001002301

Rombauer, Irma S., Marion Rombauer Becker and Ethan Becker. Laura Hartman Maestro, illus. THE JOY OF COOKING, revised. New York: Scribner, 1997.

THE ENDPAPERS

AUTHOR: Steven Guarnaccia

NOTES: My epiphany came while I was lying on my back in exercise class, looking at the bottoms of the exercise shoes/running shoes/sneakers (I do not even know what you call these things anymore—until I started the class, the last pair of sportive foot coverings I had were Jack Purcells which, not incidentally, have a totally flat, totally smooth, totally devoid-of-any-typographic-features sole) on my fellow classmates, all on their backs also.

What I noticed was that each pair of shoes had its own unique sole design, and in this room of thirty-odd people, no two were alike. Which started me thinking, who designs the sole? Is everyone's sneaker-sole design in the universe different? Are these the shoe's fingerprint? And does anyone buy their shoes for the sole design (as I assume they do for the design of the upper and the logo on the flank)?

I did not get answers, but I did begin to collect (mostly from my students) running shoe sole designs by asking people to make rubbings of their soles. Another question I left unanswered was: when did everybody start wearing running shoes? That question will have to molder in the closet along with: when did everybody start wearing baseball caps and when did we all suddenly think it was okay to spend $2.50 for a cup of coffee and $500 for a pair of eyeglasses?

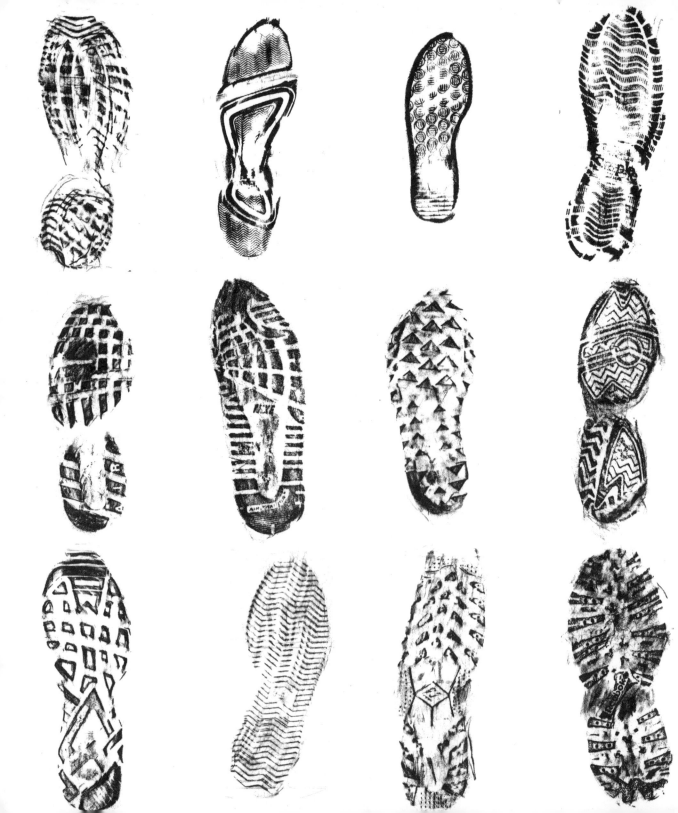

LE VENT DANS LES OREILLES!

Catalogage avant publication de Bibliothèque et Archives Canada

Brochu, Yvon

    Galoche le vent dans les oreilles!

    (Galoche; 5)
    Pour les jeunes de 8 à 12 ans.

    ISBN 2-89591-015-4

    I. Lemelin, David. II. Titre. III. Collection: Brochu, Yvon.
Galoche; 5.

PS8553.R6G345 2005   jC843'.54   C2005-940899-5
PS9553.R6G345 2005

Tous droits réservés
Dépôts légaux: 3e trimestre 2005
Bibliothèque nationale du Québec
Bibliothèque nationale du Canada
ISBN 2-89591-015-4

© 2005 Les éditions FouLire inc.
4339, rue des Bécassines
Charlesbourg (Québec) G1G 1V5
CANADA
Téléphone: (418) 628-4029
Sans frais depuis l'Amérique du Nord: 1 877 628-4029
Télécopie: (418) 628-4801
info@foulire.com

Gouvernement du Québec – Programme de crédit d'impôt
pour l'édition de livres – gestion SODEC.

LE VENT DANS LES OREILLES!

YVON BROCHU

Illustrations
David Lemelin

ÉDITIONS
FouLire

*Le premier principe
de fierté canine…
ne jamais donner
sa langue au chat!*

*N'oublie pas qu'il me fait toujours plaisir
de t'accueillir dans ma cyberniche.
www.galoche.ca*

La Famille Meloche

ÉLOÏSE LA GRANDE DIVA

MARILOU LA TRISTE SOUS-MINISTRE

FABIEN UN BIEN BON GARS

SÉBASTIEN MONSIEUR-JE-SAIS-TOUT

MOI GALOCHE SUPERCABOCHE

ÉMILIE MA DOUCE

UN VENT DE DÉTRESSE

Grand branle-bas dans la maison des Meloche !

– Toi, vieille sacoche, débarrasse !

Marilou fonce vers moi. La sous-ministre transporte une boîte de rapports remplie à ras bord. Un vrai mastodonte ! Je freine. Mes coussinets crissent sur le plancher de bois franc du corridor. Si la mère d'Émilie trébuche, elle se fracture les côtes et m'envoie *ipso canino* à la maison des chiens perdus.

Marilou est sur les nerfs : demain matin, elle quitte la maison pour un congrès international sur les arts, congrès qu'elle organise pour sa ministre.

– Maman! hurle Éloïse, dans sa chambre. Je ne trouve plus ma robe de Cléopâtre!

La sœur aînée d'Émilie est sur les nerfs: ce soir, elle part en tournée avec sa nouvelle troupe de théâtre, dans une roulotte.

– Maman?!... tempête à son tour Sébastien, au pied de l'escalier. Quelqu'un a volé mes éprouvettes!

Monsieur-je-sais-tout est sur les nerfs: comme chaque été, le frère d'Émilie va dans un camp de vacances scientifique. Son autobus quitte la ville dans moins d'une heure.

Trois hystériques!

Et moi, Galoche, suis-je sur les nerfs? Pas du tout! Bien sûr, depuis tout à l'heure, dans le corridor, je plonge à bâbord, à tribord, bref de tous les bords pour éviter la mort. Mais vont-ils me rendre fou?... Pas du tout!

Si je suis fou, c'est de joie! Imagine: je vais passer quelques jours seul à la maison en compagnie de mes deux plus grands amis: ma douce Émilie et son gros et grand barbu de père. Le paradis!

– Enlève-toi de mon chemin! crie le mastodonte, qui se rapproche dange- reusement de moi. Es-tu sourd, vieille chaussette?

IVG! Improvise vite, Galoche!...

Avec pareille fa- mille de fous, je suis passé maître dans

l'art d'im-
proviser, foi de
Galoche! Toutes griffes
dehors, je fais volte-museau
et m'élance vers l'escalier. Je
passe devant la chambre d'Éloïse, dont la
porte est grande ouverte.

– Maman, gémit la diva, nous allons
présenter *Heureux qui comme Ulysse a fait
un beau voyage*. Pourrais-tu me repasser
ma chasuble de la déesse Athéna?

Une ombre plane soudain au-dessus
de ma tête. Misère à poil ! La chasuble…
Éloïse l'a lancée dans le corridor, juste
au-dessus de moi. J'accélère ma course.
Le haut de l'escalier est tout près.

AOUUUH!!!

Trop tard: le trou noir. La chasuble
me tombe dessus. Et… horreur! impossible d'arrêter ma course. BOUM! Je
commence à débouler l'escalier. BOUM,
BOUM!

– Mamaaaaan? s'énerve Sébastien, tout en bas des marches. Mes éprouvettes!...

Monsieur-je-sais-tout n'en a que pour ses éprouvettes alors que moi, pauvre chien emprisonné dans les grands plis bleu ciel de la déesse Athéna... BOUM, BOUM, BOUM!... je déboule l'escalier. Une vraie boule de quilles. BOUM, BOUM, BOUM, BOUM!

Bien que nous, les chiens, ayons une souplesse et un sang-froid que les humains n'ont pas pour ce genre de dégringolade... BOOOUM!!!... après un dur atterrissage juste aux pieds de Sébastien, je sens encore mes os s'entrechoquer. Un vibraphone sur quatre pattes. Je l'avoue : je suis plutôt sonné.

Le frère d'Émilie lance sur un ton moqueur :

– Heureux qui comme Galoche a fait un beau voyage ! Hi, hi, hi, hi...

Brillant, mais mal élevé, ce Sébastien!

L'idée de lui mordre une fesse effleure mon esprit, mais les pas et la voix de Marilou, la déesse de la foudre, retentissent juste derrière moi:

– Encore toi, Galoche!? Quelle sangsue!... Veux-tu bien te tasser!

Toujours empêtré sous la divine chasuble d'Athéna, je tente de m'en extirper.

– Mais grouille, grosse nouille!

Bon, d'accord, j'ai peut-être la bouille en mauvais état; mais de là à la comparer à une nouille...

– Quelle andouille!

Elle exagère, la sous-ministre! Pas facile de se dépêtrer là-dessous quand on a quatre pattes. J'aimerais bien la voir à ma place, la Marilou.

– Et toi, «traîneux», fustige-t-elle maintenant Monsieur-je-sais-tout, j'ai assez de problèmes avec mon congrès et ma ministre! Alors, laisse-moi tranquille avec tes damnées éprouvettes!

«Les éprouvettes! Bien sûr! Quelle idée géniale!»

Je réussis de peine et de misère à me dégager de la chasuble et à m'éloigner en douce, laissant la mère et le fils se disputer. Ouille! Je titube. J'ai les muscles tendus et le museau bas. Je traîne de la patte. Mes oreilles balaient le plancher. Pour la première fois de ma vie, j'ai l'impression de me déplacer dans le corps d'un basset (un basset, oui; surtout pas un *chien-saucisse,* une autre horreur du langage humain à l'endroit de la race canine!).

W-ouf! Peu à peu, je retrouve mes moyens. Je me mets à trottiner vers la chambre-capharnaüm du grand «bolé». Avec mon pif légendaire, en un tour de patte, je trouve les éprouvettes dans un recoin de la penderie, sous une montagne de vêtements. Excité, je me glisse en vitesse hors de la maison, la boîte d'éprouvettes dans la gueule. Quelques secondes plus tard, je suis près de la haie, en train de creuser un trou pour les y cacher. Tout à coup, entre un coup de museau et un coup de patte, j'entends :

– Qu'est-ce que tu fais là, Galoche ?

Émilie et Fabien !?... Misère à poil ! C'est ce qui s'appelle se faire prendre la patte dans le sac... Quel os ! Le museau levé, encore tout glaiseux, je subis un interrogatoire serré.

– Serais-tu en train de cacher les éprouvettes de Sébas, Galoche ? me demande Émilie.

Je regarde ma Douce dans les yeux... une seconde.

– N'a-t-il pas un autobus à prendre dans quelques minutes pour se rendre à son camp scientifique ?

Mes yeux trottinent entre Fabien, le ciel, la haie et mon Émilie.

– Tu as raison, Mimi, intervient le père d'Émilie. Et pour Sébastien, partir à son camp sans ses fameuses éprouvettes, c'est pire que de partir sans ses « bobettes ». Pas vrai, Galoche ?

Je prends mon air le plus innocent. Rien n'y fait.

– Tu devrais avoir honte, Galoche ! Faire ça à Sébastien ; toi, un si gentil chien-chien.

– Oui ! Toi, un boooon chien ! de renchérir le gros et grand barbu de père d'Émilie. Un bon chien qui va aller reporter les éprouvettes à Sébastien...

– À moins que tu veuilles que Sébas reste avec nous ? Sans éprouvettes, pas de camp pour lui, c'est certain.

Ils ont bien raison : pas question d'avoir Monsieur-je-sais-tout dans les pattes. J'ai beau être une supercaboche, je n'avais pas pensé à ça ! Je me précipite dans la maison, dépose les éprouvettes au pied de l'escalier. Sébastien et Marilou se disputent toujours. Ils s'arrêtent et me regardent, sans parvenir à me dire

«Merci» ni l'un ni l'autre. Puis, ils poursuivent leur engueulade. Je retourne vite dehors et me retrouve face à mes deux amis.

Je suis tout piteux.

Émilie et Fabien se regardent un moment. Quel n'est pas mon étonnement de les voir éclater de rire tout à coup. Ah! ces deux-là: deux beaux moineaux difficiles à suivre!

– Ne te mets pas dans tous tes états, mon beau! intervient ma Douce. On ne va pas te gronder... et puis on a une grande nouvelle à t'annoncer.

– Ça, oui! Une nouvelle géniale, Galoche!

– Essaie de deviner? lance Émilie, rayonnante.

Aussitôt, de belles images s'imposent dans ma supercaboche. Des images qui pourraient devenir réalité au cours des prochains jours que nous passerons seuls à la maison, tous les trois: crêpes baignant dans le sirop d'érable, longues promenades au parc dans les allées fleuries, parties de soccer endiablées où je me surpasserai dans les buts avec une petite récompense à la fin – deux jolies boules de crème glacée sur un petit cornet sucré –, sieste mi-ombre, mi-soleil le midi sous le parasol avec jus exotiques pleins de ces cerises rouges qu'Émilie aime tant... Bref, j'en ai les babines frémissantes et le cœur gonflé de plaisir !

– Es-tu bien assis, Galoche ?

Très bien, merci ! Mais arrêtez de me faire languir ainsi, misère à poil : je vais y laisser ma fourrure. Jappez-moi le morceau, mes deux moineaux !

– Mon beau, commence Émilie...

Elle et son père se lancent alors un regard pétillant de complicité et s'exclament d'une seule voix :

– ON PART EN VOYAGE !

Je tombe sur le dos. Renversé, atterré, débobiné, je me rappelle aussitôt notre dernier voyage, l'hiver passé.

– Voyons, Galoche, qu'y a-t-il?

Je ne bouge plus. Pas même d'un poil. Émilie se retourne vers Fabien et dit:

– Il a l'air d'un vrai zombie, papa!... Il est peut-être malade?

Oui, je suis malade.

Les humains et leur manie de toujours partir en voyage me rendent malade. Toute l'année durant, Fabien m'écorche les oreilles: il faut rénover la maison, améliorer notre environnement. Et pourtant, dès qu'il a des vacances, pas question de profiter de toutes ces belles choses qu'il a faites. Il ne pense qu'à partir en VOYAGE. En canot, en auto, en moto, en planche à voile ou à roulettes, alouette… pas moyen de l'arrêter. Courir vers l'imprévu, les problèmes, le stress.

Ahhh! Pourquoi les humains ne sont-ils pas davantage comme nous, les chiens: *pattouflards*? On est si bien à la maison…

Le voyage est une maladie typiquement humaine. Et, comme j'ai pu le constater souvent, une maladie qui transforme les «deux pattes» en grands bébés:

- Un petit trou d'eau et un terrain sablonneux, et oups! les voilà qui se promènent la bedaine à l'air, riant comme des enfants dans une barboteuse;
- Une statue sans tête ou un vieux bâtiment qui s'écroule, et oups! les voilà qui s'émerveillent comme de petits enfants devant un joli mobile musical;
- Une colline, quelques arbres, un plan d'eau, et oups! les voilà qui s'amusent

à grimper, à courir, à plonger, inconscients comme des enfants dans un parc d'amusement.

Et la liste de comportements étranges en voyage pourrait s'allonger ainsi presque indéfiniment selon les observations faites depuis mon arrivée chez les Meloche.

Les humains disent que «les voyages forment la jeunesse». Moi, Galoche, je dirais plutôt que «les voyages déforment les humains». Et je ne parle pas à travers les poils de mon toupet! L'hiver dernier, j'ai encore été le témoin privilégié d'un voyage plutôt épuisant. Et cela a commencé exactement comme il y a un instant. Mes deux beaux moineaux devaient m'annoncer «une grande nouvelle», disaient-ils.

Revis avec moi ce fameux voyage hivernal et tu comprendras pourquoi l'idée d'un autre départ avec Fabien et ma Douce me stresse à ce point...

UN VENT DE FOLIE

Brrrrrrrr! Je suis glacé d'effroi. Rien à voir avec le froid intense qui sévit dehors ni avec la neige qui n'arrête plus de tomber en ce mois de février, misère à poil!

– Toi, le chien, t'as besoin de te tenir tranquille.

– Et de ne pas gémir d'ennui la nuit.

– Et ne t'attends pas à ce que je te fasse des crêpes comme Fabien.

Je suis assis bien droit au milieu du salon et trois humains désespérés me tombent dessus à pattes raccourcies: Marilou, Éloïse et Sébastien. Ils vont devoir me garder quelques jours, car Émilie et Fabien partent demain matin pour un camp de neige organisé par l'école. Et impossible de m'emmener.

Malgré mon aversion pour les voyages, j'aurais préféré partir avec eux plutôt que de rester à la maison, foi de Galoche!

– Vraiment, comme projet éducatif, ils auraient pu penser à autre chose, tempête Monsieur-je-sais-tout.

– Un camp de neige pour faire de l'activité physique… ils auraient pu utiliser le gymnase de l'école au lieu de s'en aller au diable vauvert, renchérit la diva.

– Ils auraient pu emmener cette vieille sacoche: regardez son gros bedon. L'exercice ne lui aurait pas fait de tort, rage la mère d'Émilie.

Un trio vraiment pas rigolo! Je me demande bien comment je vais faire pour passer quelques jours à la merci des caprices de ces trois têtes de pioche de Meloche?

Et puis, me faire ainsi traiter d'obèse par la sous-ministre Marilou, ce n'est rien pour me faire desserrer les crocs...

BANG! La porte d'entrée frappe durement le mur. Mon cœur se transforme en yoyo. Une rafale de vent et de neige s'engouffre dans la maison et vient refroidir les ardeurs du trio au salon. Avant que Marilou ne puisse ouvrir la bouche, Émilie bondit près de nous. Le visage tout blanc sous son immense capuchon, elle lance:

– Galoche, tu pars en voyage!

Je rêve ou quoi? Fabien et ma Douce m'ont expliqué, à plusieurs reprises, que les règlements de l'école défendaient à

tout animal de faire partie d'un camp de neige.

– Émilie, tes bottes…, fait Marilou d'une voix étrangement douce, avant d'ajouter : Tu es bien sûre, ma chouette ? Galoche peut vous accompagner ?

Émilie explique que Fabien, le président du comité organisateur, a convaincu tout le monde de me laisser faire partie de la grande expédition.

Derrière Émilie se profile le visage de l'abominable homme des neiges. La barbe de Fabien est toute gelée, comme s'il avait passé des heures au congélateur. Il confirme la nouvelle et, à chaque mot prononcé, de tout petits glaçons argentés éclatent sur le plancher, sans qu'une seule réprimande de Marilou ne vienne ternir ces douces nouvelles.

Je ne rêve donc pas ?

– … et je les ai convaincus. Mais c'est grâce à l'idée géniale d'Émilie que j'ai pu amadouer le comité de parents, précise

Fabien, dont le visage craque de partout, maintenant.

Ah, Émilie! Quelle grande amie!

– Oui, acquiesce-t-elle en se tournant vers moi. Galoche, tu as été nommé la mascotte de notre camp de neige.

Mascotte?

– Bravo! s'exclame une Marilou soulagée, qui retrouve vite son air et son ton de sous-ministre : Vous deux, vos bottes! Vite, dans le vestibule! Vous êtes en train d'inonder le plancher. Où est-ce que vous avez la tête? Si ça continue, on va devoir nager.

Moi, Galoche, je nage dans le bonheur.

Puis, une toute petite question se met soudain à trotter dans ma supercaboche : une mascotte, c'est quoi? Et ça fait quoi, une mascotte?

L'autobus jaune file à vive allure... et moi, je file un mauvais coton.

À l'avant, Fabien est en grande conversation avec Émilie, son amie Sophie et la grande sœur de celle-ci, Marie-Ève, notre animatrice, qui a 16 ans. Ils parlent fort, rient et s'amusent; vraiment, ils m'ont abandonné à mon triste sort.

Tout au fond, et depuis un bon moment, je me promène dans de véritables montagnes russes. Non pas à cause d'une route cahoteuse ou d'un autobus en train de tomber en ruine, mais bien à cause de mon fameux statut de «mascotte».

– Bouh!... Maxime, attrape le gros toutou!

Et je m'envole, tel un ballon de football.

– Oups! Salut, Galoche!... Tu trembles comme une feuille. Mais t'es bien peureux! Vincent? Regarde comme elle a de beaux yeux pochés, notre mascotte! On dirait un raton laveur.

Le vent dans les oreilles, je repars de plus belle au-dessus des têtes. Je retombe durement sur des genoux peu accueillants.

– Que t'es doux! On dirait la fourrure d'un ours. Est-ce que tu sers de tapis pour Émilie?... Ha, ha, ha!

Pour Émilie, la mascotte est un leader. Un rassembleur. Un amuseur public. C'est ce qu'elle m'a expliqué, hier soir, dans le lit. Mais ici, dans le dernier banc de l'autobus, une «mascotte» n'a d'autre signification qu'une vieille peluche qu'on se renvoie comme un ballon et avec laquelle on s'amuse en public...

Pourtant, il me suffirait d'un seul petit coup de crocs sur le bout du nez de chacun pour rabattre le caquet de ces garnements. Mais j'écarte cette idée. Je causerais trop de tort à Fabien, l'organisateur, ainsi qu'à Émilie.

Pendant que Vincent s'amuse à mes dépens, j'essaie de me raisonner: «Galoche, ce n'est pas pire que d'être resté coincé avec Marilou, Éloïse et Sébastien.»

– Est-ce que tu parles, toi? demande le garçon en me secouant comme une pauvre marionnette.

– HÉ! C'est pas un jouet; c'est un chien.

Pierre-Luc! Je suis rassuré. Notre jeune voisin, amoureux d'Émilie, n'est pas très fort ni habile, mais il est courageux comme dix. Et il m'aime bien. Surtout que je suis son meilleur allié pour qu'il parvienne à séduire ma Douce.

– De quoi tu te mêles, le roseau? demande Vincent, qui se lève et fait face à Pierre-Luc. C'est notre mascotte, non?

– Oui, mais c'est aussi un vrai chien.

Vincent me soulève à bout de bras. Je reste mou comme de la guenille pour éviter la chute sur le plancher de l'autobus.

– Quoi? Un vrai chien…

Il m'agite avant d'ajouter, sur un ton moqueur:

– Ça, un chien?

Trop, c'est trop! IVG!

– Ouache! Il a pissé! hurle le grand comique tandis qu'une coulée de petits critaux dorés se met à serpenter sur son beau chandail blanc.

– Oui, un vrai chien! s'amuse Pierre-Luc qui me prend vite dans ses bras, alors que tout le monde autour, même les amis du grand comique, n'en finissent plus de rire.

Un vrai amuseur public !

Foi de Galoche, je commence à mieux saisir mon rôle de mascotte… et même à lui trouver des côtés intéressants.

L'autobus jaune file toujours à vive allure; au fond, Vincent, tout blanc, file à son tour un mauvais coton et moi, Galoche, je suis de bien meilleur poil…

Je suis assis avec Pierre-Luc, à l'avant, dans le second banc; juste devant se trouvent ma douce Émilie et Sophie, une amie de sa classe. Je n'aurais pas cru qu'un simple pipi puisse me transformer en vedette, mais c'est le cas ! Je n'ai jamais reçu autant de douces caresses ni de beaux compliments. Vraiment, les humains ne cessent de me surprendre.

– Galoche, me chuchote Pierre-Luc à l'oreille, j'ai encore besoin d'un coup de pouce!

Je tourne la tête. Les yeux de notre jeune voisin brillent d'amour et d'espoir. Il ajoute d'un air suppliant:

– Je sens que cette fois, en vacances, avec la neige, dans un beau paysage d'hiver, ça va marcher.

Quel romantique, ce Pierre-Luc! Et quelle tête dure: il n'arrêtera jamais de faire la cour à ma Douce. Et moi, je n'arrêterai sûrement pas de l'aider.

– Merci, Galoche.

Eh oui! Mon regard lui fait comprendre que je viens de succomber. Je suis sensible aux beaux sentiments humains, qui sont si rares... Je peux les compter sur le bout de mes griffes.

W-ouf! Quelles vacances mouvementées en perspective!

– Attention, tout le monde! Aaaaaattention!!!

Projetée par un porte-voix, la voix de l'animatrice me fait bondir sur le siège. Marie-Ève, la grande sœur de Sophie, se tient debout, tout près du chauffeur. C'est elle, m'a dit Émilie, qui a suggéré l'Auberge du lac Dégelé, où nous allons.

Notre animatrice obtient rapidement le silence et s'écrie:

– Êtes-vous d'accord pour chanter un peu?

Un long et assourdissant «Oui!» fait vibrer les vitres de l'auto-bus ainsi que mes pauvres tympans. Deux jeunes distri-buent une feuille à chaque vacan-cier et viennent retrouver l'animatrice.

– Mes acolytes, Jonathan et Marie-Claude, ont composé une chanson facile à retenir: une chanson dédiée à notre mascotte GALOCHE!

Une chanson pour moi!? Flatté, je me redresse sur mon siège alors qu'on se prépare à chanter mon hymne.

– Attention! Je vous chante le premier couplet et...

– Ne t'en fais pas, Galoche, c'est juste pour rire! me lance Émilie. Ne prends pas ça au sérieux, mon beau.

Je n'ai pas le temps de comprendre pourquoi ma Douce semble mal à l'aise; déjà j'entends la voix puissante de l'animatrice entonner:

♪♪ *Galoche a l'air poche, poche, poche*
Mais il n'a rien d'une cloche, cloche, cloche
Sauf s'il fait sa tête de pioche,
pioche, pioche... ♪♪

Je tombe des nues.

C'est la frénésie dans l'autobus: à l'unisson, les jeunes chantent, hurlent et

massacrent la chan-
son. Je voudrais me
boucher les oreilles;
mais c'est difficile,
dans mon cas.

Et Marie-Ève d'enchaîner:

♪♪ *Malgré sa faible cote, cote, cote*
Et son petit air crotte, crotte, crotte
Galoche est notre mascotte, cotte, cotte! ♪♪

Cote, cote, cote! Misère à poil, je me sens comme une poule en cage. Mais le poulailler jaune roulant, lui, est en liesse. On n'en finit plus de reprendre la chanson, avec des élans *crescendo*, des rires *fortissimo* et des farces *allegretto*.

– Une dernière fois! lance Marie-Ève, heureuse du succès fou et de l'ambiance extraordinairement détendue.

Moi, Galoche, je suis bien d'accord pour jouer la mascotte jusqu'au bout et «amuser en public», mais mon ego canin en prend un rude coup, juré, jappé! La chanson et la poésie, c'est ce que les humains ont inventé de plus beau. Mais là, quelles rimes! Quel crime!

Pourtant, un massacre encore pire allait bientôt se produire...

Les portes métalliques de l'autobus infernal grincent et s'ouvrent enfin. Sitôt le museau dehors, je prends la poudre *d'escampatte.*

– Galoche, où cours-tu comme ça?

La mascotte-cotte-cotte a besoin d'air, misère à poil!

Je laisse derrière moi Émilie, Fabien, Pierre-Luc et tout ce jeune monde en délire; je fais voler la fameuse «capuche» dans les airs d'un grand coup de tête.

Quelques minutes avant notre arrivée, j'ai eu peur de perdre le contrôle de mes émotions. Marie-Ève, l'animatrice, a demandé à deux filles de venir me décorer de la tuque officielle de la mascotte: un genre de vieux torchon multicolore, aussi long que les collants d'Émilie, appelé «la capuche». Je veux bien faire rire à titre de mascotte, mais avoir l'air d'une cruche, pas question, foi de Galoche! J'ai droit à un peu de respect, nom d'un humain!

La capuche s'envole. W-ouf! Je me sens déjà mieux.

Je m'élance droit vers l'immensité blanche du domaine de l'Auberge du lac Dégelé: je grimpe sur les bancs de neige, plonge dans les creux de vagues blanches, saute les clôtures et slalome entre les bouleaux derrière la vieille auberge. J'en ai la langue pendante, haletante. Les frustrations du voyage fondent une à une, comme ces flocons qui tombent des branches sur ma fourrure. Je sens ma patience, tout aussi légendaire que mon flair, se régénérer peu à peu.

Une voix de garçon résonne au loin:

– À l'attaque! À l'attaque!

Je m'arrête brusquement.

– Acceptez-vous de vous rendre, les filles?

– On n'a pas peur de vous ! réplique une autre voix.

Émilie!?

Ma folle escapade m'a beaucoup éloigné de l'auberge, que je ne vois même plus.

– Aïe!

– Yééé! Touchééée!... En voilà une autre!

On dirait une bataille.

– Vous n'avez pas honte de vous en prendre aux filles?

La voix de Pierre-Luc!? IVG! Improvise vite, Galoche!

Je fais demi-tour et bondis par-dessus le premier banc de neige, en suivant les voix pour me guider. Moins d'une minute plus tard, je débouche sur un véritable champ de bataille: divers clans s'affrontent autour des valises éparpillées près de l'autobus. Des balles de neige fusent de partout. Des cris, aussi.

À l'arrière de l'autobus, j'aperçois Vincent et quelques amis qui s'en prennent à ma Douce ainsi qu'à Sophie.

– Bande de lâches !

Oh, oh ! Pierre-Luc se précipite vers Émilie. Il a flairé la bonne affaire : devenir le superhéros de ma Douce. Moi, Galoche, je flaire plutôt la catastrophe.

Émilie est debout, servant fièrement de bouclier aux deux filles occupées à refaire le plein de munitions.

– Toi, P.-L., fais pas ton brave !

– Ouais, le « bolé » ! T'es même pas capable de faire une vraie bonne balle de neige !

– On te connaît: si on te touche, tu vas te mettre à brailler!

Les sarcasmes ne semblent pas atteindre Pierre-Luc, qui se fait des balles de neige en vitesse. Notre jeune voisin ne manque vraiment pas d'audace; affronter d'aussi coriaces adversaires… avec des talents sportifs aussi limités que les siens.

«Il faut qu'il aime Émilie en misère à poil!» que je me dis, fonçant dans sa direction.

– Pierre-Luc, enlève-toi de là, imbécile!

À ma grande surprise, Émilie fustige notre brave voisin.

– Tu vas nous rendre vulnérables, crie Sophie, l'amie d'Émilie.

– On ne voit plus nos cibles! Décolle, Pierre-Luc!

– Plutôt mourir que de te laisser seule, Émilie! déclame notre jeune voisin à la façon d'un valeureux chevalier, faisant de nouveau face aux trois guerriers.

Les poches remplies de balles, Vincent et ses deux acolytes avancent de quelques pas.

– Que c'est beau, l'AMOUR! se moque Vincent. Arrête, Pierre-Luc, tu vas nous faire pleurer...

Ses deux complices éclatent de rire. Émilie, les joues rouges, riposte tout de go:

– C'est pas mon amoureux, OK?!... Toi, Pierre-Luc, va-t'en!

Sourd comme un pot, ce dernier ne bronche pas. Une seconde attaque est imminente, foi de Galoche. Je ne sais plus quoi faire. Et s'il réussissait un coup d'éclat? S'il épatait ma Douce?

Fiiiiiiiou!

Un projectile sillonne l'air. Pierre-Luc, toujours devant ma Douce, a lancé la première balle. *Fiiiiiiou!* Dans son excitation, il en propulse aussitôt une deuxième; puis *Fiiiiiou! Fiiiiiou! Fiiiiiou!* il épuise sa réserve en moins de quinze secondes, sans toucher un seul membre du trio.

– Pousse-toi! hurlent Émilie et Sophie. *FFFFIOU!!!*

La réplique ne tarde pas: un boulet de canon lancé par Vincent directement vers la tête de Pierre-Luc. J'en ai des frissons jusque dans les coussinets tellement cette balle est grosse. Il va se faire décapiter... par amour!

À la toute dernière seconde, le bouclier amoureux d'Émilie prend panique et se penche pour sauver sa peau. Catastrophe! Je vois la tuque d'Émilie entraînée au loin par la balle de neige de Vincent.

– Je m'excuse, Émilie! Je m'excuse! pleurniche Pierre-Luc, réalisant sa gaffe monumentale. Je ne me pencherai plus...

W-ouf! Je respire mieux: ma Douce n'a pas été touchée. Seulement effleurée. Mais son visage est aussi rouge que sa tuque envolée. Et Pierre-Luc est aussi blême qu'un bonhomme de neige.

– Va-t'en, Pierre-Luc!

Les humains disent souvent que l'amour est aveugle; moi, Galoche, je dirais qu'il est aussi sourd!

Le trio fait encore quelques pas vers les filles et s'approche de leur valeureux chevalier-bouclier... Tout à coup, bonheur! j'aperçois Fabien qui sort de l'auberge. Il regarde vers le champ de bataille où pleuvent maintenant des dizaines de balles. Je fonce droit sur le gros et grand barbu de père d'Émilie et lui fais mes yeux paniqués. Il comprend toujours mon regard: un vrai complice! À mon grand soulagement, il sort un sifflet de sa poche de manteau et le fait résonner.

Aussitôt, comme les personnages d'un film à la télé quand on appuie sur un bouton de la télécommande, tout le monde s'arrête. Plus une balle ne vole dans les airs. Fabien lance, de sa voix grave et puissante :

– Je vous laisse encore trente minutes avant d'entrer les bagages dans l'auberge ! Amusez-vous bien !

Et sur ce, je le vois se pencher, faire des balles et se lancer dans la mêlée.

Moi, Galoche, je reste sans *jappe*.

Décidément, il n'y a pas que l'amour qui rend aveugle et sourd…

Misère à poil ! Je commence à avoir le torticolis, moi, à force de suivre ces nuées de balles qui sifflent au-dessus de ma tête. Mais pourquoi les humains aiment-ils à ce point les batailles ? Jamais il ne viendrait à l'idée d'un chien de se faire peur pour s'amuser…

Oh, oh ! Émilie et Sophie viennent d'épuiser leurs réserves de balles, alors que le trio masculin reprend l'assaut.

«J'arrive, Émilie!»

Moi aussi, j'aime Émilie. C'est mon amie pour la vie. Et jamais je ne la laisserai tomber entre les pattes de ces trois gros garçons. Je vole à son secours et à celui de Pierre-Luc, qui ressemble davantage à une sculpture de neige qu'à un combattant tellement il est bombardé de toutes parts, tant par les gars que par les filles.

– Galoche, va-t'en! m'ordonne Émilie.

Quoi?

– Galoche, tu n'as rien à faire ici! Tu vas...

Moi, «rien à faire ici»! Quel affront! Eh bien, Émilie, tu vas voir de quel bois je me chauffe, foi de Galoche!

Bien assis devant ma Douce, j'attends l'occasion de démontrer mon ardeur canine et mon talent de chien-protecteur. L'occasion ne tarde pas.

– On n'a plus de «ba-balles», les filles? s'amuse Vincent. You-hou, Émilie *tomboy*? Essaie donc d'éviter celle-là!

Vincent décoche une balle immense dans sa direction. Ah! le sans-scrupule! La trajectoire de sa balle s'élève: elle va atteindre Émilie à la tête, foi de Galoche!

«Pas question!»

Juste au moment où la balle de neige passe au-dessus de moi, tel un clown sortant de sa boîte à surprise, je bondis. Très haut. Et… POW!

J'attrape la balle glacée dans ma gueule. Je retombe au sol comme une poche de patates.

– Galoche! s'inquiète Émilie. Tu saignes!

J'ai les crocs qui tremblent encore après ce choc incroyable; je ne me sens plus la gueule.

– Galoche! Galoche!… Est-ce qu'il est mort?

Les têtes d'Émilie, de Sophie et de Pierre-Luc apparaissent au-dessus de la mienne; puis, celles de Vincent et de ses deux complices qui ne cessent de s'excuser:

– On pouvait pas savoir qu'il sautait si haut!

– Un vrai kangourou! On pouvait pas deviner.

– Vite, lance Pierre-Luc, il faut le transporter dans le chalet!

– Je m'en occupe, intervient Émilie en repoussant notre jeune voisin.

Un petit filet de sang éclabousse la neige blanche, près de ma gueule endolorie. Je décide de demeurer aussi flasque qu'une peluche. En vérité, je joue un peu la comédie. Nous, les chiens, avons la «couenne dure», comme dit souvent Fabien. Nous tolérons le mal. Quant aux humains, au moindre petit bobo, ils ne se tolèrent plus eux-mêmes... Je suis un peu ébranlé, mais je pourrais me rendre au chalet sur quatre pattes.

– Je vais bien te soigner, mon beau. Tu vas voir !

Recroquevillé dans les bras d'Émilie, la plus affectueuse de toutes les infirmières, je ne vois toujours pas une seule bonne raison de briser ce doux moment. Et puis, la mascotte que je suis ne mérite-t-elle pas un peu de bien-être après avoir fait rire d'elle et avoir ramené, à elle seule, la paix sur le champ de bataille ? Que demander de plus à une mascotte-cotte-cotte ?

Mon infirmière privée me dépose délicatement sur la peau d'ours du grand salon de l'auberge. Brrrr !... Un ours tué par les humains. J'en ai la fourrure tout hérissée. À quand la chasse aux chiens ? Je secoue les puces de mon cerveau et réussis à éloigner cette cruelle idée. Je reviens dans ma peau... de mascotte blessée.

Étendu juste devant un immense feu de foyer, je laisse la bienfaisante chaleur me réconforter. Je soulève un peu les paupières, le temps de faire les yeux doux à Émilie, et je les referme aussitôt. Je veux prolonger cet instant merveilleux. Je reste donc aussi inerte que l'ours blanc sous moi. Je crois que j'hibernerais bien dans le salon de l'Auberge du lac Dégelé...

J'entends des pas s'approcher de l'âtre. Fabien demande d'une voix inquiète :

– Qu'est-ce qui s'est passé, Mimi ?

– Comme moi, Galoche a voulu protéger Émilie, intervient Pierre-Luc. Le pauvre a reçu une grosse balle de neige en plein dans la gueule.

Du coin de l'œil, j'observe Pierre-Luc : il a de larges rougeurs sur le visage. C'est lui qu'on devrait soigner... Mais je continue à jouer la comédie. Tant et si bien que le père d'Émilie me trouve, lui aussi, très mal en point. Il est aux petits soins pour moi.

– Que se passe-t-il ici?

L'arrivée d'un jeune homme vient briser le charme de ce moment exquis.

– Ah! Philippe! s'exclame Fabien, comme si un héros venait d'entrer dans le salon. Notre chien a été durement atteint par une balle, directement sur la gueule.

– Laissez-moi faire, j'ai mon diplôme de premiers soins…, lance-t-il, en ajoutant sur un ton moqueur: …pour chiens dans le coma!

L'instant d'après, l'intrus me tâtonne la gueule sans délicatesse aucune. J'entends le père d'Émilie rassurer ma Douce en l'informant discrètement qu'il s'agit du moniteur de l'auberge:

– La grande sœur de ton amie Sophie m'a dit beaucoup de bien de ce jeune homme, termine-t-il.

Moi, Galoche, je me demande comment Marie-Ève, notre animatrice, a pu dire du bien de cet insensible moniteur?

AÏE ! Oh !

Le faux vétérinaire continue à me scruter la gueule comme s'il s'agissait de la caverne d'Ali Baba. Avant que le fameux Philippe me déboîte la mâchoire, je décide d'ouvrir grands les yeux. Aussitôt ce dernier me pince les bajoues, les secoue allègrement et déclare sur un ton triomphal:

– Tiens ! Le revoilà parmi nous, votre gros toutou !

Gros ?! J'aimerais répondre à ce fanfaron par la gueule de mes canines; mais, comédien jusqu'au bout des griffes, je prends l'air d'un humain qui se réveille le matin... pas très beau à voir !

À la demande du moniteur, Fabien se précipite pour aller chercher un linge mouillé. Le grand Philippe s'adresse à mon Émilie:

– C'est à vous, ce chien, jolie demoiselle ?

– Oui, c'est... c'est mon chien.

– Il s'appelle Galoche, renchérit Pierre-Luc. C'est l'amour de…

– Il va s'en tirer? intervient brusquement ma Douce.

Ah! mon Émilie qui s'inquiète encore. Quel réconfort!

– Je veux dire…, poursuit-elle sur un ton soudain très mielleux, s'en tirer sans vraiment de séquelles?

Ce changement radical dans la voix de ma Douce ne m'inspire rien de bon, foi de Galoche! Méfiant, je jette un bref regard vers Émilie: horreur! Je réalise que «la jolie demoiselle» ne se préoccupe plus du tout de ma santé, mais bien des yeux du faux vétérinaire.

– Chère demoiselle, votre Taloche…

– Galoche! rectifie Pierre-Luc, tout aussi attentif que moi à ce tête-à-tête improvisé devant nous, comme si lui et moi n'existions plus.

– Votre Galoche, avec mes soins, n'aura que la gueule enflée pendant quelques jours. Sans plus.

J'aimerais bien le voir, le Philippe, avec la gueule enflée quelques jours... Quelle tête enflée, ce type!

Le moniteur serre la main d'Émilie. Il se présente, le sourire fendu jusqu'aux oreilles, offrant en spectacle deux larges rangées de dents toutes blanches. Un vrai chimpanzé. Il porte un col roulé rouge, un pantalon de ski vert avec de larges bretelles et des bouclettes blondes lui tombent sur le front. Tout pour que ma Douce tombe dans le panneau. Une fois encore, me voilà dans le pétrin. Avec, en prime, un Pierre-Luc au visage de père Noël qui ne parvient plus à respirer devant pareil spectacle.

Mais la mascotte-cotte-cotte n'avait encore rien vu...

Émilie est tombée sur la tête, misère à poil! Elle ne parle plus: elle susurre...

– Oui, oui, j'aime beaucoup les sports. Tous les sports de plein air.

– Génial! renchérit le blond moniteur. Alors, chère Émilie, j'imagine que tu vas participer au concours de planche à neige que l'auberge organise demain matin?

– Euh... oui, bien entendu, Philippe! Je compte bien décrocher les honneurs, d'ailleurs!

Ma Douce a vraiment perdu la tête: elle n'a fait de la planche à neige qu'une seule fois dans sa vie. Dans quelle galère s'est-elle encore embarquée... pour l'amour!?

Hébété, Pierre-Luc me fixe. Il semble vouloir me dire: «Fais quelque chose, Galoche: elle va se tuer!» Je le sais bien! Mais moi, Galoche, je suis fatigué de toujours improviser pour sauver Émilie de ses amourettes...

Fabien est de retour. Il tend au grand blond un linge imbibé d'eau avec lequel ce dernier commence à essuyer le sang séché sur mes babines.

– Tiens, Brioche, ça va te...

Je bondis sur mes quatre pattes si vivement que je fais sursauter tout le monde.

– GRRRRR!

– Galoche, voyons! me fustige Émilie.

Pas question de me laisser ridiculiser plus longtemps par cet individu! Le beau Philippe fait un pas vers moi.

– GRRRRRRRRRRR!!!

Il s'immobilise de peur. Je déguerpis.

– Galoche! Galoche!...

Vingt minutes plus tard, Émilie me retrouve au fond d'un placard dont la porte était restée ouverte. Et c'est là, assise par terre, en me caressant et en me parlant doucement, qu'elle m'amadoue... comme toujours. Impossible de résister à ma Douce.

– Chère mascotte de mon cœur, conclut-elle, j'ai une belle surprise pour toi.

Ah, Émilie! Pour les surprises, c'est la championne!

– Tu sais, la course de planche à neige demain...

«Tu ne vas pas y participer!» que je m'emballe, le museau bien haut.

– Eh bien, mon beau, je vais la gagner!

Mon museau redescend aussitôt.

– Je vais la gagner grâce à toi!

Mes babines tombent à leur tour.

– Avec toi dans mon sac à dos, mon beau, on sera les plus lourds et les plus rapides!

Mon museau, mes babines et le reste de mon corps s'affaissent d'un seul coup...

W-ouf! Enfin l'heure de dormir... Debout dans l'immense chambre à coucher, Fabien nous souhaite à toutes et à tous une bonne nuit.

– Je serai votre ange gardien. Dormez sur vos deux oreilles, les amis. Et surtout, faites de beaux rêves!

Dans un camp de vacances, on appelle «dortoir» cette immense chambre à coucher: d'un côté les garçons, de l'autre les filles. Sauf moi, bien sûr. Je suis étendu au pied du lit de ma Douce, sur un petit tapis. Pour une mascotte, on peut faire des exceptions. Je mérite bien un passe-droit après la dure journée que j'ai eue!

Laissant mon orgueil canin dans sa niche, j'ai joué mon rôle de mascotte à la perfection :

- petite caresse sur le museau par-ci; petite caresse sur le dos par-là;
- petite roulade par-ci; petite «ba-balle» à ramener par-là;
- petite promenade avec l'épouvantable «capuche» par-ci; petite chanson ridicule pour la mascotte par-là;
- petit *fa*-si-si par-ci; petit *fa-do-do* par-là.

Sans compter que j'ai dû faire l'espion :

- petit coup d'œil vers le fameux Philippe par-ci; petite surveillance de ma Douce par-là;
- petite incursion dans le groupe de Vincent pour prévenir toute attaque contre les filles par-ci; petite séance d'espionnage pour éviter que Pierre-Luc ne gaffe de nouveau par-là.

Bref, je suis exténué. Et j'ai bien droit, comme disent les humains, au repos du guerrier.

Fabien quitte le dortoir. Ah! quel silence bienfaisant! Les jeunes, fatigués comme moi, dorment à poings fermés. De vrais petits anges. On entendrait voler une mouche dans le dortoir. Mes paupières se ferment, aussi lourdement que la porte de l'autobus ce matin.

Et, tout à coup:

– À l'attaque! hurle une voix.

Je sursaute et me glisse sous le lit en vitesse. J'étire le cou et aperçois Vincent, qui court dans l'allée centrale en brandissant son oreiller.

– Cette fois, les filles, lancent les acolytes de Vincent, vous ne serez pas sauvées par Galoche la cloche!

Ah! les sans-cœur!

Quelle n'est pas ma surprise de voir Émilie, Sophie et leur bande se lever

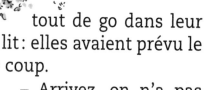

tout de go dans leur lit : elles avaient prévu le coup.

– Arrivez, on n'a pas peur de vous !

– Vous allez voir de quel oreiller on se chauffe !

Les filles attendent de patte ferme les premiers belligérants, qui s'approchent entre les petits lits tout blancs. Pas très reposants, les jeunes et leur camp de vacances, foi de Galoche !

– Ah non ! Pas encore toi !

Le cri désespéré de ma Douce me fait bondir. OUILLE ! Je me frappe la tête sur le sommier.

– Va-t'en, Pierre-Luc !

Je sors de sous le lit. J'aperçois, bien droit devant Émilie, notre héros de voisin, un oreiller dans chaque main. Il les fait tournoyer comme les hélices d'un vieil avion.

– Émilie, hurle-t-il en sautant dans le lit comme sur un trampoline.

POUF !

Le héros mal-aimé est durement touché par l'oreiller de Vincent qui éclate. Il se met à neiger des centaines de plumes.

POUF !

Un autre oreiller frappe Pierre-Luc. Le poids plume tombe du lit.

BOUM !

– Pierre-Luc ! s'écrie ma Douce.

Les deux gros acolytes de Vincent profitent de ce moment de distraction et terrassent Émilie sur son lit.

POUF! POUF!

«ÉMILIE!!!» Ah! les scélérats! Je n'y vois que du blanc avec tous ces vieux oreillers éventrés. Des dizaines et des dizaines de POUF! résonnent partout dans le dortoir. Quel étrange concert!

Moi, Galoche, à titre de mascotte-cotte-cotte, je décide d'intervenir sur-le-champ... de bataille. Ce carnage doit cesser. Il faut aller avertir Fabien.

Je me rue vers l'allée centrale: BANG! Une patte de lit... Pas facile de se frayer un chemin dans cette tempête de flocons plumés. Mais je ne suis pas une poule mouillée. Je continue. BANG! Une deuxième patte... Je me sens un peu étourdi. Mais j'ai la tête dure. Je reprends ma course, à l'aveuglette. «Courage! que je me répète. Coura...» BANG!... Je commence vraiment à tirer de la patte.

Je persiste tout de même.

La mascotte repart de plus belle, au plus fort de la bourrasque. Et quelle surprise : aucune patte de lit ne vient freiner mon élan. Je suis sûrement dans la grande allée. Tout près du but. J'accélère.

BOUM! Je m'affale au pied d'un mur. Du coin de l'œil droit, j'aperçois la porte de sortie. Euréka! Enfin, en plus des étoiles, je vois la lumière au bout du tunnel...

Le vent dans les oreilles, je dévale l'escalier, laissant des plumes sur chaque marche. Un vrai chien de conte pour enfants...

Convaincu de trouver Fabien devant le foyer, je file vers le rez-de-chaussée, sans même m'arrêter aux deux autres étages. Plus je descends, plus mes oreilles captent des ondes qui ne peuvent provenir que du grand salon. «Ah! mon flair légendaire!» que je m'enthousiasme.

Je touche enfin le dernier palier. Je bondis jusque dans le grand corridor, tout près du bureau d'accueil. Puis, je me précipite vers ces lueurs dorées qui dansent et brillent dans le noir. Mes oreilles frémissent: qu'est-ce que c'est que ces bruits étranges? Serait-ce Fabien, caché par l'énorme dossier du divan, qui fredonne, ronronne ou ronfle devant le feu?

Je contourne le vieux meuble et freine en catastrophe au pied de l'ours blanc.

– Qu'est-ce que tu viens faire ici, vieux chien fou?

Misère à poil! Sur la peau d'ours, Philippe, le moniteur, embrasse Marie-Ève, notre animatrice. De quoi jeter mon flair légendaire à la poubelle des vieux mythes...

«Ah, si Émilie pouvait voir ça: j'éviterais un dangereux concours de planche à neige...»

– Va-t'en, chien pas de médaille! ajoute le moniteur.

Avec son air renfrogné et ses bouclettes qui dansent devant ses yeux, il me fait penser à un bouc enragé.

– Voyons, Philippe, intervient Marie-Ève, ne sois pas méchant avec Galoche, c'est un bon toutou. C'est notre mascotte.

Moi, la mascotte, j'ai mieux à faire que d'écouter leurs balivernes. Le temps presse. Aussi, je reprends ma folle recherche de l'ange gardien du dortoir et je cours… et cours… et cours en vain dans tous les recoins de l'auberge sans trouver Fabien.

La queue, les oreilles et la langue par terre, je me retrouve vaincu, une heure plus tard, à la porte du dortoir. Et qui m'y accueille?

– Te revoilà enfin, Galoche, fait Fabien, un peu moqueur. Mais où étais-tu donc passé?

Je n'en crois pas mes yeux ni mes oreilles: d'abord, l'apparition de Fabien; en plus, on se croirait au ciel, dans le dortoir. Tout le monde dort paisiblement. Pas une plume à l'horizon. Pas un son. Que de beaux petits lits tout blancs avec de mignons enfants endormis.

Je rêve ou quoi?

Je fixe les yeux bleu ciel du gros et grand barbu de père d'Émilie pour essayer de comprendre. Son regard m'envoie un message pas très rassurant: «Bienvenue au paradis, mon beau!»

Je me sens tout drôle. Un instant, j'ai cru voir deux grosses ailes dans son dos... Ai-je perdu la raison?

– Bonne nuit, Galoche..., murmure Fabien.

Et il ajoute, tout sourire:

– Sache, mon beau, que je suis ton ange gardien à toi aussi.

Je me rends lentement jusqu'au lit de ma Douce. J'ai l'impression de flotter sur un nuage. Qu'est-ce qui m'arrive? J'ai les pattes molles, molles, molles... jusqu'au moment où je réalise que, dans les lits blancs, chacun des mignons petits enfants sommeille… SANS OREILLER !

D'un coup, je retrouve mon aplomb et toute ma raison. Il y a une explication simple : Fabien s'est aperçu du grabuge, a fait cesser le massacre à plumes et a obligé les jeunes à faire le ménage. Puis, il s'assure personnellement que ses petits angelots dorment à poings fermés avant de les quitter de nouveau. Et c'est alors, une heure plus tard, que je reviens, moi, la mascotte-cotte-cotte.

W-ouf ! Je suis vraiment de retour sur terre… humaine !

Je saute dans le lit de ma Douce. Elle ouvre les yeux, me sourit et me fait un clin d'œil… presque céleste. Tel père, telle fille, foi de Galoche !

UN VENT DE PANIQUE

Ce matin, sur le mont du lac Dégelé, la neige a remplacé les plumes. Émilie et moi, nous attendons le coup de sifflet pour le départ de notre descente de planche. Je suis assis dans le sac à dos de ma Douce. Nous nous trouvons tout en haut de la piste pour experts: la «Bossue».

Je me sens déjà bossu moi-même rien qu'en observant la multitude de bosses devant nous.

– Tiens-toi bien, Galoche!

Il n'y a pas que les histoires d'amour des humains qui me tuent; il y a aussi leur amour de la vitesse... misère à poil!

– Je vais lui montrer de quoi je suis capable!

Sans parler de leur amour maladif de la compétition.

– Que tu es lourd, Galoche! C'est parfait! lance ma flamboyante planchiste, en soulevant les épaules d'un coup sec pour hisser son sac à mascotte-cotte-cotte sur son dos avant notre départ imminent. Rien de mieux pour aller plus vite et s'élever plus haut!

S'élever plus haut?!... J'entends parfois certains humains dire que la foi déplace les montagnes; moi, j'aimerais seulement voir se déplacer les bosses...

– Galoche, s'écrie ma Douce, quand on chute, il faut *se laisser rouler*.

Se laisser rouler?!...

– Tu as bien compris, mon beau?

Mais pourquoi Émilie insiste-t-elle sur ces mots? Et pourquoi me parle-t-elle de chute avant même le début de notre descente?

Coup de sifflet. TRRUUUIIIIT!!!

C'est un départ. *Chhhhh!*

Oh, oh, oh! C'est parti, mon biscuit!

Nous glissons droit vers le gouffre devant nous. En quelques secondes, nous atteignons une vitesse à me faire frémir les naseaux et à me faire cligner des paupières. *Chhhhh!*

Pourtant, rien ne semble ennuyer mon Émilie. Au contraire! Elle a le vent dans les voiles, et moi, le vent dans les oreilles

plus que jamais: avec toutes ces rafales de neige, je crains de les voir se nouer au-dessus de ma tête. «Un peu d'humour me sera salutaire!» que je me dis, tentant de faire baisser mon stress, faute de voir baisser la vitesse de notre descente. Ma Douce est une experte en ski alpin, mais une débutante en planche à neige; elle achève néanmoins de contourner la première série de bosses avec brio. Bravo!

Chhhhh!

Mais le temps des réjouissances est vite passé: les plus grosses bosses, au milieu de la pente, approchent dange-reusement. Et nous prenons toujours de la vitesse. Trop, peut-être?… Je bondis et rebondis dans le sac à dos. Je m'y agrippe solidement avec mes crocs et mes griffes. Durcis et poussés par le vent froid de la montagne, les flocons de neige me pincent les bajoues sans arrêt. Une vraie torture! Mes yeux commencent à piquer alors qu'Émilie, elle, pique droit devant.

CHHHHHHH!...

Je ne vois plus rien. Que du blanc! Comme hier soir. Sauf qu'autour de moi, la plume et les petits lits ont fait place à de grosses épinettes et des bouleaux. Pas très rassurant.

– Accroche-toi bien, Galoche! hurle ma Douce. C'est le moment ou jamais!

AOUUUUUUUUH!

Ce n'est pas de la planche à neige, c'est du vol plané! Émilie ne contourne plus rien. Je ne comprends plus rien. Fait-elle exprès? J'ai les poils du visage tout rigides. Un vrai porc-épic polaire. Mes oreilles et mon museau craquent de partout. Je suis glacé d'effroi. Par surcroît, il m'est impossible d'improviser, coincé comme je suis.

AOUUUUUUUUH!

À chaque bosse, on s'élève un peu plus haut, un peu plus vite. Et à chaque envolée, je vois surgir dans ma tête la face du beau grand blond de Philippe, le vrai responsable de ce cauchemar, qui rit de toutes ses dents blanches.

«Émilie, sois raisonnable!» que je la supplie dans mes pensées.

– Ahhhh! hurle subitement ma championne, alors qu'une secousse terrible nous projette tous les deux droit au ciel.

Émilie a perdu tout contrôle.

– Yéééé!

Émilie a aussi perdu la tête.

Je me sens soudain léger, léger... comme une plume flottant dans un dortoir le soir. Jusqu'à ce que je me rende compte que j'ai été éjecté du sac à dos d'Émilie. Trois mots me reviennent en tête: «Laisse-toi rouler!» Ce que je fais aussitôt. Je ne suis plus qu'une boule de poils glacée tournoyant dans la Galaxie.

Oh! catastrophe! Que vois-je passer sur ma gauche? Ma Douce! Oui, c'est bien elle: comme moi, elle tournoie dans les airs. On dirait qu'elle fait une culbute

au ralenti, un peu à la façon d'un astro-
naute dans le vide.

Pourtant, la seconde d'après : BOUM !…
Et puis : RE-BOUM !

Comme deux astéroïdes, nous atter-
rissons très lourdement.

W-ouf ! Je sors la tête de la neige et
refais surface peu à peu. Je me félicite
d'être tombé à l'extérieur de la piste, dans
un banc de neige. Mon cœur s'arrête de
battre quand j'aperçois Émilie, à quelques
mètres de moi, étendue sur une des
bosses : elle ne bouge plus. Mes crocs
grincent, ma fourrure n'est plus que mille
et une craquelures ; peu m'importe, je suis
vite de retour sur quatre pattes et me
précipite à sa rescousse.

« Émilie ! Émilie ! Dis quelque chose !
que je m'énerve, en ne cessant de lui
lécher le visage. Quelle idée folle aussi
que de participer à ce concours… »

Je m'arrête net: Émilie a les yeux ouverts. Elle me fait son fameux clin d'œil: «Tout va bien, Galoche. Je n'ai rien de cassé. Tout va bien.» Puis, elle referme aussitôt ses paupières.

W-ouf! Quelle peur j'ai eue!

– Mimi, ça va?

– Émilie est blessée, vite, du secours! crie Pierre-Luc, paniqué.

Fabien, Pierre-Luc et plein de jeunes s'amènent en trombe. On se regroupe autour de ma Douce, qui continue à feindre le pire. Je me demande bien la raison de cette comédie. «Pas très gentil pour ses amis...» que je me dis. Je me revois hier dans les bras de ma Douce, en train de simuler le grand blessé. «Mais pourquoi donc jouerait-elle pareille scène?» Puis, je me rappelle le cri de joie poussé par Émilie, en pleine chute, il y a quelques secondes à peine: «Yéééé!» Pour une fille qui voulait gagner la compétition, c'est plutôt étrange, non?... Et là...

éclair de génie, je comprends enfin ce qui se passe dans la tête de ma rusée Émilie.

Je réagis tout de go.

– Regardez!... Galoche vient de tomber sans connaissance à son tour! Quel brave chien; il est venu au secours d'Émilie avant de tomber dans les pommes.

– Pauvre Galoche, une balle sur la gueule hier et, ce matin, une chute épouvantable!

– Il n'oubliera pas son expérience de mascotte de sitôt!

– Reculez, reculez, ordonne Fabien à tous les jeunes, il faut les laisser respirer!

J'entends le lointain ronronnement d'une motoneige. Je me félicite d'avoir joué la comédie une fois de plus. Mon flair va vite retrouver sa notoriété légendaire, foi de Galoche!

– Dégagez, dégagez!

La voix du grand moniteur blond retentit alors que le moteur de sa «motoneige-ambulance» ronronne tout près, à m'en faire trembler les tympans.

Ah, la coquine! Voilà ce qu'espérait mon Émilie. Je mettrais ma patte au feu qu'elle savait que son beau Philippe assumait la sécurité sur les pentes avec son bolide. Quel moyen parfait que la chute pour se retrouver devant le feu de foyer à son tour, dans les bras du moniteur.

Heureusement, moi, Galoche, j'ai le museau fin pour les affaires de cœur. Pas question que je la laisse seule avec ce don Juan. Si bien que, dans quelques instants, ce sera à mon tour d'être emmitouflé et allongé dans le traîneau-civière, aux côtés de ma Douce. J'ai bien hâte de lui voir la frimousse…

Le moteur de la motoneige se met à pétarader. Mais… il s'en va sans moi, cet escogriffe!

– Philippe?... lance Fabien. Tu oublies Galoche!

Quel effronté! Un peu plus et ce sans-cœur de moniteur me laissait sur cette bosse, seul comme un humain...

AÏE!

Le grand Philippe m'arrache du sol tel un pissenlit, lui qui a pris tant de précautions pour déposer ma Douce sur la civière, la couvrir et l'attacher.

– Faites attention, ce n'est pas un chien de peluche! intervient courageuse-ment Pierre-Luc.

AÏE! Oh! le grand blond me trans-porte vers la motoneige. L'instant sui-vant, il me laisse choir sur la partie arrière de son siège comme une vieille marmotte. Puis il s'assoit et met son bolide en route.

Voilà que je dévale la pente en direc-tion de l'auberge. Je suis soulevé du siège à chaque bosse. Couché sur le flanc, j'en ai les côtes tout endolories. Quel supplice!

Mais je n'ai pas le choix : je dois jouer mon rôle jusqu'au bout.

Chhhh !

Un planchiste passe dangereusement près de notre engin.

« Mais c'est... c'est Pierre-Luc ! »

On dirait un bouffon tellement il gesticule sur sa planche, le pauvre. Malgré les bosses énormes, il plonge droit devant à une vitesse vertigineuse. Un vrai fou !

« Un brave fou ! » je rectifie aussitôt dans ma tête.

Puis, je m'imagine notre jeune amoureux en train de visiter le ciel à son tour tandis que l'écho nous fait entendre un long et désespérant cri d'effroi :

– AAAAAAAAH !

« Si seulement Émilie avait pu voir son beau blondinet hier soir en train d'embrasser l'animatrice sur la peau de l'ours, je ne serais pas en si mauvaise posture!»

Depuis quelques instants, je gis sur le siège de la motoneige, juste devant l'entrée du chalet. Bien sûr, le grand Philippe m'y a oublié. Et, foi de Galoche, je suis incapable de bouger après cette descente sur… les côtes! Je suis paralysé. Encore une fois, même avec la meilleure volonté canine, impossible de me dire: «IVG». J'ai le moral… congelé.

Soudain, un bruit attire mon attention. *Chhhhhh…*

Je lève la tête. Tel un funambule sur son fil de fer, voilà Pierre-Luc sur sa planche à neige qui fonce à toute vitesse vers l'auberge. Quel héros, ce Pierre-Luc!… Ce n'est pas ce grand dadais de moniteur qui risquerait ainsi sa vie pour Émilie.

BANG!

– Aiiiiiiiie!

Un héros qui n'a pas encore appris comment freiner avec une planche…

sinon pourquoi aurait-il foncé droit dans le mur de l'auberge?

– Galoche, me voilà! lance-t-il en titubant vers moi.

Ce jeune a la «couenne» aussi dure qu'un chien, misère à poil! Voyant que je ne peux bouger sur le siège, très doucement, il me prend dans ses bras et me dépose par terre. W-ouf! Enfin...

Après quelques prudents exercices d'assouplissement, plusieurs grincements de crocs de ma part et encouragements répétés de Pierre-Luc, je reprends mon allure normale de chien athlétique – de chien athlétique bedonnant, dirait Marilou... Suivi de mon complice, je m'introduis le plus vite possible dans l'auberge et me rends directement au salon.

– Ma belle, je suis content de constater que tu ne t'es pas fait mal..., susurre une voix derrière le gros divan, devant le feu de foyer rougeoyant. Tu sais que tu m'as épaté? Quelle audace! Quelle vitesse! Quelle hauteur! Je n'avais jamais vu autant d'adresse sur la «Bossue»…

Oh, oh! Il est temps d'intervenir. Et, foi de Galoche, j'en suis davantage persuadé lorsque je contourne le divan et que je vois le blondinet penché au-dessus de la tête d'Émilie, étendue sur la peau d'ours…

«Quel ours mal léché!»

Il lui a enlevé son costume de neige, l'a recouverte d'une couverture chaude et a appuyé sa tête sur un énorme coussin. Le visage et les cheveux d'Émilie brillent sous les lueurs du feu tandis que les bouclettes blondes du vil tombeur dansent sur son front. À genoux à son chevet, le chandail attaché à sa taille, il a les yeux rivés à ceux de ma Douce. Une vraie scène de cinéma. Et, comme dans tous les films pathétiques que regardent les humains à la télévision, le docteur-moniteur va bientôt embrasser la fille…

IVG! Une idée illumine ma pensée : je dois tout de go sauter dans la mêlée, comme tout bon chien dévoué. Pourtant, je reste les quatre pattes bien au sol. J'ai une hésitation : d'accord, les yeux d'Émilie lancent des étincelles, mais pas celles qu'elle lance lorsqu'elle tombe amoureuse. Je sais de quoi je parle. À moins que mon flair légendaire me joue encore des tours ?...

Sur le côté du gros divan, la tête de Pierre-Luc surgit. Il voit la scène sur la peau d'ours. Son regard se glace. Il a le teint tout blême : un vrai vampire. Avant qu'il ne sorte ses crocs, j'oublie ces étincelles étranges dans le regard de ma Douce et je bondis droit devant moi. Comme un boulet, je passe à deux griffes du nez du grand Philippe. Ce dernier lâche un cri de peur et tombe à la renverse. Je me retourne vite. Le moniteur est sur le dos, tout près du foyer. Il se relève rapidement, dos au feu. Ses yeux me lancent des flammes aussi grosses que celles qui se balancent derrière lui. Soudain, les miens s'illuminent de peur: le bras du chandail, toujours accroché à la taille de Philippe, s'embrase. Il est resté suspendu de l'autre côté de la grille après sa chute. Je jette un regard vers Pierre-Luc et lui lance un S.O.S.: «Je viens de faire la pire gaffe de ma vie de chien, foi de Galoche!»

Je vois mon jeune complice déguerpir. Mais où se sauve-t-il?

– Wouf! wouf!

Pierre-Luc m'a abandonné. J'essaie maintenant d'avertir Philippe.

«Le feu!»

– Vieux chien de malheur! hurle le moniteur offusqué sans bouger d'un poil. T'es malade ou quoi?

– Ne t'en prends pas à mon chien, dit doucement Émilie. Il ne fait que t'avertir gentiment…

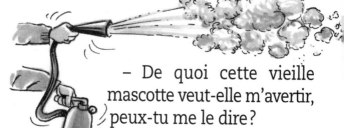

– De quoi cette vieille mascotte veut-elle m'avertir, peux-tu me le dire?

– Du feu qui grimpe sur ton chandail, derrière toi.

– Quoi?!

Un bond et voilà notre moniteur essayant de défaire le nœud qui retient son chandail à sa taille. Trop tard!... Le débrouillard Pierre-Luc l'asperge déjà avec un extincteur. En quelques secondes, le tombeur de filles a des allures de bonhomme de neige.

«Génial, Pierre-Luc! Quelle idée fantastique!»

Nos yeux se croisent: c'est la fête!... Pourtant, je reviens vite les pattes sur terre: moi, Galoche, je dois maintenant affronter le regard d'Émilie. Je tourne lentement la tête vers ma Douce. Quelle n'est pas ma stupéfaction de la voir pouffer de rire. J'en ai le poil qui danse de plaisir. Plus les bouclettes du grand Philippe se dandinent de colère, plus le fou rire d'Émilie se répercute dans l'auberge, où Fabien et plein de jeunes s'amènent en trombe; et plus le docteur-moniteur tout blanc gesticule comme un épouvantail, plus le fou rire se communique. C'est l'euphorie! Même Marie-Ève, l'animatrice, n'y échappe pas...

Ce soir, le dortoir porte bien son nom: d'abord, des oreillers sont apparus comme par enchantement – ils ne sont sûrement pas de plumes. Ensuite, tout le monde dort. Ou presque...

– Tu penses qu'il s'apprêtait vraiment à t'embrasser?

Ma Douce et son amie Sophie se murmurent des secrets, je crois bien. Au pied du lit, je reste discret... mais j'allonge tout de même un peu les oreilles.

– J'en suis certaine. Moi, je m'apprêtais à lui faire une grimace digne d'un orang-outang... mais Galoche s'est chargé de lui faire peur.

Je n'en reviens tout simplement pas: j'apprends que, avant la compétition de planche à neige, Émilie a su que le grand Philippe était l'ami de cœur de Marie-Ève, notre animatrice. C'est Sophie elle-même qui le lui a dit. Ma Douce a alors décidé de ne pas gagner la compétition mais de tendre plutôt un piège au sans-cœur de moniteur en simulant une chute dans la piste des bosses.

– Quand j'ai vu Pierre-Luc asperger Philippe avec l'extincteur, je n'ai pu me retenir plus longtemps.

– Je comprends. En tout cas, moi, à ta place, si j'avais un garçon qui démontrait autant de cran que Pierre-Luc pour venir à mon secours, je ne le repousserais pas comme toi, même s'il a l'air fou de temps à autre. Et puis, il n'est pas laid, ton voisin.

– Hum-hum…

Je suis abasourdi. Voilà l'explication de ces étincelles étranges dans le regard de ma Douce: elles ne reflétaient pas de l'amour, la taquine s'apprêtait à lui jouer un bon tour, juste avant que le beau blond ne l'embrasse.

«Galoche, tu as encore le pif, mon vieux!»

– Et ta sœur? Elle ne doit plus l'avoir dans son cœur, son Philippe?

– Euh... elle dit que... que jamais il n'a eu l'intention de t'embrasser. Que tu es beaucoup trop jeune pour lui. Elle dit aussi que... que c'est toi, Émilie, qui t'imagines plein de choses à propos de son Philippe.

– Quoi ?

– Chut !

Moi, Galoche, j'en ai ras-le-poil d'entendre parler des affaires de cœur des humains. Un vrai casse-tête. Avec beaucoup trop de morceaux. En douce, je descends du lit et quitte le dortoir. Soudain, une voix me fait sursauter :

– Tiens, si ce n'est pas Galoche !

En haut de l'escalier, je me retrouve devant l'abominable homme des neiges : Fabien, emmitouflé dans son ensemble de ski.

– Tu viens faire un tour de raquettes, mon Beau ? Le ciel doit être magnifiquement étoilé à cette heure-ci.

Je ne refuse pas l'invitation de ce grand amoureux de la nature. Foi de Galoche, la mascotte-cotte-cotte a bien besoin de se détendre après tous ces événements. Et puis, j'ai de très bons coussinets...

Quelques minutes plus tard, mes yeux se régalent: toutes ces étoiles qui scintillent dans le noir, tout là-haut, semblent briller juste pour nous deux, le gros barbu et le petit poilu. C'est dans pareil moment que j'aimerais être un «deux pattes», pour m'élever un peu plus haut vers ces étoiles...

– C'est féerique, hein, mon beau?

Mon émerveillement prend fin brusquement: le son lointain d'un moteur, que j'entendais depuis tantôt, a fait place à un bruit plus ténu, mais plus intrigant. Je m'arrête sur le sentier, laissant Fabien me devancer. Le très faible bruit se précise. Mes tympans sont en état de veille: on dirait un... un cri étouffé... un gémissement...

– Wouf ! wouf !

Le vent dans les oreilles, je suis déjà en pleine course… Un appel de détresse! Je zigzague entre les arbres touffus. Je dois prendre le chemin le plus rapide vers cette personne qui, j'en suis maintenant convaincu, s'épuise à lancer des S.O.S.

– Wouf! wouf!

Je ne cesse de japper : Fabien pourra ainsi venir me rejoindre. Mais pas question de l'attendre. Je fonce droit vers l'appel. Je saute et m'écorche les coussinets sur des bouts de rochers qui sortent de la neige comme des pics. Tête baissée, je fais voler les plus basses branches d'épinettes et de sapins qui me font obstacle. Soudain, à travers les arbres couverts de neige, devant moi, apparaît une lumière. Puis une fenêtre. Un petit bâtiment.

– Wouf! wouf!

– Au secours! Par ici!… Au secours!

Les cris s'amplifient. La personne a dû m'entendre. L'espoir lui redonne de l'énergie. Je redouble d'ardeur. Quelques secondes plus tard, je freine en catastrophe devant une motoneige enfoncée dans l'eau, tout près d'une remise. Le bout d'un lac, j'imagine. Je me précipite droit vers le petit bâtiment, contourne le bolide à moitié dans l'eau et découvre Philippe, à demi immergé, coincé entre l'engin et la glace.

Quelle horreur! Pauvre garçon!

–Va chercher de l'aide, Galoche! supplie le moniteur.

Des craquements dans la glace me font hérisser le poil.

– Wooouf! wooouf!

Je hurle comme un loup.

– Non, non, retourne à l'auberge! Retourne…

– Wooooouf! woooooouf!

Fabien? Fabien?… Mais quand va-t-il se pointer le bout de la barbe, celui-là? Moi, Galoche, je m'énerve. «Du calme. Peux-tu faire quelque chose?» IVG! Improvise vite, Galoche!

Je bondis vers la remise. D'un coup de tête, j'ouvre la porte entrebâillée. Je scrute l'intérieur en catastrophe. Rien ici qui puisse m'aider. Rien dans cette histoire de chien-héros ne peut s'arranger avec le «gars des vues». Je ne suis pas au cinéma, mais dans la réalité, misère à poil! Je ressors en vitesse et décide qu'il y a une seule solution: retrouver Fabien!

– Wouf! wouf! wouf!

Je m'élance vers le bois. Dès la première épinette, je me frappe à un mur: Fabien.

– C'est moi, Galoche! Qu'est-ce qui se passe, mon beau?

Je suis si soulagé... Pour peu, je pleurerais comme un humain.

Sous un ciel étoilé, une ambulance se dirige vers la route principale. L'Auberge du lac Dégelé est encore en émoi.

– Bon! lance Fabien. On remonte se coucher. Notre ami Philippe va s'en tirer sans séquelles graves...

– Grâce à notre mascotte! s'écrie Pierre-Luc.

– Oui, bravo, Galoche! renchérit Fabien.

– Bravo! lancent en chœur tous les jeunes vacanciers, sauf Émilie, que j'aperçois, seule dans un coin.

Bien sûr, cette reconnaissance me fait un petit velours au cœur. Mais moi,

Galoche, je sais fort bien que c'est Fabien le vrai héros! Il a trouvé une grosse corde dans la remise, l'a attachée à un arbre et il a fait un grand nœud à l'autre bout pour que Philippe s'y accroche bien. Il lui a lancé celle-ci et, tout en restant au bord du lac, il a réussi à casser un peu de glace autour de la taille du pauvre moniteur avec un long morceau de bois. Ensuite, il a tiré très fort sur la corde. Philippe a pu se laisser glisser jusqu'à nous. Quel sauvetage! Et quelle frousse: quelques secondes plus tard, des craquements terribles nous ont fait peur et on a vu s'enfoncer dans l'eau le reste de la motoneige.

– Vous avez porté le grand Philippe jusqu'ici sur vos épaules?

– Il devait être lourd?

– Bon, finies les questions! intervient Fabien, modeste. On monte. Tout de suite!

Rassurés d'avoir un pareil ange gardien, tous les jeunes regagnent le dortoir… et moi, le paradis! Car, ce soir, j'ai droit à l'oreiller et aux couvertures : je me retrouve allongé tout près d'Émilie. Elle semble encore bouleversée. La mésaventure de Philippe l'a rendue très soucieuse. Tantôt, avant que Marie-Ève ne monte dans l'ambulance, ma Douce a été lui parler. Quand elle est revenue, elle avait les yeux tout rouges et elle pleurait. Mais, pour le moment, elle me fait un sourire et me dit à l'oreille :

– Galoche, tu as été sensationnel ! Tu as sauvé la vie de Philippe.

Et elle ajoute d'une voix grave et tremblotante :

– La mienne aussi !

Je lève de grands yeux vers Émilie.

– Tu peux garder un secret ?

J'apprends que Philippe s'était rendu à la remise à la suite d'un message transmis par Émilie, message qui lui disait qu'il avait rendez-vous avec Marie-Ève à 22 h.

– Mais c'était moi...

Devant mon regard ahuri, ma Douce ajoute :

– Je voulais juste lui jouer un tour. Le faire poireauter un peu, pour m'avoir fait croire que... enfin, tu comprends.

Un tour qui a failli tourner au drame, foi de Galoche !

– Si tu n'avais pas été là, Galoche, le pire serait peut-être arrivé. Et jamais je n'aurais pu me le pardonner.

La voix d'Émilie s'étouffe. Je frissonne en pensant que si je n'avais pas entendu les cris de Philippe...

W-ouf !

Deux gouttelettes chaudes me tombent sur le museau. Ma Douce pleure. Mon cœur palpite. Sans jouer les vieux chiens sages, je me mets à espérer qu'Émilie va enfin comprendre que toutes ces histoires d'amour lui sont néfastes...

Quelle grave erreur elle a faite ! Mais elle l'a reconnue, au moins : elle s'est confiée à Marie-Ève et à moi. Elle mérite plus que jamais mon amour canin. Je remonte mes pattes arrière, me roule en boule près de son épaule et me rentre le bout du museau entre l'oreiller et son cou. Ma Douce me donne un petit baiser sur la tête.

Émilie, c'est mon amie pour la vie!

♪♪ *Galoche a une oreille croche,*
croche, croche
Mais il n'a rien d'une cloche,
cloche, cloche
C'est un héros sans reproche,
oche, oche… ♪♪

Quel retour de vacances! À l'avant de l'autobus, Vincent, le chef d'orchestre, et ses deux acolytes, les meneurs de foule, se démènent comme des poules en cage. Toujours à l'unisson, et avec toute la force de leurs poumons, les jeunes me chantent pour la xième fois, à leur façon, leur grande reconnaissance pour leur avoir évité de terminer les vacances sur une très mauvaise note.

Bon, il s'agit encore d'un joli massacre de la poésie humaine... mais on ne me massacre pas comme lors de l'aller; c'est déjà un grand progrès.

♪♪ Une petite mascotte, cotte, cotte
Qui a sauvé la vie de notre pote, pote, pote
Qui serait mort comme une marmotte,
motte, motte... ♪♪

« J'ai le vent dans le cœur... devant tant d'ardeur... à me lancer de jolies fleurs. »

Foi de Galoche, les humains ne cesseront jamais de m'étonner. Tellement que je me mets à faire de la poésie, moi aussi! Je me demande s'ils ne commencent pas à déteindre sur moi?...

– Galoche, Galoche, Galoche!

Pierre-Luc s'amène à toute vitesse dans l'allée, vers le banc arrière où je donne mes dernières prestations d'amuseur public.

– Galoche, Galoche, Galoche! continue notre jeune voisin, en s'assoyant près de moi.

Quoi? Quoi? Quoi?

– Émilie vient de m'inviter!

Ma Douce aurait-elle enfin compris qu'un premier de classe peut être un aussi bon amoureux qu'un sportif?…

– Demain soir.

Génial!

– Pour jouer au hockey!

Oups… Moi, Galoche, je ne suis plus certain de rien. Pauvre Pierre-Luc! La soirée risque d'être longue: il patine sur la bottine… Mais s'il y met autant d'énergie que sur la planche à neige, on ne sait jamais. Tout peut se produire quand un humain est en amour, foi de Galoche!

UN VENT DE SURPRISE

Nous venons de RE-partir en voyage et je ne peux éliminer de ma caboche ce fameux camp de vacances «tornade» que je viens de te raconter. C'était il y a quelques mois, mais il est encore très présent dans ma mémoire, misère à poil!

Affalé sur le siège arrière, je boude. Nous roulons vers une destination que Fabien et Émilie gardent secrète. «Une belle surprise!» s'amusent-ils à me répéter.

– Youhou! lance la copilote de Fabien, tout heureuse.

– Crois-tu, Mimi, que notre voyageur va nous faire la gueule encore longtemps?

Avec leur voyage, ils ont bousillé mes vacances de rêve. Je ne parviens pas à repousser ma colère : Marilou, Éloïse et Sébastien loin de la maison pour plusieurs jours, et nous trois, les meilleurs amis du monde, nous ne pourrons même pas en profiter !

– Papa, quand Galoche découvrira où nous l'amenons, il va bondir de joie !

– Et perdre cette attitude de vieux chien miteux, j'espère !

Depuis leur fameux «ON PART EN VOYAGE !» d'hier après-midi, ils sont restés sourds à tous mes appels à la raison. Ils sont même restés de marbre quand j'ai fait la grève de la faim. Au déjeuner seulement, mais bon, il faut le faire, tout de même : je n'ai pas touché à une seule parcelle de la crêpe que me tendait le père d'Émilie. Ils m'ont alors traité de bébé gâté et… les sans-cœur ! ils ont mangé leurs crêpes avec une double portion de sirop d'érable. Je m'en léchais les babines… de remords!

J'avais déjà essayé l'entorse à la cheville en soirée, le cauchemar en pleine nuit et la chute dans les pommes au petit matin. Rien à faire: *caninement parlant*, j'ai vraiment tout fait pour éviter ce nouveau voyage.

Toujours couché sur la banquette arrière, j'essaie tout de même de garder le moral: «Au moins, cette fois, je n'aurai pas à jouer la mascotte-cotte-cotte…»

Rapidement, nous arrivons à destination. La portière arrière s'ouvre.

– Viens voir, Galoche! lance Émilie, enthousiaste.

Je soulève le museau et feins l'indifférence. Pourtant, je suis curieux de voir enfin ce qui devrait me faire «bondir de joie». Je me mets à quatre pattes pour la première fois depuis notre départ, et je descends lentement de l'automobile.

Aussitôt, une odeur salée me fait frémir les narines. Devant moi, un quai immense. Je saute dans la voiture avant que ma Douce ne referme la portière.

– Mais, Galoche, que fais-tu ?… Redescends, voyons !… Viens, mon beau ! Nous allons vivre une expérience extraordinaire.

Je lui lance un regard incrédule. Elle ajoute, les yeux pétillants :

– Un voyage en voilier, Galoche !

Quoi ?! Je suis aussi allergique aux bateaux et à l'eau qu'à Marilou et à ses fameux rapports. Non, pas question que je monte sur un bateau ! Misère à poil ! Un simple tour de chaloupe avec Fabien me transforme en une grosse barbe à papa tellement j'ai les nerfs en boule de poils. Comment ma Douce peut-elle

m'annoncer, tout sourire, qu'elle m'em-
mène faire un voyage en voilier ? Je pré-
fère encore, et de beaucoup, devoir jouer
la mascotte-cotte-cotte que le chien
marin-rin-rin...

– Fais pas ta tête dure ! Viens, Galoche,
vite !

Aucun humain ne me fera bouger de
ce siège, foi de Galo...

AÏE !

– Salut, mon gros ! Comment vas-tu ?

Je me retrouve museau à museau
avec une énorme tête. Ricardo !? Pris par
surprise, je ne peux éviter ses deux
grosses mains poilues qui m'empoi-
gnent. Le gros et grand motard artiste
peintre et frère de Fabien me soulève
comme si j'étais une petite mésange. Il
me sort de la voiture.

– Tu te souviens de mon oncle Ricardo ?
fait Émilie.

Comment l'avoir oublié, celui-là ? Je
suis de nouveau « en état de choc »...

Surtout que je viens de constater qu'il porte une casquette, non pas de base-ball, ni de golf, ni de tennis, ni même de motard, mais bien... DE CAPITAINE! Il a aussi un grand chandail de marin bleu et blanc. Dans ses bras, moi, Galoche, je me sens aussi petit et coincé qu'un poisson rouge dans son bocal.

– Mon frérot n'est pas qu'un artiste peintre très connu à San Francisco, lance fièrement Fabien, c'est aussi un artiste... de la mer. Il nous invite à faire un voyage sur le voilier d'un de ses amis.

– Je te l'avais dit, Galoche: une belle surprise! Mais... qu'est-ce que tu as à trembler comme une feuille?

Moi, Galoche, je suis convaincu que nous coulerons à pic si Ricardo conduit son voilier aussi follement que sa moto-cyclette...

Depuis de longues minutes déjà, la coque monte et redescend sans arrêt, l'eau du fleuve éclaboussant jusque sur le pont avant où je suis avec Émilie. Elle a revêtu un imperméable avec capuchon. Moi, je joue le bouffon en essuyant une véritable douche froide à chaque grosse vague. Quel plaisir fou!…

– Ça, c'est du sport! Pas vrai, Galoche?

C'est vrai, la danse est un sport: depuis notre départ, je n'arrête pas de sauter sur trois, deux et même une patte pour ne pas me retrouver à l'eau. Un vrai chien de cirque!

Je vois soudain la grande voile tomber lentement vers l'eau, sur notre droite. Le plancher se met à s'incliner dangereusement. J'essaie de m'accrocher aux jambes de ma Douce. Trop tard! Je glisse. Droit devant, à hauteur de museau, les vagues frappent le haut du rebord du bateau. J'ai l'impression de me diriger droit dans le fleuve.

AOOOOUH!

Une main accroche mon gilet de sauvetage. W-ouf!

– Pas de danger, Galoche! s'amuse Émilie. C'est normal de tanguer sur un voilier. Ricardo contrôle tout.

Vraiment, je n'ai pas la patte marine. Et, contrairement aux humains en voyage, moi, Galoche, je n'ai nullement envie de me faire des peurs ni de jouer les héros. Finie la danse! Vive la carpette! Trempé, je m'éclipse et me dirige vers la cabine. En passant près du capitaine et de son second, à l'arrière du voilier, je les entends hurler:

– On dirait que le temps se gâte!

– Oui, tu as raison, frérot, le vent d'est se lève! reconnaît le capitaine, à la barre du bateau. Ce n'était pas prévu, ces vents. Je vais aller écouter la météo.

Très, très, très rassuré, je descends les marches en vitesse et trouve rapidement un tapis moelleux et chaud, au pied du lit,

dans la cham-
brette du capi-
taine. Et là, alors
que la barbe à papa
que je suis commence
enfin à se détendre, à
moins de trois centimè-
tres de ma truffe, je vois…
DEUX GROS YEUX JAUNES
TERRIFIANTS QUI ME FIXENT DANS
LA PÉNOMBRE.

« Victor !? »

Je lis dans le regard moqueur du
matou tigré du gros Ricardo : « Comment
se fait-il, Galoche, que tu aies aussi peur
de l'eau ? Serais-tu devenu un chat ? »

Tout un coup de barre pour mon
orgueil canin. Ce Victor, le vrai portrait de
Ricardo !

– Fabien ? Émilie ? lance soudain la
voix forte du capitaine. On fait demi-tour.
Ils annoncent du mauvais temps dans le
golfe pour quelques jours. Des vents plus

forts que prévus! Je ne peux prendre de risque, surtout qu'il s'agit du voilier de mon ami.

Voilà ce que j'appelle un bon capitaine, foi de Galoche! W-ouf! Quelle bonne nouvelle: on va sans doute retourner à la maison. Et moi, Galoche, je vais peut-être réaliser mes vacances de rêve…

Comme je l'imaginais, nous avons bel et bien repris la route vers la maison. D'ailleurs, nous approchons.

– Youhou! hurle joyeusement Émilie.

La pluie, la brume et les vents nous ont finalement rejoints. Le temps est très maussade. Mais pas autant que moi!

– Youhou! s'exclame Ricardo à son tour.

Fabien a eu la brillante idée d'inviter Ricardo à la maison. Dès que celui-ci a su que Marilou, la sous-ministre, n'y était pas, il a accepté. Et mon Émilie a eu un éclair de génie.

– Ça, c'est du sport, hein, Galoche ? crie Émilie, qui resserre ses bras autour de la taille de Ricardo.

Pauvre moi ! Me voilà de retour dans le *side-car* de la motocyclette du gros et grand oncle motard de mon Émilie. Quel choc de me retrouver sur une roue, dans cette espèce de bac à vidanges accroché au vieil engin roulant de Ricardo. Quel bruit d'enfer ! Sans compter qu'à chaque nid-de-poule, je vole dans les airs : tour à tour, je me sens comme une crêpe de Fabien, une pizza de Ricardo ou une omelette d'Émilie, qui risque de s'écrabouiller sur l'asphalte. Grâce à mes talents d'acrobate et à mon puissant instinct de survie, je réussis à retomber chaque fois sur mon siège… mais j'ai les fesses en compote, misère à poil !

Ah ! Émilie et ses idées originales !

De minute en minute, ma colère empire : je ne peux m'empêcher de penser que ce gros Victor de malheur tient compagnie à Fabien dans la voiture qui nous suit, bien au chaud sur un siège douillet.

J'en ai les crocs qui grincent de frustration.

– Galoche, même sans voilier, on va passer des vacances de rêve ! crie à tue-tête mon Émilie.

Des vacances cauchemardesques, oui ! Je vais devoir partager mon intimité avec un chat...

GRRRRrrrrrrrrrrr !!!

Foi de Galoche, je m'ennuie presque de la planche à neige et du beau et blond Philippe !

YVON BROCHU

Comme son fidèle ami Galoche, Yvon a des tonnes d'histoires à raconter! Il aime faire rire… et faire rêver. Voilà pourquoi il a écrit une trentaine de romans jeunesse. Quand il n'écrit pas, il joue au tennis, lit un roman, regarde du sport à la télé ou, en bon gourmand qu'il est, mange un petit plat… de préférence bien sucré! Pas étonnant que Galoche aime autant les crêpes au sirop d'érable!

DAVID LEMELIN

En plus d'illustrer des livres, David est aussi journaliste. Quand il ne dessine pas une nouvelle aventure de Galoche, David fait des chroniques à la radio ou présente le téléjournal, suit attentivement la politique et l'actualité, prend des cours pour apprendre le russe et, bien sûr, garde du temps pour ses deux garçons. Comme ce cher Galoche, on peut dire que notre illustrateur a le vent dans les oreilles!

Visite le site de Galoche pour t'amuser

À toi de jouer

Plusieurs jeux rigolos et activités à partir de l'univers de Galoche. Du plaisir assuré!

À toi de participer

Chaque mois, ton ami Galoche répond à une ou plusieurs questions qui lui sont posées sur le site par ses admirateurs. À toi de participer!

Les galocheries

Des textes amusants écrits par Galoche, spécialement pour le site; une fois de plus, Galoche se moque des habitudes des humains. Aussi, des fous rires avec les fameux *gagaloches*!

L'auteur

À partir d'un jeu-questionnaire, découvre Yvon Brochu, auteur de Galoche. De quoi tout savoir sur son métier et ses habitudes d'auteur!

L'illustrateur

Vois comment David Lemelin, illustrateur, procède pour dessiner et participe au jeu-questionnaire qui te permettra de mieux le connaître.

Le coin des profs

Des activités Galoche à faire en classe.

Dear Reader,

I really can't express how flattered I am and also how grateful I am to Harlequin Books for releasing this collection of my published works. It came as a great surprise. I never think of myself as writing books that are collectible. In fact, there are days when I forget that writing is work at all. What I do for a living is so much fun that it never seems like a job. And since I reside in a small community, and my daily life is confined to such mundane things as feeding the wild birds and looking after my herb patch in the backyard, I feel rather unconnected from what many would think of as a glamorous profession.

But when I read my email, or when I get letters from readers, or when I go on signing trips to bookstores to meet all of you, I feel truly blessed. Over the past thirty years I have made lasting friendships with many of you. And quite frankly, most of you are like part of my family. You can't imagine how much you enrich my life. Thank you so much.

I also need to extend thanks to my family (my husband, James, son, Blayne, daughter-in-law, Christina, and granddaughter, Selena Marie), to my best friend, Ann, to my readers, booksellers and the wonderful people at Harlequin Books—from my editor of many years, Tara, to all the other fine and talented people who make up our publishing house. Thanks to all of you for making this job, and my private life, so worth living.

Thank you for this tribute, Harlequin, and for putting up with me for thirty long years! Love to all of you.

Diana Palmer

DIANA PALMER

The prolific author of more than a hundred books, Diana Palmer got her start as a newspaper reporter. A multi–*New York Times* bestselling author and one of the top ten romance writers in America, she has a gift for telling the most sensual tales with charm and humor. Diana lives with her family in Cornelia, Georgia.

Visit her website at www.DianaPalmer.com.

THE
Essential
COLLECTION

DIANA

New York Times and USA TODAY Bestselling Author

PALMER

COLTRAIN'S PROPOSAL

TORONTO NEW YORK LONDON
AMSTERDAM PARIS SYDNEY HAMBURG
STOCKHOLM ATHENS TOKYO MILAN MADRID
PRAGUE WARSAW BUDAPEST AUCKLAND

To Darlene, Cindy and Melissa

Recycling programs
for this product may
not exist in your area.

ISBN-13: 978-0-373-36377-3

COLTRAIN'S PROPOSAL

Copyright © 1995 by Diana Palmer

All rights reserved. Except for use in any review, the reproduction or utilization of this work in whole or in part in any form by any electronic, mechanical or other means, now known or hereafter invented, including xerography, photocopying and recording, or in any information storage or retrieval system, is forbidden without the written permission of the publisher, Harlequin Enterprises Limited, 225 Duncan Mill Road, Don Mills, Ontario M3B 3K9, Canada.

This is a work of fiction. Names, characters, places and incidents are either the product of the author's imagination or are used fictitiously, and any resemblance to actual persons, living or dead, business establishments, events or locales is entirely coincidental.

This edition published by arrangement with Harlequin Books S.A.

For questions and comments about the quality of this book please contact us at Customer_eCare@Harlequin.ca.

® and TM are trademarks of the publisher. Trademarks indicated with ® are registered in the United States Patent and Trademark Office, the Canadian Trade Marks Office and in other countries.

www.eHarlequin.com

Printed in U.S.A.

AVAILABLE JUNE 2011
A Long, Tall Texan Summer
(containing "Tom," "Drew" and "Jobe")
Nora
Dream's End
Champagne Girl
Friends and Lovers
The Wedding in White

AVAILABLE JULY 2011
Heather's Song
Snow Kisses
To Love and Cherish
Long, Tall and Tempted
(containing "Redbird," "Paper Husband" and
"Christmas Cowboy")
The Australian
Darling Enemy
Trilby

AVAILABLE AUGUST 2011
Sweet Enemy
Soldier of Fortune
The Tender Stranger
Enamored
After the Music
The Patient Nurse

AVAILABLE SEPTEMBER 2011
The Case of the Mesmerizing Boss
The Case of the Confirmed Bachelor
The Case of the Missing Secretary
September Morning
Diamond Girl
Eye of the Tiger

Chapter 1

The little boy's leg was bleeding profusely. Dr. Louise Blakely knew exactly what to do, but it was difficult to get the right pressure on the cut so that the nicked artery would stop emptying onto the brown, dead December grass.

"It hurts!" the little boy, Matt, cried. "Ow!"

"We have to stop the bleeding," she said reasonably. She smiled at him, her dark eyes twinkling in a face framed by thick, medium blond hair. "Maybe your mom could get you an ice cream after we've patched you up." She glanced at the white-faced lady beside them, who nodded enthusiastically. "Okay?"

"Well…" He grimaced, holding his leg above where Lou was putting pressure to bear.

"Only a minute more," she promised, looking around for the ambulance she'd asked a bystander to call. It was on the way. She could hear the siren. Even in a small town like Jacobsville, there was an efficient ambulance service. "You're going to get to ride in a real ambulance," she told the child. "You can tell your friends all about it on Monday at school!"

"Will I have to go back?" he asked, enthusiastic now. "Maybe I could stay in the hospital for a whole week?"

"I really think the emergency room is as far as you're going to get this time." Lou chuckled. "Now pay attention while they're loading you up, so that you can remember everything!"

"I sure will!" he said.

She stood up as the ambulance pulled alongside the police car and two attendants jumped out. They started loading the boy onto a stretcher. Lou had a brief word with the female EMT and described the boy's injuries and gave instructions. She was on staff at the local hospital where he would be taken, and she planned to follow the ambulance in her own car.

The police officer who'd been citing the reckless driver for hitting the small boy on the bicycle came over to talk to Lou. "Good thing you were having lunch in the café," he remarked with a grin. "That was a bad cut."

"He'll be okay," Lou said as she closed her medical bag. She always had it in the car when she left the office, and this time it had paid off.

"You're Dr. Coltrain's partner, aren't you?" he asked suddenly.

"Yes." She didn't add anything to that. The expression on the officer's face said enough. Most people around Jacobsville knew that Dr. Coltrain had as little use for his partner as he had for alcohol. He'd made it all too evident in the months she'd been sharing his practice.

"He's a good man," the officer added. "Saved my wife when her lung collapsed." He smiled at the memory. "Nothing shakes him up. Nor you, either, judging by what I just saw. You're a good hand in an emergency."

"Thanks." She gave him a brief smile and went to her small gray Ford to follow the ambulance to the hospital.

The emergency room was full, as usual. It was Saturday and accidents always doubled on weekends. She nodded to a couple of her patients that she recognized, and she kept walking, right behind the trolley that was taking young Matt to a treatment room.

Dr. Coltrain was on his way back from surgery. They met in the hall. The green surgical uniform looked sloppy on some of the surgeons, but not on Coltrain. Despite the cap that hid most of his thick red hair, he looked elegant and formidable.

"Why are you here on Saturday? I'm supposed to be doing rounds today for both of us," he asked sharply.

Here he goes again, practicing Coltrain's First Law... jump to conclusions, she thought. She didn't grin, but she felt like it.

"I wound up at a car accident scene," she began.

"The hospital pays EMTs to work wrecks," he continued, glaring at her while hospital personnel came and went around them.

"I did not go out to—" she began hotly.

"Don't let this happen again, or I'll have a word with

Wright, and you'll be taken off staff here. Is that clear?"
he added coldly. Wright was the hospital administrator
and Coltrain was medical chief of staff. He had the
authority to carry out the threat.

"Will you listen?" she asked irritably. "I didn't go
out with the ambulance…!"

"Doctor, are you coming?" one of the EMTs called
to her.

Coltrain glanced toward the EMT and then back at
Louise, irritably jerking off his cap and mask. His pale
blue eyes were as intimidating as his stance. "If your
social life is this stale, Doctor, perhaps you need to
consider a move," he added with biting sarcasm.

She opened her mouth to reply, but he was already
walking away. She threw up her hands furiously. She
couldn't ever get a word in, because he kept talking, or
interrupted her, and then stormed off without giving
her a chance to reply. It was useless to argue with him,
anyway. No matter what she said or did, she was always
in the wrong.

"One day you'll break something," she told his re-
treating back. "And I'll put you in a body cast, so help
me God!"

A passing nurse patted her on the shoulder. "There,
there, Doctor, you're doing it again."

She ground her teeth together. It was a standing joke
in the hospital staff that Louise Blakely ended up talking to herself every time she argued with Dr. Coltrain.
That meant that she talked to herself almost constantly.
Presumably he heard her from time to time, but he never
gave a single indication that he had.

With a furious groan deep in her throat, she turned down the hall to join the EMT.

It took an hour to see to the boy, who had more than one cut that needed stitches. His mother was going to have to buy him a lot of ice cream to make up for the pain, Lou thought, and she'd been wrong about another thing, too—he did have to stay overnight in the hospital. But that would only give him status among his peers, she thought, and left him smiling with a cautionary word about the proper way to ride a bicycle in town.

"No need to worry about that," his mother said firmly. "He won't be riding his bike across city streets anymore!"

She nodded and left the emergency room, her bag in hand. She looked more like a teenager on holiday than a doctor, she mused, in her blue jeans and T-shirt and sneakers. She'd pulled her long blond hair up into its habitual bun and she wore no makeup to enhance her full mouth or her deep brown eyes. She had no man to impress, except the one she loved, and he wouldn't notice if she wore tar and feathers to the office they shared. "Copper" Coltrain had no interest in Lou Blakely, except as an efficient co-worker. Not that he ever acknowledged her efficiency; instead he found fault with her constantly. She wondered often why he ever agreed to work with her in the first place, when he couldn't seem to stand the sight of her. She wondered, too, why she kept hanging on where she wasn't wanted. The hunger her poor heart felt for him was her only excuse. And one day, even that wouldn't be enough.

Dr. Drew Morris, the only friend she had on staff,

came down the hall toward her. Like Coltrain, he'd been operating, because he was wearing the same familiar green surgical clothing. But where Coltrain did chest surgery, Drew's talents were limited to tonsils, adenoids, appendices and other minor surgeries. His speciality was pediatrics. Coltrain's was chest and lungs, and many of his patients were elderly.

"What are you doing here? It's too early or too late for rounds, depending on your schedule," he added with a grin. "Besides, I thought Copper was doing them today."

Copper, indeed. Only a handful of people were privileged to call Dr. Coltrain by that nickname, and she wasn't numbered among them.

She grimaced at him. He was about her height, although she was tall, and he had dark hair and eyes and was a little overweight. He was the one who'd phoned her at the Austin hospital where she was working just after her parents' deaths, and he'd told her about the interviews Coltrain was holding for a partner. She'd jumped at the chance for a new start, in the hometown where her mother and father had both been born. And amazingly, in light of his ongoing animosity toward her, Coltrain had asked her to join him after a ten-minute interview.

"There was an accident in front of the café," she said. "I was having lunch there. I haven't been to the grocery store yet," she added with a grimace. "I hate shopping."

"Who doesn't?" He smiled. "Doing okay?"

She shrugged. "As usual."

He stuck his hands on his hips and shook his head.

"It's my fault. I thought it would get better, but it hasn't, has it? It's been almost a year, and he still suffers you."

She winced. She didn't quite avert her face fast enough to hide it.

"You poor kid," he said gently. "I'm sorry. I suppose I was too enthusiastic about getting you here. I thought you needed a change, after...well, after your parents' deaths. This looked like a good opportunity. Copper's one of the best surgeons I've ever known, and you're a skilled family practitioner. It seemed a good match of talent, and you've taken a load off him in his regular practice so that he could specialize in the surgery he's so skilled at." He sighed. "How wrong can a man be?"

"I signed a contract for one year," she reminded him. "It's almost up."

"Then what?"

"Then I'll go back to Austin."

"You could work the E.R.," he teased. It was a standing joke between them. The hospital had to contract out the emergency room staff, because none of the local doctors wanted to do it. The job was so demanding that one young resident had walked out in the middle of the unnecessary examination of a known hypochondriac at two in the morning and never came back.

Lou smiled, remembering that. "No, thanks. I like private practice, but I can't afford to set up and equip an office of my own just yet. I'll go back to the drawing board. There's bound to be a practice somewhere in Texas."

"You're fit for this one," he said shortly.

"Not to hear my partner tell it," she said curtly. "I'm

never right, didn't you know?" She let out a long breath. "Anyway, I'm in a rut, Drew. I need a change."

"Maybe you do, at that." He pursed his lips and smiled. "What you really need is a good social life. I'll be in touch."

She watched him walk away with grave misgivings. She hoped that he didn't mean what it sounded like he meant. She wanted nothing to do with Drew in a romantic way, although she did like him. He was a kind man, a widower who'd been in love with his wife and was still, after five years, getting over her. Drew was a native of Jacobsville, and knew Lou's parents. He'd been very fond of her late mother. He'd met up with them again in Austin—that's where Lou had met him.

Lou decided not to take Drew's teasing seriously because she knew about his devotion to his wife's memory. But he'd looked very solemn when he'd remarked that her social life needed uplifting.

She was probably imagining things, she told herself. She started out to the parking lot and met Dr. Coltrain, dressed in an expensive gray vested suit, bent on the same destination. She ground her teeth together and slowed her pace, but she still reached the doors at the same time he did.

He spared her a cold glance. "You look unprofessional," he said curtly. "At least have the grace to dress decently if you're going to cruise around with the ambulance service."

She stopped and looked up at him without expression. "I wasn't cruising anywhere. I don't have a boat, so how could I cruise?"

He just looked at her. "They don't need any new EMTs…"

"You shut up!" she snapped, surprising him speechless. "Now you listen to me for a change, and don't interrupt!" she added, holding up her hand when his thin lips parted. "There was an accident in town. I was in the café, so I gave assistance. I don't need to hang out with the ambulance crew for kicks, Doctor! And how I dress on my days off is none of your—" she almost turned blue biting back the curse *"—business,* Doctor!"

He was over his shock. His hand shot out and caught the wrist of her free hand, the one that wasn't holding her black medical bag, and jerked. She caught her breath at the shock of his touch and squirmed, wrestling out of his grip. The muted violence of it brought back protective instincts that she'd almost forgotten. She stood very still, holding her breath, her eyes the size of saucers as she looked at him and waited for that hand to tighten and twist…

But it didn't. He, unlike her late father, never seemed to lose control. He released her abruptly. His blue eyes narrowed. "Cold as ice, aren't you?" he drawled mockingly. "You'd freeze any normal man to death. Is that why you never married, Doctor?"

It was the most personal thing he'd ever said to her, and one of the most insulting.

"You just think what you like," she said.

"You might be surprised at what I think," he replied. He looked at the hand he'd touched her with and laughed deep in his throat. "Frostbitten," he pronounced. "No wonder Drew Morris doesn't take you out. He'd need a blowtorch, wouldn't he?" he added with a meaningful, unblinking blue stare.

"Maybe so, but you'd need a grenade launcher," she retorted without thinking.

He lifted an eyebrow and gave her a look that held mingled contempt and distaste. "You'd be lucky."

The remark was painful, but she didn't let him see that. Her own eyebrows lifted. "Really?" She laughed and walked off to her car, happy to have seen him stiffen. She walked past his Mercedes without even a glance. Take that, she thought furiously. She didn't care what he thought about her, she told herself. She spent most of her free time telling herself that. But she did care about him, far too much. That was the whole problem.

He thought she was cold, but she wasn't. It was quite the reverse where he was concerned. She always jerked away when he came too close, when he touched her infrequently. It wasn't because she found him repulsive but because his touch excited her so much. She trembled when he was too close, her breathing changed. She couldn't control her shaky legs or her shaky voice. The only solution had been to distance herself physically from him, and that was what she'd done.

There were other reasons, too, why she avoided physical involvement. They were none of his business, or anyone else's. She did her job and avoided trouble as much as possible. But just lately, her job was becoming an ordeal.

She drove home to the small dilapidated white house on the outskirts of town. It was in a quiet neighborhood that was just beginning to go downhill. The rent was cheap. She'd spent weekends painting the walls and adding bits and pieces to the house's drab interior. She had it all but furnished now, and it reflected her own quiet personality. But there were other dimensions to the room, like the crazy cat sculpture on the mantel and the colorful serapes on the chairs, and the Indian pottery and exotic musical instruments on the bookshelf. The paintings were her own, disturbingly violent ones with reds and blacks and whites in dramatic chaos. A visitor would have found the combinations of flowers amid those paintings confusing. But, then, she'd never had a visitor. She kept to herself.

Coltrain did, too, as a rule. He had visitors to his ranch from time to time, but his invitations even when they included the medical staff invariably excluded Louise. The omission had caused gossip, which no one had been brave enough to question to his face. Louise didn't care if he never invited her to his home. After all, she never invited him to hers.

Secretly she suspected that he was grieving for Jane Parker, his old flame who'd just recently married Todd Burke. Jane was blond and blue-eyed and beautiful, a former rodeo star with a warm heart and a gentle personality.

Lou often wondered why he'd ever agreed to work with someone he disliked so much, and on such short acquaintance. He and Dr. Drew Morris were friends, and she'd tried to question Drew about her sudden acceptance, but Drew was a clam. He always changed the subject.

Drew had known her parents in Jacobsville and he had been a student of her father's at the Austin teaching hospital where he'd interned. He'd become an ally of her mother during some really tough times, but he didn't like Lou's father. He knew too much about his home life, and how Lou and her mother were treated.

There had been one whisper of gossip at the Jacobsville hospital when she'd first gone there on cases. She'd heard one of the senior nurses remark that it must disturb "him" to have Dr. Blakely's daughter practicing at this hospital and thank God she didn't do surgery. Lou had wanted to question the nurse, but she'd made herself scarce after that and eventually had retired.

Louise had never found out who "he" was or what was disturbing about having another Blakely practice at the Jacobsville hospital. But she did begin to realize that her father had a past here.

"What did my father do at this hospital, Drew?" she'd asked him one day suddenly, while they were doing rounds at the hospital.

He'd seemed taken aback. "He was a surgeon on staff, just as I am," he said after a hesitation.

"He left here under a cloud, didn't he?" she persisted.

He shook his head. "There was no scandal, no cloud on his reputation. He was a good surgeon and well respected, right until the end. You know that. Even if he was less than admirable as a husband and father, he was an exceptional surgeon."

"Then why the whispers about him when I first came here?"

"It was nothing to do with his skill as a surgeon," he replied quietly. "It's nothing that really even concerns you, except in a roundabout way."

"But what…?"

They'd been interrupted and he'd looked relieved. She hadn't asked again. But she wondered more and more. Perhaps it had affected Dr. Coltrain in some way and that was why he disliked Lou. But wouldn't he have mentioned it in a whole year?

She didn't ever expect to understand the so-controlled Dr. Coltrain or his venomous attitude toward her. He'd been much more cordial when she first became his partner. But about the time she realized that she was in love with him, he became icy cold and antagonistic. He'd been that way ever since, raising eyebrows everywhere.

The remark he'd made this morning about her coldness was an old one. She'd jerked back from him at a Christmas party, soon after she'd come to work in his office in Jacobsville, to avoid a kiss under the mistletoe. She could hardly have admitted that even then the thought of his hard, thin mouth on hers made her knees threaten to buckle. Her attraction to him had been explosive and immediate, a frightening experience to a woman whose whole life had been wrapped around academic excellence and night upon night of exhaustive studying. She had no social life at all—even in high school. It had been the one thing that kept her father's vicious sarcasm and brutality at bay, as long as she made good grades and stayed on the dean's list.

Outside achievements had been the magic key that kept the balance in her dysfunctional family. She studied and won awards and scholarships and praise, and her father basked in it. She thought that he'd never felt much for her, except pride in her ability to excel. He was a cruel man and grew crueler as his addiction climbed year after year to new heights. Drugs had caused the plane crash. Her mother had died with him. God knew, that was fitting, because she'd loved him to the point of blindness, overlooking his brutality, his addiction, his cruelty in the name of fidelity.

Lou wrapped her arms around herself, feeling the chill of fear. She'd never marry. Any woman could wake up in a relationship that damaging. All she had to do was fall in love, lose control, give in to a man's dominance. Even the best man could become a predator if he sensed vulnerability in a woman. So she would never be vulnerable, she assured herself. She would never be at a man's mercy as her mother had been.

But Copper Coltrain made her vulnerable, and that was why she avoided any physical contact with him. She couldn't give in to the feelings he roused in her, for fear of becoming a victim. Loneliness might be a disease, but it was certainly a more manageable one than love.

The ringing of the telephone caught her attention.

"Dr. Blakely?" Brenda, her office nurse, queried. "Sorry to bother you at home, but Dr. Coltrain said there's been a wreck on the north end of town and they'll be bringing the victims to the emergency room. Since he's on call, you'll have to cover the two-hour Saturday clinic at the office."

"I'll be right over," she promised, wasting no more time in conversation.

The clinic was almost deserted. There was a football game at the local high school that night, and it was sunny and unseasonably warm outside for early

December. It didn't really surprise Lou that she only needed to see a handful of patients.

"Poor Dr. Coltrain," Brenda said with a sigh as they finished the last case and closed up the office. "I'll bet he won't be in until midnight."

"It's a good thing he isn't married," Lou remarked. "He'd have no home life at all, as hard as he works."

Brenda glanced at her, but with a kind smile. "That is true. But he should be thinking about it. He's in his thirties now, and time is passing him by." She turned the key in the lock. "Pity about Miss Parker marrying that Burke man, isn't it? Dr. Coltrain was sweet on her for so many years. I always thought—I guess most people here did—that they were made for each other. But she was never more than friendly. If you saw them together, it was obvious that she didn't feel what he did."

In other words, Dr. Coltrain had felt a long and unrequited love for the lovely blond former rodeo cowgirl, Jane Parker. That much, Lou had learned from gossip. It must have hurt him very badly when she married someone else.

"What a pity that we can't love to order," Lou remarked quietly, thinking how much she'd give to be unscarred and find Dr. Coltrain as helplessly drawn to her as she was to him. That was the stuff of fantasy, however.

"Wasn't it surprising about Ted Regan and Coreen Tarleton, though?" Brenda added with a chuckle.

"Indeed it was," Lou agreed, smiling as she remembered having Ted for a patient. "She was shaking all over when she got him to me with that gored arm. He was cool. Nothing shakes Ted. But Coreen was as white as milk."

"I thought they were already married," Brenda groaned. "Well, I was new to the area and I didn't know them. I do now," she added, laughing. "I pass them at least once a week on their way to the obstetrician's office. She's due any day."

"She'll be a good mother, and Ted will certainly be a good father. Their children will have a happy life."

Brenda caught the faint bitterness in the words and glanced at Lou, but the other woman was already calling her goodbyes and walking away.

She went home and spent the rest of the weekend buried in medical journals and the latest research on the new strain of bacteria that had, researchers surmised, mutated from a deadly scarlet fever bacterium that had caused many deaths at the turn of the century.

Chapter 2

Monday morning brought a variety of new cases, and Louise found herself stuck with the most routine of them, as usual. She and Coltrain were supposed to be partners, but when he wasn't operating, he got the interesting, challenging illnesses. Louise got fractured ribs and colds.

He'd been stiff with her this morning, probably because he was still fuming over the argument they'd had about his mistaken idea of her weekend activities. Accusing her of lollygagging with the EMTs for excitement; really!

She watched his white-coated back disappear into an examination room down the hall in their small building and sighed half-angrily as she went back to check an X-ray in the files. The very worst thing about unrequited love, she thought miserably, was that it fed on itself. The more her partner in the medical practice ignored and

antagonized her, the harder she had to fight her dreams
about him. She didn't want to get married; she didn't
even want to get involved. But he made her hungry.

He'd spent a lot of time with Jane Parker until she
married that Burke man, and Lou had long ago given
up hope that he would ever notice her in the same way
he always noticed Jane. The two of them had grown up
together, though, whereas Lou had only been in partnership with him for a year. She was a native of Austin, not
Jacobsville. Small towns were like extended families.
Everybody knew each other, and some families had
been friends for more than one generation. Lou was a
true outsider here, even though she *was* a native Texan.
Perhaps that was one of many reasons that Dr. Coltrain
found her so forgettable.

She wasn't bad looking. She had long, thick blond
hair and big brown eyes and a creamy, blemish-free
complexion. She was tall and willowy, but still shorter
than her colleague. She lacked his fiery temper and his
authoritarian demeanor. He was tall and whipcord lean,
with flaming red hair and blue eyes and a dark tan from
working on his small ranch when he wasn't treating
patients. That tan was odd in a redhead, although he did
have a smattering of freckles over his nose and the backs
of his big hands. She'd often wondered if the freckles
went any farther, but she had yet to see him without his
professional white coat over his very formal suit. He
wasn't much on casual dressing at work. At home, she
was sure that he dressed less formally.

That was something Lou would probably never know.
She'd never been invited to his home, despite the fact
that most of the medical staff at the local hospital had.

Lou was automatically excluded from any social gathering that he coordinated.

Other people had commented on his less than friendly behavior toward her. It puzzled them, and it puzzled her, because she hadn't become his partner in any underhanded way. He had known from the day of her application that she was female, so it couldn't be that. Perhaps, she thought wistfully, he was one of those old-line dominating sort of men who thought women had no place in medicine. But he'd been instrumental in getting women into positions of authority at the hospital, so that theory wasn't applicable, either. The bottom line was that he simply did not like Louise Blakely, medical degree or no medical degree, and she'd never known why.

She really should ask Drew Morris why, she told herself with determination. It had been Drew, a surgeon and friend of her family, who'd sent word about the opening in Coltrain's practice. He'd wanted to help Lou get a job near him, so that he could give her some moral support in the terrible days following the deaths of her parents. She, in turn, had liked the idea of being in practice in a small town, one where she knew at least one doctor on the staff of the hospital. Despite growing up in Austin, it was still a big city and she was lonely. She was twenty-eight, a loner whose whole life had been medicine. She'd made sure that her infrequent dates never touched her heart, and she was innocent in an age when innocence was automatically looked on with disdain or suspicion.

Her nurse stuck her head in the doorway. "There's a call for you. Dr. Morris is on line two."

"Thanks, Brenda."

She picked up the receiver absently, her finger poised over the designated line. But when she pressed it, before she could say a word, the sentence she'd intercepted accidentally blared in her ear in a familiar deep voice.

"...told you I wouldn't have hired her in the first place, if I had known who she was related to. I did you a favor, never realizing she was Blakely's daughter. You can't imagine that I'll ever forgive her father for what he did to the girl I loved, do you? She's been a constant reminder, a constant torment!"

"That's harsh, Copper," Drew began.

"It's how I feel. She's nothing but a burden here. But to answer your question, hell no, you're not stepping on my toes if you ask her out on a date! I find Louise Blakely repulsive and repugnant, and an automaton with no attractions whatsoever. Take her with my blessing. I'd give real money if she'd get out of my practice and out of my life, and the sooner the better!" There was a click and the line, obviously open, was waiting for her.

She clicked the receiver to announce her presence and said, as calmly as she could, "Dr. Lou Blakely."

"Lou! It's Drew Morris," came the reply. "I hope I'm not catching you at a bad moment?"

"No." She cleared her throat and fought to control her scattered emotions. "No, not at all. What can I do for you?"

"There's a dinner at the Rotary Club Thursday. How about going with me?"

She and Drew occasionally went out together, in a friendly but not romantic way. She would have refused, but what Coltrain had said made her mad. "Yes, I would like to, thanks," she said.

Drew laughed softly. "Great! I'll pick you up at six on Thursday, then."

"See you then."

She hung up, checked the X-ray again meticulously, and put it away in its file. Brenda ordinarily pulled the X-rays for her, but it was Monday and, as usual, they were overflowing with patients who'd saved their weekend complaints for office hours.

She went back to her patient, her color a little high, but no disturbance visible in her expression.

She finished her quota of patients and then went into her small office. Mechanically she picked up a sheet of letterhead paper, with Dr. Coltrain's name on one side and hers on the other. Irrelevantly, she thought that the stationery would have to be replaced now.

She typed out a neat resignation letter, put it in an envelope and went to place it on Dr. Coltrain's desk. It was lunchtime and he'd already left the building. He made sure he always did, probably to insure that he didn't risk having Lou invite herself to eat with him.

Brenda scowled as her boss started absently toward the back door. "Shouldn't you take off your coat first?" she asked hesitantly.

Lou did, without a word, replaced it in her office, whipped her leather fanny pack around her waist and left the building.

It would have been nice if she'd had someone to talk to, she thought wistfully, about this latest crisis. She sat alone in the local café, drinking black coffee and picking at a small salad. She didn't mingle well with people. When she wasn't working, she was quiet and shy, and she kept to herself. It was difficult for strangers to approach her, but she didn't realize that. She stared into her coffee and remembered every word Coltrain had said to Drew Morris about her. He hated her. He couldn't possibly have made it clearer. She was repugnant, he'd said.

Well, perhaps she was. Her father had told her so, often enough, when he was alive. He and her mother were from Jacobsville but hadn't lived in the area for years. He had never spoken of his past. Not that he spoke to Lou often, anyway, except to berate her grades and tell her that she'd never measure up.

"Excuse me?"

She looked up. The waitress was staring at her. "Yes?" she asked coolly.

"I don't mean to pry, but are you all right?"

The question surprised Lou, and touched her. She managed a faint smile through her misery. "Yes. It's been a…long morning. I'm not really hungry."

"Okay." The waitress smiled again, reassuringly, and went away.

Just as Lou was finishing her coffee, Coltrain came in the front door. He was wearing the elegant gray suit that looked so good on him, and carrying a silver belly Stetson by the brim. He looked furiously angry as his pale eyes scanned the room and finally spotted Lou, sitting all alone.

He never hesitated, she thought, watching him walk purposefully toward her. There must be an emergency…

He slammed the opened envelope down on the table

in front of her. "What the hell do you mean by that?" he demanded in a dangerously quiet tone.

She raised her dark, cold eyes to his. "I'm leaving," she explained and averted her gaze.

"I know that! I want to know why!"

She looked around. The café was almost empty, but the waitress and a local cowboy at the counter were glancing at them curiously.

Her chin came up. "I'd rather not discuss my private business in public, if you don't mind," she said stiffly.

His jaw clenched, and his eyes grew glittery. He stood back to allow her to get up. He waited while she paid for her salad and coffee and then followed her out to where her small gray Ford was parked.

Her heart raced when he caught her by the arm before she could get her key out of her jeans pocket. He jerked her around, not roughly, and walked her over to Jacobsville's small town square, to a secluded bench in a grove of live oak and willow trees. Because it was barely December, there were no leaves on the trees and it was cool, despite her nervous perspiration. She tried to throw off his hand, to no avail.

He only loosened his grip on her when she sat down on a park bench. He remained standing, propping his boot on the bench beside her, leaning one long arm over his knee to study her. "This is private enough," he said shortly. "Why are you leaving?"

"I signed a contract to work with you for one year. It's almost up, anyway," she said icily. "I want out. I want to go home."

"You don't have anyone left in Austin," he said, surprising her.

"I have friends," she began.

"You don't have those, either. You don't have friends at all, unless you count Drew Morris," he said flatly.

Her fingers clenched around her car keys. She looked at them, biting into the flesh even though not a speck of emotion showed on her placid features.

His eyes followed hers to her lap and something moved in his face. There was an expression there that puzzled her. He reached down and opened her rigid hand, frowning when he saw the red marks the keys had made in her palm.

She jerked her fingers away from him.

He seemed disconcerted for a few seconds. He stared at her without speaking and she felt her heart beating wildly against her ribs. She hated being helpless.

He moved back, watching her relax. He took another step and saw her release the breath she'd been holding. Every trace of anger left him.

"It takes time for a partnership to work," he said abruptly. "You've only given this one a year."

"That's right," she said tonelessly. "*I've* given it a year."

The emphasis she placed on the first word caught his attention. His blue eyes narrowed. "You sound as if you don't think I've given it any time at all."

She nodded. Her eyes met his. "You didn't want me in the practice. I suspected it from the beginning, but it wasn't until I heard what you told Drew on the phone this morning that—"

His eyes flashed oddly. "You heard what I said?" he asked huskily. "You heard…all of it!" he exclaimed.

Her lips trembled just faintly. "Yes," she said.

He was remembering what he'd told Drew Morris in a characteristic outburst of bad temper. He often said things in heat that he regretted later, but this he regretted most of all. He'd never credited his cool, unflappable partner with any emotions at all. She'd backed away from him figuratively and physically since the first day she'd worked at the clinic. Her physical withdrawal had maddened him, although he'd always assumed she was frigid.

But in the past five minutes, he'd learned disturbing things about her without a word being spoken. He'd hurt her. He didn't realize she'd cared that much about his opinion. Hell, he'd been furious because he'd just had to diagnose leukemia in a sweet little boy of four. It had hurt him to do that, and he'd lashed out at Morris over Lou in frustration at his own helplessness. But he'd had no idea that she'd overheard his vicious remarks. She was going to leave and it was no less than he deserved. He was genuinely sorry. She wasn't going to believe that, though. He could tell by her mutinous expression, in her clenched hands, in the tight set of her mouth.

"You did Drew a favor and asked me to join you, probably over some other doctor you really wanted," she said with a forced smile. "Well, no harm done. Perhaps you can get him back when I leave."

"Wait a minute," he began shortly.

She held up a hand. "Let's not argue about it," she said, sick at knowing his opinion of her, his real opinion. "I'm tired of fighting you to practice medicine here. I haven't done the first thing right, according to you. I'm a burden. Well, I just want out. I'll go on working until you can replace me." She stood up.

His hand tightened on the brim of his hat. He was losing this battle. He didn't know how to pull his irons out of the fire.

"I had to tell the Dawes that their son has leukemia," he said, hating the need to explain his bad temper. "I say things I don't mean sometimes."

"We both know that you meant what you said about me," she said flatly. Her eyes met his levelly. "You've hated me from almost the first day we worked together. Most of the time, you can't even be bothered to be civil to me. I didn't know that you had a grudge against me from the outset..."

She hadn't thought about that until she said it, but there was a subtle change in his expression, a faint distaste that her mind locked on.

"So you heard that, too." His jaw clenched on words he didn't want to say. But maybe it was as well to say them. He'd lived a lie for the past year.

"Yes." She gripped the wrought-iron frame of the park bench hard. "What happened? Did my father cause someone to die?"

His jaw tautened. He didn't like saying this. "The girl I wanted to marry got pregnant by him. He performed a secret abortion and she was going to marry me anyway." He laughed icily. "A fling, he called it. But the medical authority had other ideas, and they invited him to resign."

Lou's fingers went white on the cold wrought iron. Had her mother known? What had happened to the girl afterward?

"Only a handful of people knew," Coltrain said, as if he'd read her thoughts. "I doubt that your mother did.

She seemed very nice—hardly a fit match for a man like that."

"And the girl?" she asked levelly.

"She left town. Eventually she married." He rammed his hands into his pockets and glared at her. "If you want the whole truth, Drew felt sorry for you when your parents died so tragically. He knew I was looking for a partner, and he recommended you so highly that I asked you. I didn't connect the name at first," he added on a mocking note. "Ironic, isn't it, that I'd choose as a partner the daughter of a man I hated until the day he died."

"Why didn't you tell me?" she asked irritably. "I would have resigned!"

"You were in no fit state to be told anything," he replied with reluctant memories of her tragic face when she'd arrived. His hands clenched in his pockets. "Besides, you'd signed a one-year contract. The only way out was if you resigned."

It all made sense immediately. She was too intelligent not to understand why he'd been so antagonistic. "I see," she breathed. "But I didn't resign."

"You were made of stronger stuff than I imagined," he agreed. "You wouldn't back down an inch. No matter how rough it got, you threw my own bad temper back at me." He rubbed his fingers absently over the car keys in his pocket while he studied her. "It's been a long time since anyone around here stood up to me like that," he added reluctantly.

She knew that without being told. He was a holy terror. Even grown men around Jacobsville gave him a wide berth when he lost his legendary temper. But Lou never had. She stood right up to him. She wasn't fiery by nature, but her father had been viciously cruel to her. She'd learned early not to show fear or back down, because it only made him worse. The same rule seemed to apply to Coltrain. A weaker personality wouldn't have lasted in his office one week, much less one year, male or female.

She knew now that Drew Morris had been doing what he thought was a good deed. Perhaps he'd thought it wouldn't matter to Coltrain after such a long time to have a Blakely working for him. But he'd obviously underestimated the man. Lou would have realized at once, on the shortest acquaintance, that Coltrain didn't forgive people.

He stared at her unblinkingly. "A year. A whole year, being reminded every day I took a breath what your father cost me. There were times when I'd have done anything to make you leave. Just the sight of you was painful." He smiled wearily. "I think I hated you, at first."

That was the last straw. She'd loved him, against her will and all her judgment, and he was telling her that all he saw when he looked at her was an ice woman whose father had betrayed him with the woman he loved. He hated her.

It was too much all at once. Lou had always had impeccable control over her emotions. It had been dangerous to let her father know that he was hurting her, because he enjoyed hurting her. And now here was the one man she'd ever loved telling her that he hated her because of her father.

What a surprise it would be for him to learn that her

father, at the last, had been little more than a high-class drug addict, stealing narcotics from the hospital where he worked in Austin to support his growing habit. He'd been as high as a kite on narcotics, in fact, when the plane he was piloting went down, killing himself and his wife.

Tears swelled her eyelids. Not a sound passed her lips as they overflowed in two hot streaks down her pale cheeks.

He caught his breath. He'd seen her tired, impassive, worn-out, fighting mad, and even frustrated. But he'd never seen her cry. His lean hand shot out and touched the track of tears down one cheek, as if he had to touch them to make sure they were real.

She jerked back from him, laughing tearfully. "So that was why you were so horrible to me." She choked out the words. "Drew never said a word…no wonder you suffered me! And I was silly enough to dream…!" The laughter was harsher now as she dashed away the tears, staring at him with eyes full of pain and loss. "What a fool I've been," she whispered poignantly. "What a silly fool!"

She turned and walked away from him, gripping the car keys in her hand. The sight of her back was as eloquently telling as the words that haunted him. She'd dreamed…what?

For the next few days, Lou was polite and remote and as courteous as any stranger toward her partner. But something had altered in their relationship. He was aware of a subtle difference in her attitude toward him, in a distancing of herself that was new. Her eyes had always followed him, and he'd been aware of it at some subconscious level. Perhaps he'd been aware of more than covert glances, too. But Lou no longer watched him or went out of her way to seek him out. If she had questions, she wrote them down and left them for him on his desk. If there were messages to be passed on, she left them with Brenda.

The one time she did seek him out was Thursday afternoon as they closed up.

"Have you worked out an advertisement for someone to replace me?" she asked him politely.

He watched her calm dark eyes curiously. "Are you in such a hurry to leave?" he asked.

"Yes," she said bluntly. "I'd like to leave after the Christmas holidays." She turned and would have gone out the door, but his hand caught the sleeve of her white jacket. She slung it off and backed away. "At the first of the year."

He glared at her, hating the instinctive withdrawal that came whenever he touched her. "You're a good doctor," he said flatly. "You've earned your place here."

High praise for a man with his grudges. She looked over her shoulder at him, her eyes wounded. "But you hate me, don't you? I heard what you said to Drew, that every time you looked at me you remembered what my father had done and hated me all over again."

He let go of her sleeve, frowning. He couldn't find an answer.

"Well, don't sweat it, Doctor," she told him. "I'll be gone in a month and you can find someone you like to work with you."

She laughed curtly and walked out of the office.

* * *

She dressed sedately that evening for the Rotary Club dinner, in a neat off-white suit with a pink blouse. But she left her blond hair long around her shoulders for once, and used a light dusting of makeup. She didn't spend much time looking in the mirror. Her appearance had long ago ceased to matter to her.

Drew was surprised by it, though, and curious. She looked strangely vulnerable. But when he tried to hold her hand, she drew away from him. He'd wanted to ask her for a long time if there were things in her past that she might like to share with someone. But Louise was an unknown quantity, and she could easily shy away. He couldn't risk losing her altogether.

Drew held her arm as they entered the hall, and Lou was disconcerted to find Dr. Coltrain there. He almost never attended social functions unless Jane Parker was in attendance. But a quick glance around the room ascertained that Jane wasn't around. She wondered if the doctor had brought a date. It didn't take long to have that question answered, as a pretty young brunette came up beside him and clung to his arm as if it was the ticket to heaven.

Coltrain wasn't looking at her, though. His pale, narrow eyes had lanced over Lou and he was watching her closely. He hadn't seen her hair down in the year they'd worked together. She seemed more approachable tonight than he'd ever noticed, but she was Drew's date. Probably Drew's woman, too, he thought bitterly, despite her protests and reserve.

But trying to picture Lou in Drew's bed was more difficult than he'd thought. It wasn't at all in character.

She was rigid in her views, just as she was in her mode of dress and her hairstyle. Just because she'd loosened that glorious hair tonight didn't mean that she'd suddenly become uninhibited. Nonetheless, the change disturbed him, because it was unexpected.

"Copper's got a new girl, I see," Drew said with a grin. "That's Nickie Bolton," he added. "She works as a nurse's aide at the hospital."

"I didn't recognize her out of uniform," Lou murmured.

"I did," he said. "She's lovely, isn't she?"

She nodded amiably. "Very young, too," she added with an indulgent smile.

He took her hand gently and smiled down at her. "You aren't exactly over the hill yourself," he teased.

She smiled up at him with warm eyes. "You're a nice man, Drew."

Across the room, a redheaded man's grip tightened ominously on a glass of punch. For over a year, Louise had avoided even his lightest touch. A few days ago, she'd thrown off his hand violently. But there she stood not only allowing Drew to hold her hand, but actually smiling at him. She'd never smiled at Coltrain that way; she'd never smiled at him any way at all.

His companion tapped him on the shoulder.

"You're with me, remember?" she asked with a pert smile. "Stop staring daggers at your partner. You're off duty. You don't have to fight all the time, do you?"

He frowned slightly. "What do you mean?"

"Everyone knows you hate her," Nickie said pleasantly. "It's common gossip at the hospital. You rake her over the coals and she walks around the corridors, red in the face and talking to herself. Well, most of the time, anyway. Once, Dr. Simpson found her crying in the nursery. But she doesn't usually cry, no matter how bad she hurts. She's pretty tough, in her way. I guess she's had to be, huh? Even if there are more women in medical school these days, you don't see that many women doctors yet. I'll bet she had to fight a lot of prejudice when she was in medical school."

That came as a shock. He'd never seen Lou cry until today, and he couldn't imagine her being upset at any temperamental display of his. Or was it, he pondered uneasily, just that she'd learned how not to show her wounds to him?

Chapter 3

At dinner, Lou sat with Drew, as far away from Coltrain and his date as she could get. She listened attentively to the speakers and whispered to Drew in the spaces between speakers. But it was torture to watch Nickie's small hand smooth over Coltrain's, to see her flirt with him. Lou didn't know how to flirt. There were a lot of things she didn't know. But she'd learned to keep a poker face, and she did it very well this evening. The one time Coltrain glanced down the table toward her, he saw nothing on her face or in her eyes that could tell him anything. She was unreadable.

After the meeting, she let Drew hold her hand as they walked out of the restaurant. Behind them, Coltrain was glaring at her with subdued fury.

When they made it to the parking lot, she found that the other couple had caught up with them.

"Nice bit of surgery this morning, Copper," Drew

remarked. "You do memorable stitches. I doubt if Mrs. Blake will even have a scar to show around."

He managed a smile and held Nickie's hand all the tighter. "She was adamant about that," he remarked. "It seems that her husband likes perfection."

"He'll have a good time searching for it in this imperfect world," Drew replied. "I'll see you in the morning. And I'd like your opinion on my little strep-throat patient. His mother wants the whole works taken out, tonsils and adenoids, but he doesn't have strep often and I don't like unnecessary surgery. Perhaps she'd listen to you."

"Don't count on it," Copper said dryly. "I'll have a look if you like, though."

"Thanks."

"My pleasure." He glanced toward Lou, who hadn't said a word. "You were ten minutes late this morning," he added coldly.

"Oh, I overslept," she replied pleasantly. "It wears me out to follow the EMTs around looking for work."

She gave him a cool smile and got into the car before he realized that she'd made a joke, and at his expense.

"Be on time in the morning," he admonished before he walked away with Nickie on his arm.

"On time," Lou muttered beside Drew in the comfortable Ford he drove. Her hands crushed her purse. "I'll give him on time! I'll be sitting in *his* parking spot at eight-thirty on the dot!"

"He does it on purpose," he told her as he started the car. "I think he likes to make you spark at him."

"He's overjoyed that I'm leaving," she muttered. "And so am I!"

He gave her a quick glance and hid his smile. "If you say so."

She twisted her small purse in her lap, fuming, all the way back to her small house.

"I haven't been good company, Drew," she said as he walked her to the door. "I'm sorry."

He patted her shoulder absently. "Nothing wrong with the company," he said, correcting her. He smiled down at her. "But you really do rub Copper the wrong way, don't you?" he added thoughtfully. "I've noticed that antagonism from a distance, but tonight is the first time I've seen it at close range. Is he always like that?"

She nodded. "Always, from the beginning. Well, not quite," she confessed, remembering. "From last Christmas."

"What happened last Christmas?"

She studied him warily.

"I won't tell him," he promised. "What happened?"

"He tried to kiss me under the mistletoe and I, well, I sort of ducked and pulled away." She flushed. "He rattled me. He does, mostly. I get shaky when he comes too close. He's so forceful, and so physical. Even when he wants to talk to me, he's forever trying to grab me by the wrist or a sleeve. It's as if he knows how much it disturbs me, so he does it on purpose, just to make me uncomfortable."

He reached down and caught her wrist very gently, watching her face distort and feeling the instinctive, helpless jerk of her hand.

He let go at once. "Tell me about it, Lou."

With a wan smile, she rubbed her wrist. "No. It's history."

"It isn't, you know. Not if it makes you shaky to have people touch you…"

"Not everyone, just him," she muttered absently.

His eyebrows lifted, but she didn't seem to be aware of what she'd just confessed.

She sighed heavily. "I'm so tired," she said, rubbing the back of her neck. "I don't usually get so tired from even the longest days."

He touched her forehead professionally and frowned. "You're a bit warm. How do you feel?"

"Achy. Listless." She grimaced. "It's probably that virus that's going around. I usually get at least one every winter."

"Go to bed and if you aren't better tomorrow, don't go in," he advised. "Want me to prescribe something?"

She shook her head. "I'll be okay. Nothing does any good for a virus, you know that."

He chuckled. "Not even a sugarcoated pill?"

"I can do without a placebo. I'll get some rest. Thanks for tonight. I enjoyed it."

"So did I. I haven't done much socializing since Eve died. It's been five long years and I still miss her. I don't think I'll ever get over her enough to start a new relationship with anyone. I only wish we'd had a child. It might have made it easier."

She was studying him, puzzled. "It's said that many people marry within months of losing a mate," she began.

"I don't fit that pattern," he said quietly. "I only loved once. I'd rather have my memories of those twelve years with Eve than a hundred years with someone else. I suppose that sounds old-fashioned."

She shook her head. "It sounds beautiful," she said softly. "Lucky Eve, to have been loved so much."

He actually flushed. "It was mutual."

"I'm sure it was, Drew. I'm glad to have a friend like you."

"That works both ways." He smiled ruefully. "I'd like to take you out occasionally, so that people will stop thinking of me as a mental case. The gossip is beginning to get bad."

"I'd love to go out with you," she replied. She smiled. "I'm not very worldly, you know. It was books and exams and medicine for eight long years, and then internship. I was an honor student. I never had much time for men." Her eyes darkened. "I never wanted to have much time for them. My parents' marriage soured me. I never knew it could be happy or that people could love each other enough to be faithful—" She stopped, embarrassed.

"I knew about your father," he said. "Most of the hospital staff did. He liked young girls."

"Dr. Coltrain told me," she said miserably.

"He what?"

She drew in a long breath. "I overheard what he said to you on the telephone the other day. I'm leaving. My year is up after New Year's, anyway," she reminded him. "He told me what my father had done. No wonder he didn't want me here. You shouldn't have done it, Drew. You shouldn't have forced him to take me on."

"I know. But it's too late, isn't it? I thought I was help-ing, if that's any excuse." He searched her face. "Maybe I hoped it would help Copper, too. He was infatuated with Jane Parker. She's a lovely, sweet woman, and she has a temper, but she was never a match for Copper. He's the sort who'd cow a woman who couldn't stand up to him."

"Just like my father," she said shortly.

"I've never mentioned it, but one of your wrists looks as if it's suffered a break."

She flushed scarlet and drew back. "I have to go in now. Thanks again, Drew."

"If you can't talk to me, you need to talk to someone," he said. "Did you really think you could go through life without having the past affect the future?"

She smiled sweetly. "Drive carefully going home."

He shrugged. "Okay. I'll drop it."

"Good night."

"Good night."

She watched him drive away, absently rubbing the wrist he'd mentioned. She wouldn't think about it, she told herself. She'd go to bed and put it out of her mind.

Only it didn't work that way. She woke up in the middle of the night in tears, frightened until she remembered where she was. She was safe. It was over. But she felt sick and her throat was dry. She got up and found a pitcher, filling it with ice and water. She took a glass along with her and went back to bed. Except for frequent trips to the bathroom, she finally slept soundly.

There was a loud, furious knock at the front door. It kept on and on, followed by an equally loud voice. What a blessing that she didn't have close neighbors, she thought drowsily, or the police would be screaming up the driveway.

She tried to get up, but surprisingly, her feet wouldn't

support her. She was dizzy and weak and sick at her stomach. Her head throbbed. She lay back down with a soft groan.

A minute later, the front door opened and a furious redheaded man in a lab coat came in the bedroom door.

"So this is where you are," he muttered, taking in her condition with a glance. "You couldn't have called?"

She barely focused on him. "I was up most of the night…"

"With Drew?"

She couldn't even manage a glare. "Being sick," she corrected. "Have you got anything on you to calm my stomach? I can't keep down anything to stop the nausea."

"I'll get something."

He went back out, grateful that she kept a key under the welcome mat. He didn't relish having to break down doors, although he had in the past to get to a patient.

He got his medical bag and went back into the bedroom. She was pale and she had a fever. He turned off the electronic thermometer and checked her lungs. Clear, thank God.

Her pulse was a little fast, but she seemed healthy enough. "A virus," he pronounced.

"No!" she exclaimed with weak sarcasm.

"You'll live."

"Give me the medicine, please," she asked, holding out a hand.

"Can you manage?"

"If you'll get me to the bathroom, sure."

He helped her up, noticing the frailty of her body.

She didn't seem that thin in her clothing, but she was wearing silky pajamas that didn't conceal the slender lines of her body. He supported her to the door, and watched the door close behind her.

Minutes later, she opened the door again and let him help her back into bed.

He watched her for a minute and then, with resolution, he picked up the telephone. He punched in a number. "This is Dr. Coltrain. Send an ambulance out to Dr. Blakely's home, 23 Brazos Lane. That's right. Yes. Thank you."

She glared at him. "I will not…!"

"Hell, yes, you will," he said shortly. "I'm not leaving you out here alone to dehydrate. At the rate you're losing fluids, you'll die in three days."

"What do you care if I die?" she asked furiously.

He reached down to take her pulse again. This time, he caught the left wrist firmly, but she jerked it back. His blue eyes narrowed as he watched her color. Drew had been holding her right hand. At the table, it was her right hand he'd touched. But most of the time, Copper automatically reached for the left one…

He glanced down to where it lay on the coverlet and he noticed what Drew had; there was a definite break there, one which had been set but was visible.

She clenched her fist. "I don't want to go to the hospital."

"But you'll go, if I have to carry you."

She glared at him. It did no good at all. He went into the kitchen to turn off all the appliances except the refrigerator. On his way back, he paused to look around the living room. There were some very disturbing paintings on her walls, side by side with beautiful pastel drawings of flowers. He wondered who'd done them.

The ambulance arrived shortly. He watched the paramedics load her up and he laid the small bag she'd asked him to pack on the foot of the gurney.

"Thank you so much," she said with her last lucid breath. The medicine was beginning to take effect, and it had a narcotic in it to make her sleep.

"My pleasure, Dr. Blakely," he said. He smiled, but it didn't reach his eyes. They were watchful and thoughtful. "Do you paint?" he asked suddenly.

Her dark eyes blinked. "How did you know?" she murmured as she drifted off.

She awoke hours later in a private room, with a nurse checking her vital signs. "You're awake!" the nurse said with a smile. "Feeling any better?"

"A little." She touched her stomach. "I think I've lost weight."

"No wonder, with so much nausea. You'll be all right now. We'll take very good care of you. How about some soup and Jell-O and tea?"

"Coffee?" she asked hopefully.

The nurse chuckled. "Weak coffee, perhaps. We'll see." She charted her observations and went to see about supper.

It was modest fare, but delicious to a stomach that had hardly been able to hold anything. Imagine being sent to the hospital with a twenty-four-hour virus, Lou thought irritably, and wanted to find Dr. Coltrain and hit him.

Drew poked his head in the door while he was doing

rounds. "I told you you felt feverish, didn't I?" he teased, smiling. "Better?"

She nodded. "But I would have been just fine at home."

"Not to hear your partner tell it. I expected to find your ribs sticking through your skin," he told her, chuckling. "I'll check on you later. Stay put."

She groaned and lay back. Patients were stacking up and she knew that Brenda had probably had to deal with angry ones all day, since Dr. Coltrain would have been operating in the morning. Everyone would be sitting in the waiting room until long after dark, muttering angrily.

It was after nine before he made rounds. He looked worn, and she felt guilty even if it couldn't be helped.

"I'm sorry," she said irritably when he came to the bedside.

He cocked an eyebrow. "For what?" He reached down and took her wrist—the right one—noticing that she didn't react while he felt her pulse.

"Leaving you to cope with my patients as well as your own," she said. The feel of his long fingers was disturbing. She began to fidget.

He leaned closer, to look into her eyes, and his hand remained curled around her wrist. He felt her pulse jump as his face neared hers and suddenly a new thought leaped into his shocked mind and refused to be banished.

She averted her gaze. "I'm all right," she said. She sounded breathless. Her pulse had gone wild under his searching fingers.

He stood up, letting go of her wrist. But he noticed the

quick rise and fall of her chest with new interest. What an odd reaction for a woman who felt such antagonism toward him.

He picked up her chart, still frowning, and read what was written there. "You've improved. If you're doing this well in the morning, you can go home. Not to work," he added firmly. "Drew's going to come in and help me deal with the backlog in the morning while he has some free time."

"That's very kind of him."

"He's a kind man."

"Yes. *He* is."

He chuckled softly. "You don't like me, do you?" he asked through pursed lips. "I've never given you any reason to. I've been alternately hostile and sarcastic since the day you came here."

"Your normal self, Doctor," she replied.

His lips tugged up. "Not really. You don't know me."

"Lucky me."

His blue eyes narrowed thoughtfully. She'd reacted to him from the first as if he'd been contagious. Every approach he'd made had been met with instant withdrawal. He wondered why he'd never questioned her reactions. It wasn't revulsion. Oh, no. It was something much more disturbing on her part. She was vulnerable, and he'd only just realized it, when it was too late. She would leave before he had the opportunity to explore his own feelings.

He stuck his hands into his pockets and his eyes searched her pale, worn face. She wasn't wearing a trace of makeup. Her eyes held lingering traces of fever and her hair was dull, lackluster, disheveled by sleep. But even in that condition, she had a strange beauty.

"I know how I look, thanks," she muttered as she saw how he was looking at her. "You don't need to rub it in."

"Was I?" He studied her hostile eyes.

She dropped her gaze to her slender hands on the sheets. "You always do." Her eyes closed. "I don't need you to point out my lack of good looks, Doctor. My father never missed an opportunity to tell me what I was missing."

Her father. His expression hardened as the memories poured out. But even as they nagged at his mind, he began to remember bits and pieces of gossip he'd heard about the way Dr. Fielding Blakely treated his poor wife. He'd dismissed it at the time, but now he realized that Mrs. Blakely had to be aware of her husband's affairs. Had she not minded? Or was she afraid to mind…

He had more questions about Lou's family life than he had answers, and he was curious. Her reticence with him, her broken wrist, her lack of self-esteem—they began to add up.

His eyes narrowed. "Did your mother know that your father was unfaithful to her?" he asked.

She stared at him as if she didn't believe what she'd heard. "What?"

"You heard me. Did she know?"

She drew the sheet closer to her collarbone. "Yes." She bit off the word.

"Why didn't she leave him?"

She laughed bitterly. "You can't imagine."

"Maybe I can." He moved closer to the bed. "Maybe

I can imagine a lot of things that never occurred to me before. I've looked at you for almost a year and I've never seen you until now."

She fidgeted under the cover. "Don't strain your imagination, Doctor," she said icily. "I haven't asked for your attention. I don't want it."

"Mine, or any other man's, right?" he asked gently.

She felt like an insect on a pin. "Will you stop?" she groaned. "I'm sick. I don't want to be interrogated."

"Is that what I'm doing? I thought I was showing a belated interest in my partner," he said lazily.

"I won't be your partner after Christmas."

"Why?"

"I've resigned. Have you forgotten? I even wrote it down and gave it to you."

"Oh. That. I tore it up."

Her eyes popped. "You what?"

"Tore it up," he said with a shrug. "I can't do without you. You have too many patients who won't come back if they have to see me."

"You had a fine practice…"

"Too fine. I never slept or took vacations. You've eased the load. You've made yourself indispensable. You have to stay."

"I do not." She shot her reply back instantly. "I hate you!"

He studied her, nodding slowly. "That's healthy. Much healthier than withdrawing like a frightened clam into a shell every time I come too close."

She all but gasped at such a blunt statement. "I do not…!"

"You do." He looked pointedly at her left wrist.

"You've kept secrets. I'm going to worry you to death until you tell me every last one of them, beginning with why you can't bear to have anyone hold you by the wrist."

She couldn't get her breath. She felt her cheeks becoming hot as he stared down at her intently. "I'm not telling you any secrets," she assured him.

"Why not?" he replied. "I don't ever tell what I know."

She knew that. If a patient told him anything in confidence, he wouldn't share it.

She rubbed the wrist absently, wincing as she remembered how it had felt when it was broken, and how.

Coltrain, watching her, wondered how he could ever have thought her cold. She had a temper that was easily the equal of his own, and she never backed away from a fight. She'd avoided his touch, but he realized now that it was the past that made her afraid, not the present.

"You're mysterious, Lou," he said quietly. "You hold things in, keep things back. I've worked with you for a year, but I know nothing about you."

"That was your choice," she reminded him coolly. "You've treated me like a leper in your life."

He started to speak, took a breath and finally, nodded. "Yes. Through no fault of your own, I might add. I've held grudges."

She glanced at his hard, lean face. "You were entitled," she admitted. "I didn't know about my father's past. I probably should have realized there was a reason he never went back to Jacobsville, even to visit, while his brother was still alive here. Afterward, there wasn't even a cousin to write to. We all lost touch. My mother never seemed to mind that we didn't come back." She looked up at him. "She probably knew…" She flushed and dropped her eyes.

"But she stayed with him," he began.

"She had to!" The words burst out. "If she'd tried to leave, he'd have…" She swallowed and made a futile gesture with her hand.

"He'd have what? Killed her?"

She wouldn't look at him. She couldn't. The memories came flooding back, of his violence when he used narcotics, of the threats, her mother's fear, her own. The weeping, the cries of pain…

She sucked in a quick breath, and all the suffering was in the eyes she lifted to his when he took her hand.

His fingers curled hard around hers and held them, as if he could see the memories and was offering comfort.

"You'll tell me, one day," he said abruptly, his eyes steady on her own. "You'll tell me every bit of it."

She couldn't understand his interest. She searched his eyes curiously and suddenly felt a wave of feeling encompass her like a killing tide, knocking her breathless. Heat surged through her slender body, impaling her, and in his hard face she saw everything she knew of love, would ever know of it.

But he didn't want her that way. He never would. She was useful to the practice, but on a personal level, he was still clutching hard at the past; at the girl her father had taken from him, at Jane Parker. He was sorry for her, as he would be for anyone in pain, but it wasn't a personal concern.

She drew her hand away from his slowly and with a

faint smile. "Thanks," she said huskily. "I...I think too hard sometimes. The past is long dead."

"I used to think so," he said, watching her. "Now, I'm not so sure."

She didn't understand what he was saying. It was just as well. The nurse came in to do her round and any personal conversation was banished at once.

Chapter 4

The next day, Lou was allowed to go home. Drew had eaten breakfast with her and made sure that she was well enough to leave before he agreed with Copper that she was fit. But when he offered to drive her home, Coltrain intervened. His partner, he said, was his responsibility. Drew didn't argue. In fact, when they weren't looking, he grinned.

Copper carried her bag into the house and helped her get settled on the couch. It was lunchtime and he hesitated, as if he felt guilty about not offering to take her out for a meal.

"I'm going to have some soup later," she murmured without looking at him. "I'm not hungry just yet. I expect you are."

"I could eat." He hesitated again, watching her with vague irritation. "Will you be all right?"

"It was only a virus," she said, making light of it. "I'm fine. Thank you for your concern."

"You might as well enjoy it, for novelty value if nothing else," he said without smiling. "It's been a long time since I've given a damn about a woman's comfort."

"I'm just a colleague," she replied, determined to show him that she realized there was nothing personal in their relationship. "It isn't the same thing."

"No, it isn't," he agreed. "I've been very careful to keep our association professional. I've never even asked you to my home, have I?"

He was making her uneasy with that unblinking stare. "So what? I've never asked you to mine," she replied. "I wouldn't presume to put you in such an embarrassing situation."

"Embarrassing? Why?"

"Well, because you'd have to find some logical excuse to refuse," she said.

He searched her quiet face and his eyes narrowed thoughtfully. "I don't know that I'd refuse. If you asked me."

Her heart leaped and she quickly averted her eyes. She wanted him to go, now, before she gave herself away. "Forgive me, but I'm very tired," she said.

She'd fended him off nicely, without giving offense. He wondered how many times over the years she'd done exactly that to other men.

He moved closer to her, noticing the way she tensed, the telltale quickening of her breath, the parting of her soft lips. She was affected by his nearness and trying valiantly to hide it. It touched him deeply that she was so vulnerable to him. He could have cursed himself for the way he'd treated her, for the antagonism that made her wary of any approach now.

He stopped when there was barely a foot of space between them, with his hands in his pockets so that he wouldn't make her any more nervous.

He looked down at her flushed oval face with curious pleasure. "Don't try to come in tomorrow if you don't feel like it. I'll cope."

"All right," she said in a hushed tone.

"Lou."

He hadn't called her by her first name before. It surprised her into lifting her eyes to his face.

"You aren't responsible for anything your father did," he said. "I'm sorry that I've made things hard for you. I hope you'll reconsider leaving."

She shifted uncomfortably. "Thank you. But I think I'd better go," she said softly. "You'll be happier with someone else."

"Do you think so? I don't agree." His hand lowered slowly to her face, touching her soft cheek, tracing it down to the corner of her mouth. It was the first intimate contact she'd ever had with him, and she actually trembled.

Her reaction had an explosive echo in his own body. His breath jerked into his throat and his teeth clenched as he looked at her mouth and thought he might die if he couldn't have it. But it was too soon. He couldn't…!

He drew back his hand as if she'd burned it. "I have to go," he said tersely, turning on his heel. Her headlong response had prompted a reaction in him that he could barely contain at all. He had to distance himself before he reached for her and ruined everything.

Lou didn't realize why he was in such a hurry to leave. She assumed that he immediately regretted that unexpected caress and wanted to make sure that she didn't read anything into it.

"Thank you for bringing me home," she said formally.

He paused at the door and looked back at her, his eyes fiercely intent on her slender body in jeans and sweatshirt, on her loosened blond hair and exquisite complexion and dark eyes. "Thank your lucky stars that I'm leaving in time." He bit off the words.

He closed the door on her puzzled expression. He was acting very much out of character lately. She didn't know why, unless he was sorry he'd tried to talk her out of leaving the practice. Oh, well, she told herself, it was no longer her concern. She had to get used to the idea of being out of his life. He had nothing to offer her, and he had good reason to hate her, considering the part her father had played in his unhappy past.

She went into the kitchen and opened a can of tomato soup. She'd need to replenish her body before she could get back to work.

The can slipped in her left hand and she grimaced. Her dreams of becoming a surgeon had been lost overnight in one tragic act. A pity, her instructor had said, because she had a touch that few surgeons ever achieved, almost an instinctive knowledge of the best and most efficient way to sever tissue with minimum loss of blood. She would have been famous. But alas, the tendon had been severed with the compound fracture. And the best efforts of the best orthopedic surgeon hadn't been able to repair the damage. Her father hadn't even been sorry....

She shook her head to clear away the memories and went back to her soup. Some things were better forgotten.

She was back at work the day after her return home, a bit shaky, but game. She went through her patients efficiently, smiling at the grievance of one small boy whose stitches she'd just removed.

"Dr. Coltrain doesn't like little kids, does he?" he muttered. "I showed him my bad place and he said he'd seen worse!"

"He has," she told the small boy. She smiled at him. "But you've been very brave, Patrick my boy, and I'm giving you the award of honor." She handed him a stick of sugarless chewing gum and watched him grin. "Off with you, now, and mind you don't fall down banks into any more creeks!"

"Yes, ma'am!"

She handed his mother the charge sheet and was showing them out the door of the treatment cubicle just as Coltrain started to come into it. The boy glowered at him, smiled at Lou and went back to his waiting mother.

"Cheeky brat," he murmured, watching him turn the corner.

"He doesn't like you," she told him smugly. "You didn't sympathize with his bad place."

"Bad place." He harrumphed. "Two stitches. My God, what a fuss he made."

"It hurt," she informed him.

"He wouldn't let me take the damn stitches out, either. He said that I didn't know how to do it, but you did."

She grinned to herself at that retort while she dealt with the mess she'd made while working with Patrick.

"You don't like children, do you?" she asked.

He shrugged. "I don't know much about them, except what I see in the practice," he replied. "I deal mostly with adults since you came."

He leaned against the doorjamb and studied her with his hands in the pockets of his lab coat, a stethoscope draped around his neck. His eyes narrowed as he watched her work.

She became aware of the scrutiny and turned, her eyes meeting his and being captured there. She felt her heart race at the way he looked at her. Her hands stilled on her preparations for the next patient as she stood helplessly in thrall.

His lips compressed. He looked at her mouth and traced the full lower lip, the soft bow of the upper, with her teeth just visible where her lips parted. The look was intimate. He was wondering how it would feel to kiss her, and she knew it.

Muffled footsteps caught them unawares, and Brenda jerked open the sliding door of the cubicle. "Lou, I've got the wrong… Oh!" She bumped into Coltrain, whom she hadn't seen standing there.

"Sorry," he muttered. "I wanted to ask Lou if she'd seen the file on Henry Brady. It isn't where I left it."

Brenda grimaced as she handed it to him. "I picked it up mistakenly. I'm sorry."

"No harm done." He glanced back at Lou and went out without another word.

"Not another argument," Brenda groaned. "Honestly, partners should get along better than this."

Lou didn't bother to correct that assumption. It was much less embarrassing than what had really happened. Coltrain had never looked at her in that particular way before. She was glad that she'd resigned; she wasn't sure that she could survive any physical teasing from him. If he started making passes, she'd be a lot safer in Austin than she would be here.

After all he was a confirmed bachelor and there was no shortage of women on his arm at parties. Nickie was the latest in a string of them. And according to rumor, before Nickie, apparently he'd been infatuated with Jane Parker. He might be nursing a broken heart as well, since Jane's marriage.

Lou didn't want to be anybody's second-best girl. Besides, she never wanted to marry. It had been better when Coltrain treated her like the enemy. She wished he'd go back to his former behavior and stop looking at her mouth that way. She still tingled remembering the heat in his blue eyes. A man like that would be just plain hell to be loved by. He would be addictive. She had no taste for addictions and she knew already that Coltrain would break her heart if she let him. No, it was better that she leave. Then she wouldn't have the anguish of a hopeless relationship.

The annual hospital Christmas party was scheduled for Friday night, two weeks before Christmas so that the staff wouldn't be too involved with family celebrations to attend.

Lou hadn't planned to go, but Coltrain cornered her in his office as they prepared to leave that afternoon for the weekend.

"The Christmas party is tonight," he reminded her.

"I know. I'm not going."

"I'll pick you up in an hour," he said, refusing to listen when she tried to protest. "I know you still tire easily after the virus. We won't stay long."

"What about Nickie?" she asked irritably. "Won't she mind if you take your partner to a social event?"

Her antagonism surprised him. He lifted an indignant eyebrow. "Why should she?" he asked stiffly.

"You've been dating her."

"I escorted her to the Rotary Club meeting. I haven't proposed to her. And whatever you've heard to the contrary, she and I are not an item."

"You needn't bite my head off!" She shot the words at him.

His eyes dropped to her mouth and lingered there. "I know something I'd like to bite," he said deep in his throat.

She actually gasped, so stunned by the remark that she couldn't even think of a reply.

His eyes flashed back up to catch hers. He was a bulldozer, she thought, and if she didn't stand up to him, he'd run right over her.

She stiffened her back. "I'm not going to any hospital dance with you," she said shortly. "You've given me hell for the past year. Do you think you can just walk in here and wipe all that out with an invitation? Not even an invitation, at that—a command!"

"Yes, I do," he returned curtly. "We both belong to the hospital staff, and nothing will start gossip quicker than having one of us stay away from an annual event. I do not plan to have any gossip going around here at my expense. I had enough of that in the past, thanks to your philandering father!"

She gripped her coat, furious at him. "You just got through saying that you didn't blame me for what he did."

"And I don't!" he said angrily. "But you're being blind and stupid."

"Thank you. Coming from you, those are compliments!"

He was all but vibrating with anger. He stared at her, glared at her, until her unsteady movement made him realize that she'd been ill.

He became less rigid. "Ben Maddox is going to be there tonight. He's a former colleague of ours from Canada. He's just installed a massive computer system with linkups to medical networks around the world. I think it's too expensive for our purposes, but I agreed to hear him out about it. You're the high-tech expert," he added with faint sarcasm. "I'd like your opinion."

"My opinion? I'm honored. You've never asked for it before."

"I've never given a damn about it before," he retorted evenly. "But maybe there's something to this electronic revolution in medicine." He lifted his chin in a challenge. "Or so you keep telling me. Put your money where your mouth is, Doctor. Convince me."

She glared at him. "I'll drive my own car and see you there."

It was a concession, of sorts. He frowned slightly. "Why don't you want to ride with me? What are you afraid of?" he taunted softly.

She couldn't admit what frightened her. "It wouldn't

look good to have us arrive together," she said. "It would give people something to talk about."

He was oddly disappointed, although he didn't quite know why. "All right, then."

She nodded, feeling that she'd won something. He nodded, too, and quietly left her. It felt like a sort of truce. God knew, they could use one.

Ben Maddox was tall, blond and drop-dead gorgeous. He was also married and the father of three. He had photographs, which he enjoyed showing to any of his old colleagues who were willing to look at them. But in addition to those photographs, he had information on a networking computer system that he used extensively in his own practice. It was an expensive piece of equipment, but it permitted the user instant access to medical experts in every field. As a diagnostic tool and a means of getting second opinions from recognized authorities, it was breathtaking. But so was the price.

Lou had worn a black silk dress with a lace overlay, a demure rounded neckline and see-through sleeves. Her hairstyle, a topknot with little tendrils of blond hair slipping down to her shoulders, looked sexy. So did her long, elegant legs in high heels, under the midknee fitted skirt. She wore no jewelry at all, except for a strand of pearls with matching earrings.

Watching her move, Coltrain was aware of old, un-wanted sensations. At the party a year ago, she'd worn something a little more revealing, and he'd deliberately maneuvered her under the mistletoe out of mingled cu-riosity and desire. But she'd evaded him as if he had the plague, then and since. His ego had suffered a sharp blow. He hadn't felt confident enough to try again, so antagonism and anger had kept her at bay. Not that his memories of her father's betrayal hadn't added to his enmity.

She was animated tonight, talking to Ben about the computer setup as if she knew everything there was to know about the machines.

"Copper, you've got a savvy partner here," Ben remarked when he joined them. "She's computer literate!"

"She's the resident high-tech expert," Copper replied. "I like old-fashioned, hands-on medicine. She'd rather reach for a machine to make diagnoses."

"High tech is the way of the future," Ben said coaxingly.

"It's also the reason medical costs have gone through the roof," came the predictable reply. "The money we spend on these outrageously expensive machines has to be passed on to the patients. That raises our fees, the hospital's fees, the insurance companies' fees…"

"Pessimist!" Ben accused.

"I'm being realistic," Copper told him, lifting his highball glass in a mock toast. He drained it, feeling the liquor.

Ben frowned as his old colleague made his way past the dancers back to the buffet table. "That's odd," he remarked. "I don't remember ever seeing Copper take more than one drink."

Neither did Lou. She watched her colleague pour himself another drink and she frowned.

Ben produced a card from the computer company for her, and while he was explaining the setup procedure, she noticed Nickie going up to Coltrain. She was wearing an electric blue dress that could have started a riot. The woman was pretty anyway, but that dress certainly revealed most of her charms.

Nickie laughed and dragged Coltrain under the mistletoe, looking up to indicate it there, to the amusement of the others standing by. Coltrain laughed softly, whipped a lean arm around Nickie's trim waist and pulled her against his tall body. He bent his head, and the way he kissed her made Lou go hot all over. She'd never been in his arms, but she'd dreamed about it. The fever in that thin mouth, the way he twisted Nickie even closer, made her breath catch. She averted her eyes and flushed at the train of her own thoughts.

"Leave it to Coltrain to draw the prettiest girls." Ben chuckled. "The gossip mill will grind on that kiss for a month. He's not usually so uninhibited. He must be over his limit!"

She could have agreed. Her hand clenched around the piña colada she was nursing. "This computer system, is it reliable?" she asked through tight lips, forcing a smile.

"Yes, except in thunderstorms. Always unplug it, regardless of what they tell you about protective spikes. One good hit, and you could be down for days."

"I'll remember, if we get it."

"The system I have is expensive," Ben agreed, "but there are others available that would be just right for a small practice like yours and Copper's. In fact…"

His voice droned on and Lou tried valiantly to pay attention. She was aware at some level that Coltrain and Nickie were dancing and making the rounds of guests together. It was much later, and well into her second piña colada, when the lavish mistletoe began to get serious workouts.

Lou wasn't in the mood to dance. She refused Ben's offer, and several others. A couple of hours had passed and it felt safe to leave now, before her spirit was totally crushed by being consistently ignored by Coltrain. She put down her half-full glass. "I really do have to go," she told Ben. "I've been ill and I'm not quite back up to par yet." She shook his hand. "It was very nice to have met you."

"Same here. I wonder why Drew Morris didn't show up? I had hoped to see him again while I was here."

"I don't know," she said, realizing that she hadn't heard from Drew since she was released from the hospital. She had no idea where he was, and she hadn't asked.

"I'll check with Copper. He's certainly been elusive this evening. Not that I can blame him, considering his pretty companion over there." He raised his hand to catch the other man's eyes, to Lou's dismay.

Coltrain joined them with Nickie hanging on his arm. "Still here?" he asked Lou with a mocking smile. "I thought you'd be out the door and gone by now."

"I'm just about to leave. Do you know where Drew is?"

"He's in Florida at that pediatric seminar. Didn't Brenda tell you?"

"She was so busy she probably forgot," she said.

"So that's where the old devil has gone," Ben said ruefully. "I'm sorry I missed him."

"I'm sure he will be, too," Lou said. The sight of

Nickie and Coltrain together was hurting her. "I'd better be off—"

"Oh, not yet," Copper said with glittery blue eyes. "Not before you've been kissed under the mistletoe, Doctor."

She flushed and laughed nervously. "I'll forgo that little ritual, I think."

"No, you won't." He sounded pleasant enough, but the expression on his face was dangerous. He moved away from Nickie and his lean arm shot around Lou's waist, maneuvering her under a low-hanging sprig of mistletoe tied with a red velvet bow. "You're not getting away this time," he said huskily.

Before she could think, react, protest, his head bent and his thin, cruel mouth fastened on hers with fierce intent. He didn't close his eyes when he kissed, she thought a bit wildly, he watched her all through it. His arm pressed her closer to the length of his muscular body, and his free hand came up so that his thumb could rub sensuously over her mouth while he kissed it, parting her lips, playing havoc with her nerves.

She gasped at the rough pleasure, and inadvertently gave him exactly what he wanted. His open mouth ground into hers, pressing her lips apart. She tasted him in an intimacy that she'd never shared with a man, in front of the amused hospital staff, while his cold eyes stared straight into hers.

She made a faint sound and he lifted his head, looking down at her swollen lips. His thumb traced over them with much greater tenderness than his mouth had given her, and he held her shocked eyes for a long moment before he reluctantly let her go.

"Merry Christmas, Dr. Blakely," he said in a mocking tone, although his voice was husky.

"And you, Dr. Coltrain," she said shakily, not quite meeting his eyes. "Good night, Ben…Nickie."

She slid away from them toward the door, on shaky legs, with a mouth that burned from his cold, fierce kiss. She barely remembered getting her coat and saying goodbye to the people she recognized on her way to the car park.

Coltrain watched her go with feelings he'd never encountered in his life. He was burning up with desire, and he'd had enough whiskey to threaten his control.

Nickie tugged on his sleeve. "You didn't kiss me like that," she protested, pouting prettily. "Why don't you take me home and we can…"

"I'll be back in a minute," he said, shaking her off.

She glared at him, coloring with embarrassment when she realized that two of the staff had overheard her. Rejection in private was one thing, but it hurt to have him make it so public. He hadn't called her since the night of the Rotary Club meeting. He'd just kissed her very nicely, but it looked different when he'd done it with his partner. She frowned. Something was going on. She followed at a distance. She was going to find out what.

Coltrain, unaware of her pursuit, headed after Lou with no real understanding of his own actions. He couldn't get the taste of her out of his head. He was pretty sure that she felt the same way. He couldn't let her leave until he knew…

Lou kept walking, but she heard footsteps behind her as she neared her car. She knew them, because she heard them every day on the slick tile of the office floor. She walked faster, but it did no good. Coltrain reached her car at the same time she reached it.

His hand came around her, grasping her car key and her fingers, pulling, turning her. She was pressed completely against the car by the warm weight of his body, and she looked up into a set, shadowy face while his mouth hovered just above her own in the starlit darkness.

"It wasn't enough," he said roughly. "Not nearly enough."

He bent and his mouth found hers expertly. His hands smoothed into hers and linked with her fingers. His hips slid sensuously over hers, seductive, refusing to entertain barriers or limits. His mouth began to open, brushing in soft strokes over her lips until they began to part, but she stiffened.

"Don't you know how to kiss?" he whispered, surprised. "Open your mouth, little one. Open it and fit it to mine... Yes, that's it."

She felt his tongue dance at the opening he'd made, felt it slowly ease into her mouth and penetrate, teasing, probing, tasting. Her fingers clutched helplessly at his and she shivered. It was so intimate, so...familiar! She moaned sharply as his hips began to caress hers. She felt him become aroused and her whole body vibrated.

His mouth grew more insistent then. He released one of her hands and his fingers played with her mouth, as they had inside, but now there was the heat and the magic they were generating, and it was no cold, clinical experiment. He groaned against her mouth and she felt his body go rigid all at once.

He bit her lower lip, hard, when her teeth clenched at the soft probing of his tongue. Suddenly she came to her senses and realized what was happening. He tasted blatantly of whiskey. He'd had too much to drink and he'd forgotten which woman he was with. Did he think she was Nickie? she wondered dizzily. Was that why he was making love to her? And that was what it was, she realized with a shock. Only a lover would take such intimacy for granted, be so blind to surroundings and restraint.

Chapter 5

Despite the pleasure she felt, the whiskey on his breath brought back unbearable memories of another man who drank; memories not of kisses, but of pain and fear. Her hands pressed against his warm shirtfront under the open dinner jacket and she pushed, only vaguely aware of thick hair under the silkiness of the fabric.

"No," she whispered into his insistent mouth.

He didn't seem to hear her. His mouth hardened and a sound rumbled out of the back of his throat. "For God's sake, stop fighting me," he whispered fiercely. "Open your mouth!"

The intimacy he was asking for frightened her. She twisted her face, breathing like a runner. "Jebediah... no!" she whispered frantically.

The fear in her voice got through the intoxication. His mouth stilled against her cheek, but his body didn't withdraw. She could feel it against every inch of her like a warm, steely brand. His breathing wasn't steady, and over her breasts, his heart was beating like a frenzied bass drum.

It suddenly dawned on him what he was doing, and with whom.

"My God!" he whispered fiercely. His hands tightened for an instant before they fell away from her. A faint shudder went through his powerful body as he slowly, so slowly, pushed himself away from her, balancing his weight on his hands against the car doorframe.

She felt his breath on her swollen mouth as he fought for control. He was still too close.

"You haven't used my given name before," he said as he levered farther away from her. "I didn't know you knew it."

"It's…on our contract," she said jerkily.

He removed his hands from the car and stood upright, dragging in air. "I've had two highballs," he said on an apologetic laugh. "I don't drink. It hit me harder than I realized."

He was apologizing, she thought dazedly. That was unexpected. He wasn't that kind of man. Or was he? She hadn't thought he was the type to get drunk and kiss women in that intimate, fierce way, either. Especially her.

She tried to catch her own breath. Her mouth hurt from the muted violence of his kisses and her legs felt weak. She leaned back against the car, only now noticing its coldness. She hadn't felt it while he was kissing her. She touched her tongue to her lips and she tasted him on them.

She eased away from the car a little, shy now that he was standing back from her.

She was so shaky that she wondered how she was going to drive home. Then she wondered, with even more concern, how *he* was going to drive home.

"You shouldn't drive," she began hesitantly.

In the faint light from the hospital, she saw him smile sardonically. "Worried about me?" he chided.

She shouldn't have slipped like that. "I'd worry about anyone who'd had too much to drink," she began.

"All right, I won't embarrass you. Nickie can drive. She doesn't drink at all."

Nickie. Nickie would take him home and she'd probably stay to nurse him, too, in his condition. God only knew what might happen, but she couldn't afford to interfere. He'd had too much to drink and he'd kissed her, and she'd let him. Now she was ashamed and embarrassed.

"I have to go," she said stiffly.

"Drive carefully," he replied.

"Sure."

She found her keys where they'd fallen to the ground when he kissed her and unlocked the car door. She closed it once she was inside and started it after a bad fumble. He stood back from it, his hands in his pockets, looking dazed and not quite sober.

She hesitated, but Nickie came out the door, calling him. When he turned and raised a hand in Nickie's direction and answered her, laughing, Lou came to her senses. She lifted a hand toward both of them and drove away as quickly as she could. When she glanced back in the rearview mirror, it was to see Nickie holding Coltrain's hand as they went toward the building again.

So much for the interlude, she thought miserably. He'd probably only just realized who he'd kissed and was in shock.

That was close to the truth. Coltrain's head was spinning. He'd never dreamed that a kiss could be so explosive or addictive. There was something about Lou Blakely that made his knees buckle. He had no idea why he'd reacted so violently to her that he couldn't even let her leave. God knew what would have happened if she hadn't pushed him away when she did.

Nickie held on to him as they went back inside. "You've got her lipstick all over you," she accused.

He paused, shaken out of his brooding. Nickie was pretty, he thought, and uncomplicated. She already knew that he wasn't going to get serious however long they dated, because he'd told her so. It made him relax. He smiled down at her. "Wipe it off."

She pulled his handkerchief out of his pocket and did as he asked, smiling pertly. "Want to sample mine again?"

He tapped her on the nose. "Not tonight," he said. "We'd better leave. It's getting late."

"I'm driving," she told him.

"Yes, you are," he agreed.

She felt better. At least she was the one going home with him, not Lou. She wasn't going to give him up without a struggle, not when he was the best thing that had ever happened to her. Wealthy bachelor surgeons didn't come along every day of the week.

* * *

Lou drove home in a similar daze, overcome by the fervor of Coltrain's hard kisses. She couldn't understand why a man who'd always seemed to hate her had suddenly become addicted to her mouth; so addicted, in fact, that he'd followed her to her car. It had been the sweetest night of her life, but she had to keep her head and realize that it was an isolated incident. If Coltrain hadn't been drinking, it would never have happened. Maybe by Monday, she thought, he'd have convinced himself that it hadn't. She wished she could. She was more in love with him than ever, and he was as far out of her reach as he had ever been. Except that now he'd probably go even farther out of reach, because he'd lost his head and he wouldn't like remembering it.

She did her usual housework and answered emergency calls. She got more than her share because Dr. Coltrain had left word with their answering service that he was going to be out of town until Monday and Dr. Blakely would be covering for him.

Nice of him to ask her first, she thought bitterly, and tell her that he was going to be out of town. But perhaps he'd been reluctant to talk to her after what had happened. If the truth were known, he was more than likely as embarrassed as she was and just wanted to forget the whole thing.

She did his rounds and hers at the hospital, noticing absently that she was getting more attention than usual. Probably, she reasoned, because people were remembering the way Coltrain had kissed her. Maybe they thought something was going on between them.

"How's it going?" Drew asked on Sunday afternoon,

grinning at her. "I hear I missed a humdinger of a kiss at the Christmas party," he added wickedly.

She blushed to her hairline. "Lots of people got kissed."

"Not like you did. Not so that he followed you out to the parking lot and damn near made love to you on the hood of your car." He chuckled.

"Who...?"

"Nickie," he said, confirming her worst nightmare. "She was watching, apparently, and she's sweet on Copper. I guess she thought it might turn him off you if there was a lot of gossip about what happened. Rumors fly, especially when they're about two doctors who seem to hate each other."

"He'll walk right into it when he comes back," she said uneasily. "What can I do?"

"Nothing, I'm afraid."

Her eyes narrowed. "That's what you think."

She turned on her heel and went in search of Nickie. She found her in a patient's room and waited calmly while the girl, nervous and very insecure once she saw Lou waiting for her, finished the chore she was performing.

She went out into the hall with Lou, and she looked apprehensive.

Lou clutched a clipboard to her lab jacket. She didn't smile. "I understand you've been feeding the rumor mill. I'll give you some good advice. Stop it while you can."

By now, Nickie's face had gone puce. "I never meant...I was kidding!" she burst out. "That's all, just kidding!"

Lou studied her without emotion. "I'm not laughing. Dr. Coltrain won't be laughing, either, when he hears about it. And I'll make sure he knows where it came from."

"That's spiteful!" Nickie cried. "I'm crazy about him!"

"No, you aren't," Lou said shortly. "You'd never subject him to the embarrassment you have with all this gossip if you really cared."

Nickie's hands locked together. "I'm sorry," she said on a long sigh. "I really am. I was just jealous," she confessed, avoiding Lou's eyes. "He wouldn't even kiss me good-night, but he'd kiss you that way, and he hates you."

"Try to remember that he'd had too much to drink," Lou said quietly. "Only a fool would read anything into a kiss under the mistletoe."

"I guess so," Nickie said, but she wasn't really convinced. "I'm sorry. You won't tell him it was me, will you?" she added worriedly. "He'll hate me. I care so much, Dr. Blakely!"

"I won't tell him," Lou said. "But no more gossip!"

"Yes, ma'am!" Nickie brightened, grinned and went off down the hall, irrepressibly young and optimistic. Watching her, Lou felt ancient.

The next morning was Monday, and Lou went into the office to come face-to-face with a furious partner, who blocked her doorway and glared at her with blue eyes like arctic ice.

"Now what have I done?" she asked before he could

speak, and slammed her bag down on her desk, ready to do battle.

"You don't know?" he taunted.

She folded her arms over her breasts and leaned back against the edge of the desk. "There's a terrible rumor going around the hospital," she guessed.

His eyebrow jerked, but the ice didn't leave his eyes. "Did you start it?"

"Of course," she agreed furiously. "I couldn't wait to tell everybody on staff that you bent me back over the hood of my car and ravished me in the parking lot!"

Brenda, who'd started in the door, stood there with her mouth open, intercepted a furious glare from two pairs of eyes, turned on her heel and got out.

"Could you keep your voice down?" Coltrain snapped.

"Gladly, when you stop making stupid accusations!"

He glared at her and she glared back.

"I was drinking!"

"That's it, announce it to everyone in the waiting room, why don't you, and see how many patients run for their cars!" she raged.

He closed her office door, hard, and leaned back against it. "Who started the rumor?" he asked.

"That's more like it," she replied. "Don't accuse until you ask. I didn't start it. I have no wish to become the subject of gossip."

"Not even to force me to do something about the rumors?" he asked. "Such as announce our engagement?"

Her eyes went saucer-wide. "Please! I've just eaten!"

His jaw went taut. "I beg your pardon?"

"And so you should!" she said enthusiastically. "Marry you? I'd rather chain myself to a tree in an alligator swamp!"

He didn't answer immediately. He stared at her instead while all sorts of impractical ideas sifted through his mind.

A buzzer sounded on her desk. She reached over and pressed a button. "Yes?"

"What about the patients?" Brenda prompted.

"He doesn't *have* any patience," Lou said without thinking.

"Excuse me?" Brenda stammered.

"Oh. That sort of patients. Send my first one in, will you, Brenda? Dr. Coltrain was just leaving."

"No, he wasn't," he returned when her finger left the intercom button. "We'll finish this discussion after office hours."

"After office hours?" she asked blankly.

"Yes. But, don't get your hopes up about a repeat of Friday evening," he said with a mocking smile. "After all, I'm not drunk today."

Her eyes flashed murderously and her lips compressed. But he was already out the door.

Lou was never sure afterward how she'd managed to get through her patients without revealing her state of mind. She was furiously angry at Coltrain for his accusations and equally upset with Brenda for hearing what she'd said in retaliation. Now it would be all over the office as well as all over the hospital that she and Coltrain had something going. And they didn't! Despite Lou's helpless attraction to him, it didn't take much imagination to see that Coltrain didn't feel the same. Well, maybe physically he felt something for her, but emotionally he still hated her. A few kisses wouldn't change that!

She checked Mr. Bailey's firm, steady heartbeat, listened to his lungs and pronounced him over the pneumonia she'd been treating him for.

As she started to go, leaving Brenda to help him with his shirt, he called to her.

"What's this I hear about you and Doc Coltrain?" he teased. "Been kissing up a storm at the hospital Christmas party, they say. Any chance we'll be hearing wedding bells?"

He didn't understand, he told Brenda on his way out, why Dr. Blakely had suddenly screamed like that. Maybe she'd seen a mouse, Brenda replied helpfully.

When the office staff went home, Coltrain was waiting at the front entrance for Lou. He'd stationed himself there after checking with the hospital about a patient, and he hadn't moved, in case Lou decided to try to sneak out.

He was wearing the navy blue suit that looked so good on him, lounging against the front door with elegant carelessness, when she went out of her office. His red hair caught the reflection of the overhead light and seemed to burn like flames over his blue, blue eyes. They swept down over her neat gray pantsuit to her long legs encased in slacks with low-heeled shoes.

"That color looks good on you," he remarked.

"You don't need to flatter me. Just say what's on your mind, please, and let me go home."

"All right." His eyes fell to her soft mouth and lingered there. "Who started the rumors about us?"

She traced a pattern on her fanny pack. "I promised I wouldn't tell."

"Nickie," he guessed, nodding at her shocked expression.

"She's young and infatuated," she began.

"Not that young," he said with quiet insinuation.

Her eyes flashed before she could avert them. Her hand dug into the fanny pack for her car keys. "It's a nine-days wonder," she continued. "People will find something else to talk about."

"Nothing quite this spicy has happened since Ted Regan went chasing off to Victoria after Coreen Tarleton and she came home wearing his engagement ring."

"There's hardly any comparison," she said, "considering that everyone knows how we feel about each other!"

"How *do* we feel about each other, Lou?" he replied quietly, and watched her expression change.

"We're enemies," she returned instantly.

"Are we?" He searched her eyes in a silence that grew oppressive. His arms fell to his sides. "Come here, Lou."

She felt her breathing go wild. That could have been an invitation to bypass him and leave the building. But the look in his eyes told her it wasn't. Those eyes blazed like flames in his lean, tanned face, beckoning, promising pleasures beyond imagination.

He lifted a hand. "Come on, coward," he chided softly, and his lips curled at the edges. "I won't hurt you."

"You're sober," she reminded him.

"Cold sober," he agreed. "Let's see how it feels when I know what I'm doing."

Her heart stopped, started, raced. She hesitated, and he laughed softly and started toward her, with that slow, deliberate walk that spoke volumes about his intent.

"You mustn't," she spoke quickly, holding up a hand.

He caught the hand and jerked her against him, imprisoning her there with a steely arm. "I must." He corrected her, letting his eyes fall to her mouth. "I *have* to know." He bit off the words against her lips.

She never found out what he had to know, because the instant she felt his lips probing her mouth, she went under in a blaze of desire unlike anything she'd felt before. She gasped, opened her lips, yielded to his enveloping arms without a single protest. If anything, she pushed closer into his arms, against that steely body that was instantly aroused by the feel of her.

She tried to speak, to protest, but he pushed his tongue into her mouth with a harsh groan, and his arms lifted her so that she fit perfectly against him from breast to thigh. She fought, frightened by the intimacy and the sensations kindled in her untried body.

Her frantic protest registered at once. He remembered she'd had the same reaction the night of the Christmas party. His mouth lifted, and his searching eyes met hers.

"You couldn't be a virgin," he said, making it sound more like an accusation than a statement of fact.

She bit her lip and dropped her eyes, shamed and embarrassed. "Rub it in," she growled.

"My God." He eased her back onto her feet and held her by the upper arms so that she wouldn't fall. "My God! How old are you, thirty?"

"Twenty-eight," she said unsteadily, gasping for breath. Her whole body felt swollen. Her dark eyes glowered up at him as she pushed back her disheveled hair. "And you needn't look so shocked, you of all people should know that some people still have a few principles! You're a doctor, after all!"

"I thought virgins were a fairy tale," he said flatly. "Damn it!"

Her chin lifted. "What's wrong, Doctor, did you see me as a pleasant interlude between patients?"

His lips compressed. He rammed his hands into his trouser pockets, all too aware of a throbbing arousal that wouldn't go away. He turned to the door and jerked it open. All weekend he'd dreamed of taking Louise Blakely home with him after work and seducing her in his big king-size bed. She was leaving anyway, and the hunger he felt for her was one he had to satisfy or go mad. It had seemed so simple. She wanted him; he knew she did. People were already talking about them, so what would a little more gossip matter? She'd be gone at the first of the year, anyway.

But now he had a new complication, one he'd never dreamed of having. She was no young girl, but it didn't take an expert to know why she backed away from intimacy like a repressed adolescent. He'd been baiting her with that accusation of virginity, but she hadn't realized it. She'd taken it at face value and she'd given him a truth he didn't even want. She was innocent. How could he seduce her now? On the other hand, how was he going to get rid of this very inconvenient and noticeable desire for her?

Watching him, Lou was cursing her own headlong response. She hated having him know how much she wanted him.

"Any man could have made me react that way!" she flared defensively, red-faced. "Any experienced man!"

His head turned and he stared at her, seeing through the flustering words to the embarrassment.

"It's all right," he said gently. "We're both human. Don't beat your conscience to death over a kiss, Lou."

She went even redder and her hands clenched at her sides. "I'm still leaving!"

"I know."

"And I won't let you seduce me!"

He turned. "I won't try," he said solemnly. "I don't seduce virgins."

She bit her lip and tasted him on it. She winced.

"Why?" he asked quietly.

She glared at him.

"Why?" he persisted.

Her eyes fell under that piercing blue stare. "Because I don't want to end up like my mother," she said huskily.

Of all the answers he might have expected, that was the last. "Your mother? I don't understand."

She shook her head. "You don't need to. It's personal. You and I are business partners until the end of the month, and then nothing that happened to me will be any concern of yours."

He didn't move. She looked vulnerable, hurt. "Counseling might be of some benefit," he said gently.

"I don't need counseling."

"Tell me how your wrist got broken, Lou," he said matter-of-factly.

She stiffened.

"Oh, a layman wouldn't notice, it's healed nicely. But surgery is my business. I know a break when I see one. There are scars, too, despite the neat stitching job. How did it happen?"

She felt weak. She didn't want to talk to him, of all people, about her past. It would only reinforce what he already thought of her father, though God only knew why she should defend such a man.

She clasped her wrist defensively, as if to hide what had been done to it. "It's an old injury," she said finally.

"What sort of injury? How did it happen?"

She laughed nervously. "I'm not your patient."

He absently jingled the change in his pocket, watching her. It occurred to him that she was a stranger. Despite their heated arguments over the past year, they'd never come close to discussing personal matters. Away from the office, they were barely civil to each other. In it, they never discussed anything except business. But he was getting a new picture of her, and not a very reassuring one. This was a woman with a painful past, so painful that it had locked her up inside an antiseptic prison. He wondered if she'd ever had the incentive to fight her way out, or why it should matter to him that she hadn't.

"Can you talk to Drew about it?" he asked suddenly.

She hesitated and then shook her head. Her fingers tightened around her wrist. "It doesn't matter, I tell you."

His hand came out of his pocket and he caught the damaged wrist very gently in his long fingers, prepared for her instinctive jerk. He moved closer, drawing that hand to his chest. He pressed it gently into the thick fabric of his vest.

"There's nothing you can't tell me," he said solemnly. "I don't carry tales, or gossip. Anything you say to me will remain between the two of us. If you want to talk, ever, I'll listen."

She bit her bottom lip. She'd never been able to tell anyone. Her mother knew, but she defended her husband, trying desperately to pretend that Lou had imagined it, that it had never happened. She excused her husband's affairs, his drinking bouts, his drug addiction, his brutality, his sarcasm…everything, in the name of love, while her marriage disintegrated around her and her daughter turned away from her. Obsessive love, one of her friends had called it—blind, obsessive love that refused to acknowledge the least personality flaw in the loved one.

"My mother was emotionally crippled," she said, thinking aloud. "She was so blindly in love with him that he could do no wrong, no wrong at all…" She remembered where she was and looked up at him with the pain still in her eyes.

"Who broke your wrist, Lou?" he asked gently.

She remembered aloud. "He was drinking and I tried

to take the bottle away from him, because he'd hit my mother. He hit my wrist with the bottle, and it broke," she added, wincing at the memory of the pain. "And all the while, when they operated to repair the damage, he kept saying that I'd fallen through a glass door, that I'd tripped. Everyone believed him, even my mother. I told her that he did it, and she said that I was lying."

"He? Who did it, Lou?"

She searched his curious eyes. "Why...my father," she said simply.

Chapter 6

Coltrain searched her dark eyes, although the confession didn't really surprise him. He knew too much about her father to be surprised.

"So that was why the whiskey on my breath bothered you Friday night," he remarked quietly.

She averted her head and nodded. "He was a drunkard at the last, and a drug addict. He had to stop operating because he almost killed a patient. They let him retire and act in an advisory capacity because he'd been such a good surgeon. He was, you know," she added. "He might have been a terrible father, but he was a wonderful surgeon. I wanted to be a surgeon, to be like him." She shivered. "I was in my first year of medical school when it happened. I lost a semester and afterward, I knew I'd never be able to operate. I decided to become a general practitioner."

"What a pity," he said. He understood the fire for

surgical work because he had it. He loved what he did for a living.

She smiled sadly. "I'm still practicing medicine. It isn't so bad. Family practice has its place in the scheme of things, and I've enjoyed the time I've spent in Jacobsville."

"So have I," he admitted reluctantly. He smiled at her expression. "Surprised? You've been here long enough to know how a good many people react to me. I'm the original bad boy of the community. If it hadn't been for the scholarship one of my teachers helped me get, I'd probably be in jail by now. I had a hard childhood and I hated authority in any form. I was in constant trouble with the law."

"You?" she asked, aghast.

He nodded. "People aren't always what they seem, are they?" he continued. "I was a wild boy. But I loved medicine and I had an aptitude for it and there were people who were willing to help me. I'm the first of my family to escape poverty, did you know?"

She shook her head. "I don't know anything about your family," she said. "I wouldn't have presumed to ask anyone something so personal about you."

"I've noticed that," he returned. "You avoid sharing your feelings. You'll fight back, but you don't let people close, do you?"

"When people get too close, they can hurt you," she said.

"A lesson your father taught you, no doubt."

She wrapped her arms around her chest. "I'm cold," she said dully. "I want to go home."

He searched her face. "Come home with me."

She hesitated warily.

He made a face. "Shame on you for what you're thinking. You should know better. You're off the endangered list. I'll make chili and Mexican corn bread and strong coffee and we can watch a Christmas special. Do you like opera?"

Her eyes brightened. "Oh, I love it."

His own eyes brightened. "Pavarotti?"

"And Domingo." She looked worried. "But people will talk…"

"They're already talking. Who cares?" he asked. "We're both single adults. What we do together is nobody's business."

"Yes, well, the general consensus of opinion is that we're public property, or didn't you hear what Mr. Bailey said?"

"I heard you scream," he mused.

She cleared her throat. "Well, it was the last straw."

He caught her hand, the undamaged one, and locked her fingers into his, tugging her out the door.

"Dr. Coltrain," she began.

He locked the office door. "You know my name."

She looked wary. "Yes."

He glanced at her. "My friends call me Copper," he said softly, and smiled.

"We're not friends."

"I think we're going to be, though, a year too late." He tugged her toward his car.

"I can drive mine," she protested.

"Mine's more comfortable. I'll drive you home, and give you a lift to work in the morning. Is it locked?"

"Yes, but…"

"Don't argue, Lou. I'm tired. It's been a long day and we've still got to make rounds at the hospital later."

We. He couldn't know the anguish of hearing him link them together when she had less than two weeks left in Jacobsville. He'd said that he'd torn up her resignation, but she was levelheaded enough to know that she had to go. It would be pure torment to be around him all the time and have him treat her as a friend and nothing more. She couldn't have an affair with him, either, so what was left?

He glanced down at her worried face and his fingers contracted. "Stop brooding. I promised not to seduce you."

"I know that!"

"Unless you want me to," he chided, chuckling at her expression. "I'm a doctor," he added in a conspiratorial whisper. "I know how to protect you from any consequences."

"Damn you!"

She jerked away from him, furiously. He laughed at her fighting stance.

"That was wicked," he acknowledged. "But I do love to watch you lose that hot temper. Are you Irish, by any chance?"

"My grandfather was," she muttered. She dashed a strand of blond hair out of her eyes. "You stop saying things like that to me!"

He unlocked her door, still smiling. "All right. No more jokes."

She slid into the leather seat and inhaled the luxurious scent of the upholstery while he got in beside her and started the car. It was dark. She sat next to him in perfect peace and contentment as they drove out to his ranch, not breaking the silence as they passed by farms and ranches silhouetted against the flat horizon.

"You're very quiet," he remarked when he pulled up in front of the Spanish-style adobe house he called home.

"I'm happy," she said without thinking.

He was quiet, then. He helped her out and they walked a little apart on the flagstone walkway that led to the front porch. It was wide and spacious, with gliders and a porch swing.

"It must be heaven to sit out here in the spring," she remarked absently.

He glanced at her curiously. "I never pictured you as the sort to enjoy a porch swing."

"Or walks in the woods, or horseback riding, or baseball games?" she asked. "Because I like those things, too. Austin does have suburbs, and I had friends who owned ranches. I know how to ride and shoot, too."

He smiled. She'd seemed like such a city girl. He'd made sure that he never looked too closely at her, of course. Like father, like daughter, he'd always thought. But she was nothing like Fielding Blakely. She was unique.

He unlocked the door and opened it. The interior was full of Spanish pieces and dark furniture with creams and beiges and browns softened by off-white curtains. It had the look of professional decorating, which it probably was.

"I grew up sitting on orange crates and eating on

cracked plates," he commented as she touched a bronze sculpture of a bronc rider. "This is much better."

She laughed. "I guess so. But orange crates and cracked plates wouldn't be so bad if the company was pleasant. I hate formal dining rooms and extravagant place settings."

Now he was getting suspicious. They really couldn't have that much in common! His eyebrow jerked. "Full of surprises, aren't you? Or did you just take a look at my curriculum vitae and tell me what I wanted to hear?" he added in a crisp, suspicious tone.

Her surprise was genuine, and he recognized it immediately. She searched his face. "This was a mistake," she said flatly. "I think I'd like to go…"

He caught her arm. "Lou, I'm constantly on the defensive with women," he said. "I never know, you see…" He hesitated.

"Yes, I understand," she replied. "You don't have to say it."

"All that, and you read minds, too," he said with cool sarcasm. "Well, well."

She drew away from him. She seemed to read his mind quite well, she thought, because she usually knew what he was going to say.

That occurred to him, too. "It used to make me mad as hell when you handed me files before I asked for them," he told her.

"It wasn't deliberate," she said without thinking.

"I know." His jaw firmed as he looked at her. "We know too much about each other, don't we, Lou? We know things we shouldn't, without ever saying them."

She looked up, feeling the bite of his inspection all

the way to her toes. "We can't say them," she replied. "Not ever."

He only nodded. His eyes searched hers intently. "I don't believe in happily ever after," he said. "I did, once, until your father came along and shattered all my illusions. She wouldn't let me touch her, you see. But she slept with him. She got pregnant by him. The hell of it was that she was going to marry me without telling me anything." He sighed. "I lost my faith in women on the spot, and I hated your father enough to beat him to his knees. When you came here, and I found out who you were…" He shook his head. "I almost decked Drew for not telling me."

"I didn't know, either," she said.

"I realize that." He smiled. "You were an asset, after I got over the shock. You never complained about long hours or hard work, no matter how much I put on you. And I put a lot on you, at first. I thought I could make you quit. But the more I demanded, the more you gave. After a while, it occurred to me that I'd made a good bargain. Not that I liked you," he added sardonically.

"You made that perfectly clear."

"You fought back," he said. "Most people don't. They knuckle under and go home and fume about it, and think up things they wish they'd said. You just jump in with both feet and give it all you've got. You're a hell of an adversary, Lou. I couldn't beat you down."

"I always had to fight for things," she recalled. "My father was like you." Her face contorted and she turned away.

"I don't get drunk as a rule, and I've never hurt a woman!" he snapped.

"I didn't mean that," she said quickly. "It's just that you're forceful. You demand, you push. You don't ever give up or give in. Neither did he. If he thought he was right, he'd fight the whole world to prove it. But he fought the same when he was wrong. And in his later years, he drank to excess. He wouldn't admit he had a problem. Neither would my mother. She was his slave," she added bitterly. "Even her daughter was dispensable if the great man said so."

"Didn't she love you?"

"Who knows? She loved him more. Enough to lie for him. Even to die for him. And she did." She turned, her face hard. "She got into a plane with him, knowing that he was in no condition to fly. Maybe she had a premonition that he would go down and she wanted to go with him. I'm almost sure that she still would have gone with him if she'd known he was going to crash the plane. She loved him that much."

"You sound as if you can't imagine being loved that much."

"I can't," she said flatly, lifting her eyes. "I don't want that kind of obsessive love. I don't want to give it or receive it."

"What do you want?" he persisted. "A lifetime of loneliness?"

"That's what you're settling for, isn't it?" she countered.

He shrugged. "Maybe I am," he said after a minute. His blue eyes slid over her face and then averted. "Can you cook?" he asked on the way into the kitchen. Like the rest of the house, it was spacious and contained every modern device known to man.

"Of course," she said.

He glanced at her with a grin. "How well do you do chili?" he persisted.

"Well…"

"I've won contests with mine," he said smugly. He slid out of his jacket and vest and tie, opened the top buttons of his shirt and turned to the stove. "You can make the coffee."

"Trusting soul, aren't you?" she murmured as he acquainted her with the coffeemaker and the location of filters, coffee and measuring spoons.

"I always give a fellow cook the benefit of the doubt once," he replied. "Besides, you drink coffee all the time, just like I do. That means you must know how to make it."

She laughed. "I like mine strong," she warned.

"So do I. Do your worst."

Minutes later, the food was on the small kitchen table, steaming and delicious. Lou couldn't remember when she'd enjoyed a meal more.

"That's good chili," she had to admit.

He grinned. "It's the two-time winner of the Jacobsville Chili Cookoff."

"I'm not surprised. The corn bread was wonderful, too."

"The secret to good corn bread is to cook it in an iron skillet," he confessed. "That's where the crispness comes from."

"I don't own a single piece of iron cookware. I'll have to get a pan."

He leaned back, balancing his coffee mug in one

hand as he studied her through narrow eyes. "It hasn't all been on my side," he remarked suddenly.

Her eyes lifted to his. "What hasn't?"

"All that antagonism," he said. "You've been as prickly as I have."

Her slender shoulders rose and fell. "It's instinctive to recoil from people when we know they don't like us. Isn't it?"

"Maybe so." He checked his watch and finished his coffee. "I'll get these things in the dishwasher, then we'd better get over to the hospital and do rounds before the Christmas concert comes on the educational channel."

"I don't have my car," she said worriedly.

"We'll go together."

"Oh, that will certainly keep gossip down," she said on a sigh.

He smiled at her. "Damn gossip."

"Was that an adjective or a verb?"

"A verb. I'll rinse, you stack."

They loaded the dishes and he started the dishwasher. He slid back into his jacket, buttoned his shirt and fixed his tie. "Come on. We'll get the chores out of the way."

The hospital was crowded, and plenty of people noticed that Drs. Coltrain and Blakely came in together to make rounds. Lou tried not to notice as she went from patient to patient, checking charts and making conversation.

But when she finished, Coltrain was nowhere in sight. She glanced out the window into the parking lot. His car was still there in his designated space. She went to the doctors' lounge looking for him, and turned the corner just in time to see him with a devastating blond woman in a dress that Lou would love to have been able to afford.

Coltrain saw Lou and he looked grim. He turned toward her with his hands in his pockets, and Lou noticed that the woman was clutching one of his arms tightly in both hands.

"This is my partner," he said, without giving her name. "Lou, this is Dana Lester, an old…friend."

"His ex-fiancée." The woman corrected him in a sweet tone. "How nice to meet you! I've just accepted an appointment as nursing director here, so we'll be seeing a lot of each other!"

"You're a nurse?" Lou asked politely, while she caved in inside.

"A graduate nurse," she said, nodding. "I've been working in Houston, but this job came open and was advertised in a local paper. I applied for it, and here I am! How lovely it will be to come home. I was born here, you know."

"Oh, really?" Lou said.

"Darling," she told Copper, "you didn't tell me your partner's name."

"It's Blakely," he said evenly. "Dr. Louise Blakely."

"Blakely?" the woman queried, her blue eyes pensive. "Why does that name sound so familiar…." She suddenly went pale. "No," she said, shaking her head. "No, that would be too coincidental."

"My father," Lou said coolly, "was Dr. Fielding Blakely. I believe you…knew him?" she added pointedly.

Dana's face looked like rice paper. She drew away from Coltrain. "I...I must fly, darling," she said. "Things to do while I get settled! I'll have you over for supper one night soon!"

She didn't speak to Lou again, not that it was expected. Lou watched her go with cold, angry eyes.

"You didn't want to tell her my name," Lou accused softly.

His face gave away nothing. "The past is best left alone."

"Did you know about her job here?"

His jaw clenched. "I knew there was an opening. I didn't know she'd been hired. If Selby Wills hadn't just retired as hospital administrator, she wouldn't have gotten the job."

She probed into the pocket of her lab coat without really seeing it. "She's pretty."

"She's blond, too, isn't that what you're thinking?"

She raised her face. "So," she added, "is Jane Parker."

"Jane Burke, now." He corrected her darkly. "I like blondes."

His tone dared her to make another remark. She lifted a shoulder and turned. "Some men do. Just don't expect me to welcome her with open arms. I'm sure that my mother suffered because of her. At least my father was less careless with women in his later years."

"It was over a long time ago," Copper said quietly. "If I can overlook your father, you can overlook her."

"Do you think so?"

"What happened between them was nothing to do with you," he persisted.

"He betrayed my mother with her, and it's nothing to do with me?" she asked softly.

He rammed his hands into his pockets, his face set and cold. "Are you finished here?"

"Oh, yes, I'm finished here," she agreed fervently. "If you'll drop me off at my car, I'd like to go home now. We'll have to save the TV Special for another time."

He hesitated, but only for a minute. Her expression told him everything he needed to know, including the futility of having an argument with her right now.

"All right," he agreed, nodding toward the exit. "Let's go."

He stopped at her car in the office parking lot and let her out.

"Thanks for my supper," she said politely.

"You're welcome."

She closed the door and unlocked her own car. He didn't drive away until she was safely inside and heading out toward home.

Dana Lester's arrival in town was met with another spate of gossip, because there were people in Jacobsville who remembered the scandal very well. Lou tried to pay as little attention to it as possible as she weathered the first few days with the new nursing supervisor avoiding her and Coltrain barely speaking to her.

It was, she told herself, a very good thing that she was leaving after the first of January. The situation was strained and getting worse. She couldn't work out if Dana was afraid of her or jealous of her. Gossip about herself and Coltrain had been lost in the new rumors about his ex-fiancée's return, which did at least spare

Lou somewhat. She couldn't help but see that Dana spent a fair amount of time following Coltrain around the hospital, and once or twice she phoned him at the office. Lou pretended not to notice and not to mind, but it was cutting her up inside.

The night she'd had supper with her taciturn partner had been something of a beginning. But Dana's arrival had nipped it all in the bud. He'd turned his back on Lou and now he only spoke to her when it was necessary and about business. If he'd withdrawn, so had she. Poor Brenda and the office receptionist worked in an armed camp, walking around like people on eggshells. Coltrain's temper strained at the bit, and every time he flared up, Lou flared right back.

"We hear that Nickie and Dana almost came to blows the other night about who got to take Dr. Coltrain a file," Brenda remarked a few days later.

"Too bad someone didn't have a hidden camera, isn't it?" Lou remarked. She sipped her coffee.

Brenda frowned. "I thought... Well, it did seem that you and the doctor were getting along better."

"A temporary truce, nothing more," she returned. "I'm still leaving after the first of the year, Brenda. Nothing's really changed except that Coltrain's old flame has returned."

"She was poison," Brenda said. "I heard all about her from some of the older nurses at the hospital. Did you know that at least two threatened to quit when they knew she was taking over as head nurse at the hospital? One of the nurses she worked with in Houston has family here. They said she was about to be fired when she grabbed this job. Her credentials look impressive, but she's not a good administrator, regardless of her college background, and she plays favorites. They'll learn that here, the hard way."

"It's not my problem."

"Isn't it?" Brenda muttered. "Well, they also say that her real purpose in applying for this job was to see if Copper was willing to take her back and try again. She's looking for a husband and he's number one on her list."

"Lucky him," she said blithely. "She's very pretty."

"She's a blond tarantula," she said hotly. "She'll suck him dry!"

"He's a big boy, Brenda," Lou returned imperturbably. "He can take care of himself."

"No man is immune to a beautiful face and figure and having a woman absolutely worship him. You take my word for it, there's going to be trouble."

"I won't be here to see it," Lou reminded her. And for the first time, she was glad. Nickie and Dana could fight over Coltrain and may the best woman win, she thought miserably. At least she wouldn't have to watch the struggle. She'd always known that Coltrain wasn't for her. She might as well accept defeat with good grace and get out while she could.

She went back to work, all too aware of Coltrain's deep voice in one of the cubicles she passed. She wondered how her life was going to feel when this was all a bad memory, and she wouldn't hear his voice again.

Drew invited her out to eat and she went, gratefully, glad for the diversion. But the restaurant he chose, Jacobsville's best, had two unwelcome diners: Coltrain and his ex-fiancée.

"I'm sorry," Drew said with a smile and a grimace of apology. "I didn't know they'd be here or I'd have chosen another place to take you for supper."

"Oh, I don't mind," she assured him. "I have to see them at the hospital every day, anyway."

"Yes, *see* them being the key word here," he added knowingly. "I understand that they both avoid you."

"God knows why," she agreed. "She's anywhere I'm not when I need to ask her a question, and he only talks to me about patients. I'm glad I'm leaving, Drew. And with all respect to you, I'm sorry I came."

He smiled ruefully. "I'm sorry I got you into this," he said. "Nothing went as I planned."

"What exactly did you plan?" she asked probingly.

He lifted his water glass and took a sip. "Well, I had hoped that Copper would see something in you that he hadn't found anywhere else. You're unique, Lou. So is he, in some respects. You seemed like a match."

She glared at him. "We're chalk and cheese," she said, ignoring the things she and the redheaded doctor did have in common. "And we can't get along for more than five minutes."

"So I see." He looked around and made a face. "Oh, God, more complications!"

She followed his gaze. A determined Nickie, in a skintight dress cut almost to the navel, was dragging an embarrassed intern to a table right beside Coltrain and Dana's.

"That won't do," she remarked, watching Coltrain's blue eyes start to glitter. "He won't like that. And if she thinks he'll forgo a scene, she's very wrong. Any minute now he's going to get up and walk out."

When he did exactly that, leaving an astonished Dana at one table and a shocked Nickie at the other, Drew whistled through his teeth and gave Lou a pointed stare.

"You know him very well," was all he said, though.

"I know him," Lou said simply. "He says I read his mind. Maybe I do, on some level."

He frowned. "Do you realize how rare a rapport that is?"

She shrugged. "Not really. He seems to read my mind, too. I shouldn't feel sorry for him, but I do. Imagine shuffling two women in one restaurant."

He didn't add that it was really three, and that Copper had been watching Lou surreptitiously ever since she and Drew entered the restaurant. But of the three women, Lou was the only one who wasn't blatantly chasing him.

"He's paying the check," he remarked. "And, yes, there he goes, motioning to Dana. Good thing they'd finished dessert, wasn't it? Poor Nickie. She won't forget this in a while."

"I told her she was pushing too hard," Lou remarked. "Too bad. She's so young. I suppose she hasn't learned that you can chase a man too relentlessly and lose him."

"Some women never chase a man at all," he said.

She looked up and saw the teasing expression on his face. She laughed. "Drew, you are a dear," she said genuinely.

He chuckled. "My wife always said that I was," he agreed. "What are you going to do?"

"Me? What do you mean? What am I going to do about what?"

"About Copper."

"Nothing," she replied. "Right after the holidays, I leave for Austin."

He pursed his lips as he lifted his coffee cup. "You know," he said, "I have a feeling you'll never get out of town."

Chapter 7

Saturday morning, Lou woke to the sound of someone hammering on her front door. Half-asleep, with a pale pink satin robe whipped around her slender body and her hair disheveled, she made her way to open it.

The sight that met her eyes was shocking. Coltrain was standing there, dressed in jeans and boots and a faded cotton shirt under a fleece-lined jacket, with a weather-beaten gray Stetson in one lean hand.

She blinked. "Are we filming a new series called 'Cowboy Doctor'?"

"Cute," he remarked, but he wasn't smiling. "I have to talk to you."

She opened the door, still drowsy. "Come on in. I'll make coffee," she said, stifling a yawn as she shuffled toward the kitchen. She could have gone immediately to change, but she was more than adequately covered and he was a doctor. Besides, she reminded herself, he had two women chasing him relentlessly anyway.

"I'll make the coffee. How about some toast to go with it?"

"Plain or cinnamon?"

"Suit yourself."

She got out butter and cinnamon and, just as the coffee finished brewing, she had the toast ready—piping hot from the oven.

He watched her moving about the kitchen. He was sitting leaning back in one of her kitchen chairs with one booted foot on the floor and the chair propped against the wall. He looked out of humor and wickedly handsome all at the same time.

In the position he was occupying, his jeans clung closely to every powerful line of his long legs. He was muscular without being exaggerated, and with his faded shirt unbuttoned at the throat and his red hair disheveled from the hat, he looked more relaxed than she'd ever seen him.

It occurred to her that this was the way he usually was, except when he was working. It was like a private look into his secret life, and she was unexpectedly pleased to have been given it before she left town for good.

"Here." She put the toast on the table, handed him a plate, put condiments on the spotless white tablecloth and then poured coffee into two cups.

"The Christmas concert was nice," he remarked.

"Was it?" she replied. "I went to bed."

"I had nothing to do with getting Dana down here," he said flatly. "In case you wondered."

"It's none of my business."

"Yes, I know," he said heavily. He sipped coffee and munched toast, but he was preoccupied. "Nickie and Dana are becoming an embarrassment."

"Leave it to you to be irritated when two lovely women compete for your attention," she remarked dryly.

His eyes narrowed on her face. "Irritation doesn't quite cover it. I feel like the stud of the month," he said disgustedly.

She burst out laughing. "Oh, I'm sorry!" she said when he glared at her. "It was the way you said it."

He was ruffled, and looked it. He sipped more coffee. "I wasn't trying to make a joke."

"I know. It must be difficult, especially when you have to make rounds at the hospital, with both of them working there."

"I understand you're having some problems of your own in that regard."

"You might say that," she agreed. "I can't find Dana or Nickie when I need them. I seem to have the plague."

"You know that it can't continue?"

"Of course I do," she assured him. "And when I leave, things will settle down, I'm sure."

He scowled. "What do you mean, when you leave? How will that help? Anyway, we'd already agreed that you were staying."

"We agreed on nothing," she returned. "I gave you my resignation. If you tore it up, that's your problem. I consider it binding."

He stared down into his coffee cup, deep in thought. "I had no idea that you meant it."

"Amazing," she mused, watching him. "You have such a convenient memory, Dr. Coltrain. I can't forget a single word you said to Drew about me, and you can't remember?"

His face hardened. "I didn't know you were listening."

"That makes everything all right?" she asked with mock solemnity.

He ran a hand through his already disheveled hair. "Things came to a head," he replied. "I'd just had to diagnose leukemia in a child who should have had years of happiness to look forward to. I'd had a letter from my father asking for money…"

She shifted against the table. "I didn't know that your parents were still alive."

"My mother died ten years ago," he replied. "My father lives in Tucson. He wrangles horses, but he likes to gamble. When he gets in too deep, he always comes to me for a grubstake." He said it with utter contempt.

"Is that all you mean to him? Money?" she asked gently.

"It was all I ever meant to him." He lifted cold blue eyes to hers. He smiled unpleasantly. "Who do you think put me up to breaking and entering when I was a teenager? I was a juvenile, you know. Juveniles don't go to jail. Oh, we didn't do it here," he added. "Not where he lived. We always went to Houston. He cased the houses and sent me in to do the actual work."

Her gasp was audible. "He should have been arrested!"

"He was," he replied. "He served a year and got probation. We haven't spent any time together since I was placed with a foster family when I was thirteen, long before I started medical school. I put all that behind me. Apparently so did he. But now that I'm making a comfortable living, he doesn't really see any good reason not to ask me for help when he needs it."

What sort of family life had *he* grown up in? she wondered. It was, in some ways, like her own upbringing. "What a pity that we can't choose our parents," she remarked.

"Amen." His broad shoulders shifted against the wall. "I was in a temper already, and Drew's phone call was the last straw. It irritated the hell out of me that you liked him, but you jerked away from my slightest touch as if I might contaminate you."

She hadn't thought he'd noticed. He took her reaction as a sign of her distaste for him, when it was a fierce, painful attraction. It was ironic.

She lowered her eyes. "You said when I first came to work with you that we would have a business relationship."

"So I did. But that didn't mean you should treat me like a leper," he remarked. Oddly, he didn't seem to be concerned about it anymore. He smiled, in fact, his blue eyes sparkling. "But I wouldn't have had you overhear what I told Drew for all the world, Lou. It shamed me when you asked to end our partnership."

She toyed with a fingernail. "I thought it would make you happy."

Her choice of words delighted him. He knew exactly what she felt for him. He'd had suspicions for a while now, but he hadn't been certain until he kissed her. He couldn't let her leave until he was sure about what he felt for her. But how was he going to stop her? His blue eyes ran searchingly over her face and a crazy idea popped into his mind. "If you and I were engaged," he mused aloud, "Dana and Nickie would give up."

The words rambled around in her mind like marbles as she stared at him. The sun was out. It was a nice December day. Her Christmas decorations lined the windows and the tinsel on the Christmas tree in the living room caught the sun through the curtains and glittered.

"Did you hear me?" he asked when she didn't react.

Her cheeks burned. "I don't think that's very funny," she remarked, turning away.

He got to his feet with an audible thud and before she could move three feet, he had her by the waist from behind. Steely hands pulled her back against him and when she caught them, she felt their warm strength under her cool fingers. She felt his breath against her hair, felt it as his chest moved at her back.

"Shall we stop dancing around it?" he asked roughly. "You're in love with me. I've pretended not to see it, but we both know it's why you're leaving."

She gasped aloud. Frozen in his arms, she hadn't even a comeback, a face-saving reply. She felt his hands contract under hers, as if he thought she might pull away and run for it.

"Don't panic," he said quietly. "Dodging the issue won't solve it."

"I...didn't realize you could tell," she whispered, her pride in ashes at his feet.

His lean arms contracted, bringing her soft warmth closer to his taut body. "Take it easy. We'll deal with it."

"You don't have to deal with anything," she began huskily. "I'm going to…"

He turned her while she was speaking and his mouth was on hers before she could finish. She fought him for an instant, as he anticipated. But he was slow and very gentle, and she began to melt into him like ice against a flame.

He brought her closer, aware of her instant response when she felt his body harden. He made a rough sound against her mouth and deepened the kiss.

Her fingers caught in the cool flames of his hair, holding on for dear life as his ardor burned high and wild. He kissed her as he'd kissed Nickie at the party, not an inch of space between their bodies, no quarter in the thin lips devouring her open mouth. This time when his tongue penetrated, she didn't pull away. She accepted the intimate contact without a protest, shivering a little as it ignited new fires in her own taut body. The sensation was unlike anything she'd known. She held on tight, moaning, aware somewhere in the back of her mind that his hand was at the base of her spine, rubbing her against him, and that she should say something.

She was incapable of anything except blind response.

She didn't resist even when he eased her back onto her feet and, still kissing her hungrily, slid his hand under her robe against the soft, tight curve of her breast. He felt her heartbeat run away. With a groan, he fought his way under the gown, against the petal-soft warmth of her skin, and cupped her tenderly, dragging his thumb against the small hardness he found. She shivered again. Reeling, he traced the tight nub with his thumb and forefinger, testing its hardness. She sobbed against his mouth. Probably, he thought dizzily, she'd never had such a caress. And he could give her something more; another pleasure that she didn't know yet.

His mouth left hers and found its way down past her collarbone to the softness under his hand. It opened on her body, and he drank in the scented warmth of her while his tongue took the place of his thumb. She gasped and struggled, but he began to suckle her, his arms swallowing her, and she shuddered once and gave in. He felt her body go lax in his arms, so that if he hadn't supported her, she would have fallen. She caressed his nape with trembling hands, gasping a little as he increased the pressure, but clinging, not pushing.

When he thought he might explode from the pleasure it was giving him, he forced his mouth to release her and he stood erect, pulling her up abruptly.

His face was ruddy with high color, his eyes blazing as they met her half-open, dazed ones. She was oblivious to everything except the taste of him. Her lips were swollen. Even her tongue felt swollen. She couldn't say a word.

He searched over her face and then dropped his eyes to her bodice. He moved it out of the way and looked at the small, firm breast he'd been tasting. She looked like a rosebud there, the nipple red from his mouth.

He traced around it lazily and then looked back up at the shocked pleasure in her dark, dark eyes.

"I could have you on the kitchen table, right now," he

said in a deep, quiet tone. "And you think you're leaving in two weeks?"

She blinked. It was all so unreal. He'd all but seduced her. His hand was still on her breast and he'd pulled the robe and gown aside. He was looking at her...!

She gasped, horrified, jerking back from him. Her hands grappled with the unruly fabric before she finally got her body covered. She backed away, blushing, glaring at him accusingly.

He didn't move, except to lean back against the kitchen counter and cross his long legs. That action drew her eyes to something she'd felt earlier, and she blushed scarlet before she managed to look away. What had she done? What had she let him do?

"You look outraged," he mused. "I think I like having you blush when I look at you."

"Would you leave, please?" she asked tightly.

"No, I don't think so," he said pleasantly. "Get dressed. Wear jeans and boots. I'm taking you riding."

"I don't want to go anywhere with you!"

"You want to go to bed with me," he corrected, smiling gently. "I can't think of anything I'd enjoy more, but I saddled the horses and left them in the stable before I came over here."

She huddled in her robe, wincing as it rubbed against her body.

"Breast sore?" he asked softly. "I'm sorry. I lost my head a little."

She flushed more and the robe tightened. "Dr. Coltrain..."

"Copper," he reminded her. "Or you can call me Jeb, if you like." He pursed his lips and his eyes were hot and possessive. "You'd really better get dressed, Lou," he murmured. "I'm still pretty hot, and aroused men are devious."

She moved back. "I have things to do…"

"Horseback riding or…?" He moved toward her.

She turned and ran for the bedroom. She couldn't believe what had just happened, and he'd said something about them becoming engaged. She must be losing her mind. Yes, that was it, she'd worried over leaving so much that she was imagining things. The whole thing had probably been a hallucination.

He'd cleared away the breakfast things by the time she washed, dressed, pulled her hair back into a pony-tail with a blue ribbon and came into the kitchen with a rawhide jacket on.

He smiled. "You look like a cowgirl."

She'd felt a bit uneasy about facing him after that torrid interlude, but apparently he wasn't embarrassed. She might as well follow his lead. She managed a smile in return. "Thanks. But I may not quite merit the title. I haven't ridden in a long time."

"You'll be all right. I'll look after you."

He opened the door and let her out, waiting for her to lock it. Then he helped her into the Jaguar and drove her to his ranch.

The woods were lovely, despite their lack of leaves. The slow, easy rhythm of the horses was relaxing, even if the company wasn't. She was all too aware of Coltrain beside her, tall and elegant even on horseback. With the

Stetson pulled low over his eyes, he looked so handsome that he made her toes tingle.

"Enjoying yourself?" he asked companionably.

"Oh, yes," she admitted. "I haven't been riding in a long time."

"I do more of it than I like sometimes," he confessed. "This isn't a big ranch, but I run about fifty head of pedigree cattle. I have two married cowhands who help out."

"Why do you keep cattle?" she asked.

"I don't know. It was always a dream of mine, I guess, from the time I was a boy. My grandfather had one old milk cow and I'd try to ride her." He chuckled. "I fell off a lot."

She smiled. "And your grandmother?"

"Oh, she was a cook of excellent proportions," he replied. "She made cakes that were the talk of the county. When my dad went wrong, it broke her heart, and my grandfather's. I think they took it harder because he lured me into it with him." He shook his head. "When a kid goes bad, everyone blames it on the upbringing. But my grandparents were kind, good people. They were just poor. A lot of people were...still are."

She'd noticed that he had a soft spot for his needy patients. He made extra time for them, acting as counselor and even helping them get in touch with the proper government agencies when they needed help. At Christmas, he was the first to pledge a donation to local charities and contribute to parties for children who wouldn't otherwise have presents. He was a good man, and she adored him.

"Do you want children, eventually?" she asked.

"I'd like a family," he said noncommittally. He glanced at her. "How about you?"

She grimaced. "I don't know. It would be hard for me to juggle motherhood and medicine. I know plenty of people do, but it seems like begging from Peter to pay Paul, you know? Children need a lot of care. I think plenty of social problems are caused by parents who can't get enough time off from work to look after their children. And good day care is a terrible financial headache. Why isn't day care free?" she asked abruptly. "It should be. If women are going to have to work, companies should provide access to day care for them. I know of hospitals and some companies that do it for their employees. Why can't every big company?"

"Good question. It would certainly take a burden off working parents."

"All the same, if I had kids, I'd want to be with them while they were young. I don't know if I could give up practice for so long…."

He reined in his horse and caught her bridle, bringing her horse gently around so that they were facing each other at the side. "That's not the reason. Talk to me," he said quietly. "What is it?"

She huddled into her jacket. "I hated being a child," she muttered. "I hated my father and my mother and my life."

His eyebrows lifted. "Do you think a child would hate me?"

She laughed. "Are you kidding? Children love you. Except that you don't do stitches as nicely as I do," she added.

He smiled ruefully. "Thanks for small favors."

"The secret is the chewing gum I give them afterward."

"Ah, I see. Trade a few stitches for a few cavities."

"It's sugarless gum," she said smugly.

He searched her face with warm eyes. "Touché."

He wheeled his horse and led her off down a pasture path to where the big barn was situated several hundred yards away from the house. He explained the setup, and how he'd modernized his small operation.

"I'm not as up-to-date as a lot of ranchers are, and this is peanut scale," he added. "But I've put a lot of work and time into it, and I'm moderately proud of what I've accomplished. I have a herd sire who's mentioned in some of the bigger cattle magazines."

"I'm impressed. Do I get to see him?"

"Do you want to?"

"You sound surprised. I like animals. When I started out, it was a toss-up between being a doctor and being a vet."

"What swayed you?"

"I'm not really sure. But I've never regretted my choice."

He swung out of the saddle and waited for her to dismount. He tied the horses to the corral rail and led the way into the big barn.

It was surprisingly sanitary. The walkway was paved, the stalls were spacious with metal gates and fresh hay. The cows were sleek and well fed, and the bull he'd mentioned was beautiful even by bovine standards.

"Why, he's gorgeous," she enthused as they stood at the gate and looked at him. He was red-coated, huge, streamlined and apparently docile, because he came up to let Coltrain pet his muzzle.

"How are you, old man?" he murmured affectionately. "Had enough corn, have you?"

"He's a Santa Gertrudis, isn't he?" she asked curiously.

His hand stilled on the bull's nose. "How did you know that?" he asked.

"Ted Regan is one of my patients. He had a breeder's edition of some magazine with him one day, and he left it behind. I got a good idea of coat colors, at least. We have a lot of cattlemen around here," she added. "It never hurts to know a little bit about a good bull."

"Why, Lou," he mused. "I'm impressed."

"That's a first."

He chuckled. His blue eyes twinkled down at her as he propped one big boot on the low rail of the gate. "No, it's not. You impressed me the first week you were here. You've grown on me."

"Good heavens, am I a wart?"

He caught a strand of her hair and wound it around his finger. "You're a wonder," he corrected, searching her eyes. "I didn't realize we had so much in common. Funny, isn't it? We've worked together for a year, but I've found out more about you in the past two weeks than I ever knew."

"That goes for me, too."

She dropped her eyes to his chest, where the faded shirt clung to the hard muscles. She loved the way he stood, the way he walked, the way he looked with that hat tilted rakishly over one eye. She remembered the feel of his warm arms around her and she felt suddenly cold.

Her expressions fascinated him. He watched them change, saw the hunger filter into her face.

She drew a wistful breath and looked up at him with a wan smile.

He frowned. Without understanding why, he held out a lean arm.

She accepted the invitation without question. Her body went against his, pressing close. Her arms went under his and around him, so that her hands could flatten on the muscles of his long back. She closed her eyes and laid her cheek against his chest, and listened to his heart beat.

He was surprised, yet he wasn't. It felt natural to have Lou in his arms. He drew her closer, in a purely nonsexual way, and absently stroked her hair while he watched his bull eat corn out of the trough in his pen.

"Next week is Christmas," he said above her head.

"Yes, I know. What do you do for Christmas? Do you go to friends, or invite people over?"

He laughed gently. "I used to have it with Jane, before she married," he recalled, feeling her stiffen without really thinking much about it. "But last year, since she married, I cooked a TV dinner and watched old movies all day."

She didn't answer for a minute. Despite what she'd heard about Coltrain and Jane Parker in the past year, she hadn't thought that he and Jane had been quite so close. But it seemed that they were. It depressed her more than anything had in recent weeks.

He wasn't thinking about Christmases past. He was thinking about the upcoming one. His hand explored her hair strand by strand. "Where are we going to have

Christmas dinner, and who's going to cook it?" he asked matter-of-factly.

That was encouraging, that he wanted to spend Christmas with her. She couldn't refuse, even out of hurt pride. "We could have it at my house," she offered.

"I'll help cook it."

She smiled. "It would be nice to have someone to eat it with," she confessed.

"I'll make sure we're on call Christmas Eve, not Christmas Day," he promised. His arm slid down her back and drew her closer. He was aware of a kind of contentment he'd never experienced before, a belonging that he hadn't known even with Jane. Funny, he thought, until Lou came along, it had never occurred to him that he and Jane couldn't have had a serious relationship even if Todd Burke hadn't married her.

It was a sobering thought. This woman in his arms had come to mean a lot to him, without his realizing it until he'd kissed her for the first time. He laid his cheek against her head with a long sigh. It was like coming home. He'd been searching all his life for something he'd never found. He was closer to it than he'd ever been right now.

Her arms tightened around his lean waist. She could feel the wall of his chest hard against her breasts, the buckle of his belt biting into her. But it still wasn't quite close enough. She moved just a little closer, so that her legs brushed his.

He moved to accommodate her, sliding one boot higher on the fence so that she could fit against him more comfortably. But the movement aroused him and he caught his breath sharply.

"Sorry," she murmured and started to step away.

But his hand stayed her hips. "I can't help that," he said at her temple, secretly delighted at his headlong physical response to her. "But it isn't a threat."

"I didn't want to make you uncomfortable."

He smiled lazily. "I wouldn't call it that." He brushed a kiss across her forehead. "Relax," he whispered. "It's pretty public here, and I'm sure you know as well as I do that making love in a hay barn is highly unsanitary."

She laughed at his humor. "Oh, but this barn is very clean."

"Not that clean," he murmured dryly. "Besides," he added, "it's been a long, dry spell. When I'm not in the market for a companion, I don't walk around prepared for sweet interludes."

She lifted her face and searched his mocking eyes demurely. "A long, dry spell? With Nickie prancing around half-naked to get your attention?"

He didn't laugh, as she expected him to. He traced her pert nose. "I don't have affairs," he said. "And I'm the soul of discretion in my private life. There was a widow in a city I won't name. She and I were good friends, and we supplied each other with something neither of us was comfortable spreading around. She married year before last. Since then, I've concentrated on my work and my cattle. Period."

She was curious. "Can you...well, do it...without love?"

"I was fond of her," he explained. "She was fond of me. We didn't have to be in love."

She moved restlessly.

"It would have to be love, for you, wouldn't it, Lou?"

he asked. "Even desperate desire wouldn't be enough." He traced her soft lips with deliberation. "But you and I are an explosive combination. And you do love me."

She laid her forehead at his collarbone. "Yes," she admitted. "I love you. But not enough to be your mistress."

"I know that."

"Then it's hopeless."

He laughed mirthlessly. "Is it? I thought I mentioned that we could get engaged."

"Engaged isn't married," she began.

He put a finger over her lips, and he looked solemn. "I know that. Will you let me finish? We can be engaged until the first of the year, when I can afford to take a little time off for a honeymoon. We could have a New Year's wedding."

Chapter 8

"You mean, get married? Us?" she echoed blankly.

He tilted up her chin and searched her dark, troubled eyes. "Sex doesn't trouble you half as much as marriage does, is that it? Marriage means commitment, and to you, that's like imprisonment."

She grimaced. "My parents' marriage was horrible. I don't want to become like my mother."

"So you said." He traced her cheek. "But I'm not like your father. I don't drink. Well," he murmured with a sheepish grin, "maybe just once, and I had justification for that. You were letting Drew hold your hand, when you always jerked back if I touched you at all."

She was surprised. She smiled. "Was *that* why?"

He chuckled. "Yes, that was why."

"Imagine that!"

"Take one day at a time, okay?" he asked. "Let's

rock along for a couple of weeks, and spend Christmas together. Then we'll talk about this again."

"All right."

He bent and kissed her softly. She pressed up against him, but he stepped back.

"None of that," he said smartly. "We're going to get to know each other before we let our glands get in the way."

"Glands!"

"Don't you remember glands, Doctor?" He moved toward her threateningly. "Let me explain them to you."

"I think I've got the picture," she said on a laugh. "Keep away, you lecher!"

He laughed, too. He caught her hand and tangled her fingers with his as they walked back to where the horses were tied. He'd never been quite this interested in marriage, even if he'd once had it in the back of his mind when he'd dated Jane. But when he'd had Lou close in his arms, in the barn, he'd wanted it with a maddening desire. It wasn't purely physical, although she certainly attracted him that way. But despite the way she felt about him, he had a feeling that she'd have to be carefully coaxed down the aisle. She was afraid of everything marriage stood for because of her upbringing. Their marriage wouldn't be anything like her parents', but he was going to have to convince her of that first.

They made rounds together the next morning at the hospital, and as usual, Dana was lying in wait for Coltrain.

But this time, he deliberately linked Lou's hand in his as he smiled at her.

"Good morning," he said politely.

Dana was faintly startled. "Good morning, doctors," she said hesitantly, her eyes on their linked hands.

"Lou and I became engaged yesterday," he said.

Dana's face paled. She drew a stiff breath and managed the semblance of a smile. "Oh, did you? Well, I suppose I should offer my congratulations!" She laughed. "And I had such high hopes that you and I might regain something of the past."

"The past is dead," he said firmly, his blue eyes steady on her face. "I have no inclination whatsoever to revive it."

Dana laughed uncomfortably. "So I see." She glanced at Lou's left hand. "Quite a sudden engagement, was it?" she added slyly. "No ring yet?"

Lou's hand jerked in his, but he steadied it. "When Lou makes up her mind what sort she wants, I'll buy her one," he said lazily. "I'd better get started. Wait for me in the lounge when you finish, sweet," he told Lou and squeezed her fingers before he let them go.

"I will," she promised. She smiled at Dana carelessly and went down the hall to begin her own rounds.

Dana followed her. "Well, I hope you fare better than I did," she muttered. "He's had the hots for Jane Parker for years. He asked me to marry him because he wanted me and I wouldn't give in, but even so, I couldn't compete with dear Jane," she said bitterly. "Your father was willing, so I indulged in a stupid affair, hoping I might make him jealous. That was the lunatic act of the century!"

"So I heard," Lou said stiffly, glaring at the other woman.

"I guess you did," the older woman said with a grimace. "He hated me for it. There's one man who doesn't move with the times, and he never forgets a wrong you do him." Her eyes softened as she looked at Lou's frozen face. "Your poor mother must have hated me. I know your father did. He was livid that I'd been so careless, and of course, I ruined his chances of staying here. But he didn't do so bad in Austin."

Lou had different memories of that. She couldn't lay it all at Dana's door, however. She paused at her first patient's door. "What do you mean about Jane Parker?" she asked solemnly.

"You must have heard by now that she was his first love, his only love, for years. I gave up on him after my fling with your father. I thought it was surely over between them until I came back here. She's married, you know, but she still sees Copper socially." Her eyes glittered. "They say he sits and stares at her like an oil painting when they're anywhere together. You'll find that out for yourself. I should be jealous, but I don't think I am. I feel sorry for you, because you'll always be his second choice, even if he marries you. He may want you, but he'll never stop loving Jane."

She walked away, leaving a depressed, worried Lou behind. Dana's former engagement to Coltrain sounded so much like her own "engagement" with him that it was scary. She knew that he wanted her, but he didn't show any signs of loving her. Did he still love Jane? If he did, she couldn't possibly marry him.

Nickie came up the hall when Lou had finished her rounds and was ready to join Coltrain in the lounge.

"Congratulations," she told Lou with a resigned smile. "I guess I knew I was out of the running when I saw him kiss you in the car park. Good luck. From what I hear, you'll need it." She kept walking.

Lou was dejected. It was in her whole look when she went into the doctors' lounge, where Coltrain had just finished filling out a form at the table near the window. He looked up, frowning.

"What is it?" he asked curtly. "Have Dana and Nickie been giving you a hard time?"

"Not at all," she said. "I'm just a little tired." She touched her back and winced, to convince him. "Horse-back riding takes some getting used to, doesn't it?"

He smiled, glad that he'd mistaken soreness for depression. "Yes, it does. We'll have to do more of it." He picked up the folder. "Ready to go?"

"Yes."

He left the form at the nurses' station, absorbing more congratulations from the nurses, and led Lou out to his Jaguar.

"We'll take some time off this afternoon for lunch and shop for a ring," he said.

"But I don't need…"

"Of course you do," he said. "We can't let people think I'm too miserly to buy you an engagement ring!"

"But what if…?"

"Lou, it's my money," he declared.

She grimaced. Well, if he wanted to be stuck with a diamond ring when she left town, that was his business. The engagement, as far as she was concerned, was nothing more than an attempt to get his life back on an even keel and discourage Nickie and Dana from hounding him.

She couldn't forget what had been said about Jane Parker, Jane Burke now, and she was more worried than ever. She knew how entangled he'd been with Jane, all right, because she'd considered her a rival until the day Jane married Todd Burke. Coltrain's manner even when he spoke to the woman was tender, solicitous, almost reverent.

He'd proposed. But even though he knew Lou loved him, he'd never mentioned feeling anything similar for her. He was playing make-believe. But she wondered what would happen if Jane Burke suddenly became a free woman. It would be a nightmare to live with a man who was ever yearning for someone else, someone he'd loved most of his life. Jane was a habit he apparently couldn't break. She was married. But could that fact stop him from loving her?

"You're very quiet," he remarked.

"I was thinking about Mr. Bailey," she hedged. "He really needs to see a specialist about that asthma. What do you think of referring him to Dr. Jones up in Houston?"

He nodded, diverted. "A sound idea. I'll give you the number."

They worked in harmony until the lunch hour. Then, despite her arguments, they drove to a jewelry shop in downtown Jacobsville. As bad luck would have it, Jane Burke was in there, alone, making a purchase.

She was so beautiful, Lou thought miserably. Blond,

blue-eyed, with a slender figure that any man would covet.

"Why hello!" Jane said enthusiastically, and hugged Copper as if he was family.

He held her close and kissed her cheek, his smile tender, his face animated. "You look terrific," he said huskily. "How's the back? Still doing those exercises?"

"Oh, yes," she agreed. She held him by the arms and searched his eyes. "You look terrific yourself." She seemed only then to notice that he wasn't alone. She glanced at Lou. "Dr. Blakely, isn't it?" she asked politely, and altered the smile a little. "Nice to see you again."

"What are you doing here?" Coltrain asked her.

"Buying a present for my stepdaughter for Christmas. I thought she might like a nice strand of pearls. Aren't these lovely?" she asked when the clerk had taken them out of the case to show them. "I'll take them," she added, handing him her credit card.

"Is she staying with you and Todd all the time now?"

She nodded. "Her mother and stepfather and the baby are off to Africa to research his next book," she said with a grin. "We're delighted to have her all to ourselves."

"How's Todd?"

Lou heard the strained note in his voice with miserable certainty that Dana had been telling the truth.

"He's as impossible as ever." Jane chuckled. "But we scratch along, me with my horses and my clothing line and he with his computer business. He's away so much these days that I feel deserted." She lifted her eyes to his and grinned. "I don't guess you'd like to come to supper tonight?"

"Sure I would," he said without thinking. Then he made a sound. "I can't. There's a hospital board meeting."

"Oh, well," she muttered. "Another time, then." She glanced at Lou hesitantly. "Are you two out Christmas shopping—together?" she added as if she didn't think that was the case.

Coltrain stuck his hands deep into his pockets. "We're shopping for an engagement ring," he said tersely.

Her eyes widened. "For whom?"

Lou wanted to sink through the floor. She flushed to the roots of her hair and clung to her shoulder bag as if it were a life jacket.

"For Lou," Coltrain said. "We're engaged."

He spoke reluctantly, which only made Lou feel worse.

Jane's shocked expression unfroze Lou's tongue. "It's just for appearances," she said, forcing a smile. "Dana and Nickie have been hounding him."

"Oh, I see!" Jane's face relaxed, but then she frowned. "Isn't that a little dishonest?"

"It was the only way, and it's just until my contract is up, the first of the year," Lou forced herself to say. "I'll be leaving then."

Coltrain glared at her. He wasn't certain what he'd expected, but she made the proposal sound like a hoax. He hadn't asked her to marry him to ward off the other women; he'd truly wanted her to be his wife. Had she misunderstood totally?

Jane was as startled as Coltrain was. She knew that

Copper wasn't the sort of man to give an engagement ring lightly, although Lou seemed to think he was. Since Dana's horrible betrayal, Copper had been impervious to women. But even Jane had heard about the hospital Christmas party and the infamous kiss. She'd hoped that Copper had finally found someone to love, although it was surprising that it would be the partner with whom he fought with so enthusiastically. Now, looking at them together, she was confused. Lou looked as if she were being tortured. Copper was taciturn and frozen. And they said it was a sham. Lou didn't love him. She couldn't, and be so lighthearted about it. Copper looked worn.

Jane glared at Lou and put a gentle hand on Coltrain's arm. "This is a stupid idea, Copper. You'll be the butt of every joke in town when Lou leaves, don't you realize it? It could even damage your reputation, hurt your practice," she told Copper intently.

His jaw tautened. "I appreciate your concern," he said gently, even as it surprised him that Jane should turn on Lou, who was more an innocent bystander than Coltrain's worst enemy.

That got through to Lou, too. She moved restlessly, averting her gaze from the diamond rings in the display case. "She's right. It *is* stupid. I can't do this," she said suddenly, her eyes full of torment. "Please, excuse me, I have to go!"

She made it out the door before the tears were visible, cutting down an alley and ducking into a department store. She went straight to the women's rest room and burst into tears, shocking a store clerk into leaving.

In the jewelry store, Coltrain stood like a statue,

unspeakably shocked at Lou's rash departure and furious at having her back out just when he'd got it all arranged.

"For God's sake, did you have to do that?" Coltrain asked harshly. He rammed his hands into his pockets. "It's taken me days just to get her to agree on any pretext…!"

Jane realized, too late, what she'd done. She winced. "I didn't know," she said miserably. "It's my fault that she's bolted," Jane said quickly. "Copper, I'm sorry!"

"Not your fault," he said stiffly. "I used Dana and Nickie to accomplish this engagement, but she was reluctant from the beginning." He sighed heavily. "I guess she'll go, now, in spite of everything."

"I don't understand what's going on."

He moved a shoulder impatiently. "She's in love with me," he said roughly, and rammed his hands deeper into his pockets.

"Oh, dear." Jane didn't know what to say. She'd lashed out at the poor woman, and probably given Lou a false picture of her relationship with Copper to boot. They were good friends, almost like brother and sister, but there had been rumors around Jacobsville for years that they were secret lovers. Until she married Todd, that was. Now, she wondered how much Lou had heard and if she'd believed it. And Jane had brazenly invited him to supper, ignoring Lou altogether.

She grimaced. "I've done it now, haven't I? I would have included her in my invitation if I'd had any idea. I thought she was just tagging along with you on her lunch hour!"

"I'd better go after her," he said reluctantly.

"It might be best if you didn't," she replied. "She's hurt. She'll want to be alone for a while, I should think."

"I can't strand her in town." He felt worse than he could ever remember feeling. "Maybe you're both right, and this whole thing was a stupid idea."

"If you don't love her, it certainly was," she snapped at him. "What are you up to? Is it really just to protect you from a couple of lovesick women? I'm shocked. A few years ago, you'd have cussed them both to a fare-thee-well and been done with it."

He didn't reply. His face closed up and his blue eyes glittered at her. "My reasons are none of your business," he said, shutting her out.

Obviously Lou had to mean something to him. Jane felt even worse. She made a face. "We were very close once. I thought you could talk to me about anything."

"Anything except Lou," he said shortly.

"Oh." Her eyes were first stunned and then amused.

"You can stop speculating, too," he added irritably, turning away.

"She sounds determined to leave."

"We'll see about that."

Despite Jane's suggestion, he went off toward the department store where Lou had vanished and strode back to the women's rest room. He knew instinctively that she was there. He caught the eye of a female clerk.

"Could you ask Dr. Blakely to come out of there, please?"

"Dr. Blakely?"

"She's so high—" he indicated her height with his

hand up to his nose "—blond hair, dark eyes, wearing a beige suit."

"Oh, her! She's a doctor? Really? My goodness, I thought doctors never showed their emotions. She was crying as if her heart would break. Sure, I'll get her for you."

He felt like a dog. He'd made her cry. The thought of Lou, so brave and private a person, with tears in her eyes made him hurt inside. And it had been so unnecessary. If Jane had only kept her pretty mouth shut! She was like family, and she overstepped the bounds sometimes with her comments about how Coltrain should live his life. He'd been more than fond of her once, and he still had a soft spot for her, but it was Lou who was disrupting his whole life.

He leaned against the wall, his legs and arms crossed, and waited. The female clerk reappeared, smiled reassuringly, and went to wait on a customer.

A minute later, a subdued and dignified Lou came out of the small room, her chin up. Her eyes were slightly red, but she didn't look as if she needed anyone's pity.

"I'm ready to go if you are," she said politely.

He searched her face and decided that this wasn't the time for a row. They still had to get lunch and get back to the office.

He turned, leaving her to follow. "I'll stop by one of the hamburger joints and we can get a burger and fries."

"I'll eat mine at the office, if you don't mind," she said wearily. "I'm not in the mood for a crowd."

Neither was he. He didn't argue. He opened the car

door and let her in, then he went by the drive-in window of the beef place and they carried lunch back.

Lou went directly into her office and closed the door. She hardly tasted what she was eating. Her heart felt as if it had been burned alive. She knew what Dana meant now. Jane Parker was as much a part of Coltrain's life as his cattle, his practice. No woman, no matter how much she loved him, could ever compete with his love for the former rodeo star.

She'd been living in a fool's paradise, but fortunately there was no harm done. They could say that the so-called "engagement" had been a big joke. Surely Coltrain could get Nickie and Dana out of his hair by simply telling them the truth, that he wasn't interested. God knew, once he got started, he wasn't shy about expressing his feelings any other time, regardless of who was listening. Which brought to mind the question of why he'd asked her to marry him. He wasn't in love with her. He wanted her. Had that been the reason? Was he getting even with Jane because she'd married and deserted him? She worried the question until she finished eating. Then her patients kept her occupied for the rest of the day, so that she had no time to think.

Jane had wondered if she could help undo the damage she'd already done to Copper's life, and at last she came up with a solution. She decided to give a farewell party for Lou. She called Coltrain a few days later to tell him the news.

"Christmas is next week," he said shortly. "And I doubt if she'd come. She only speaks to me when she has to. I can't get near her anymore."

That depressed Jane even more. "Suppose I phone her?" she asked.

"Oh, I know she won't talk to you." He laughed without humor. "We're both in her bad books."

Jane sighed. "Then who can we have talk to her?"

"Try Drew Morris," he said bitterly. "She likes him."

That note in his voice was disturbing. Surely he knew that Drew was still mourning his late wife. If he and Lou were friends, it was nothing more than that, despite any social outings together.

"You think she'd listen to Drew?" she asked.

"Why not?"

"I'll try, then."

"Don't send out any invitations until she gives you an answer," he added. "She's been hurt enough, one way or the other."

"Yes, I know," Jane said gently. "I had no idea, Copper. I really meant well."

"I know that. She doesn't."

"I guess she's heard all the old gossip, too."

He hadn't considered that. "What old gossip?"

"About us," she persisted. "That we had something going until I married Todd."

He smoothed his fingers absently over the receiver. "She might have, at that," he said slowly. "But she must know that—" He stopped dead. She'd have heard plenty from Dana, who had always considered Jane, not her affair with Fielding Blakely, the real reason for their broken engagement. Others in the hospital knew those old rumors, too, and Jane had given Lou the wrong impression of their relationship in the jewelry store.

"I'm right, aren't I?" Jane asked.

"You might be."

"What are you going to do?"

"What can I do?" he asked shortly. "She doesn't really want to marry anyone."

"You said she loves you," she reminded him.

"Yes, and she does. It's the only thing I'm sure of. But she doesn't want to marry me. She's so afraid that she'll become like her mother, blindly accepting faults and abuse without question, all in the name of love."

"Poor girl," she said genuinely. "What a life she must have had."

"I expect it was worse than we'll ever know," he agreed. "Well, call Drew and see if he can get through to her."

"If he can, will you come, too?"

"It would look pretty bad if I didn't, wouldn't it?" he asked dryly. "They'd say we were so antagonistic toward each other that we couldn't even get along for a farewell party. And coming on the heels of our 'engagement,' they'd really have food for thought."

"I'd be painted as the scarlet woman who broke it up, wouldn't I?" Jane groaned. "Todd would love that! He's still not used to small-town life."

"Maybe Drew can reach her. If he can't, you'll have to cancel it. We can't embarrass her."

"I wouldn't dream of it."

"I know that. Jane, thanks."

"For what?" she asked. "I'm the idiot who got you into this mess in the first place. The least I owe is to try to make amends for what I said to her. I'll let you know what happens."

"Do that."

He went back to work, uncomfortably aware of Lou's calm demeanor. She didn't even look ruffled after all the turmoil. Of course, he remembered that she'd been crying like a lost child in the department store after Jane's faux pas. But that could have been so much more than a broken heart.

She hadn't denied loving him, but could love survive a year of indifference alternating with vicious antagonism, such as he'd given her? Perhaps loving him was a sort of habit that she'd finally been cured of. After all, he'd given her no reason to love him, even to like him. He'd missed most of his chances there. But if Drew could convince her to come to a farewell party, on neutral ground, Coltrain had one last chance to change her mind about him. That was his one hope; the only one he had.

Chapter 9

Drew invited Lou to lunch the next day. It was Friday, the week before the office closed for Christmas holidays. Christmas Eve would be on a week from Saturday night, and Jane had changed her mind about dates. She wanted to give the farewell party the following Friday, the day before New Year's Eve. That would, if Lou didn't reconsider her decision, be Lou's last day as Coltrain's partner.

"I'm surprised," Lou told him as they ate quiche at a local restaurant. "You haven't invited me to lunch in a long time. What's on your mind?"

"It could be just on food."

She laughed. "Pull the other one."

"Okay. I'm a delegation of one."

She held her fork poised over the last morsel of quiche on her plate. "From whom?"

"Jane Burke."

She put the fork down, remembering. Her expression hardened. "I have nothing to say to her."

"She knows that. It's why she asked me to talk to you. She got the wrong end of the stick and she's sorry. I'm to make her apologies to you," he added. "But she also wants to do something to make up for what she said to you. She wants to give you a farewell party on the day before New Year's Eve."

She glared at Drew. "I don't want anything to do with any parties given by that woman. I won't go!"

His eyebrows lifted. "Well! You are miffed, aren't you?"

"Accusing me of trying to ruin Jebediah's reputation and destroy his privacy...how dare she! I'm not the one who's being gossiped about in connection with him! And she's married!"

He smiled wickedly. "Lou, you're as red as a beet."

"I'm mad," she said shortly. "That...woman! How dare she!"

"She and Copper are friends. Period. That's all they've ever been. Are you listening?"

"Sure, I'm listening. Now," she added, leaning forward, "tell me he wasn't ever in love with her. Tell me he isn't still in love with her."

He wanted to, but he had no idea of Coltrain's feelings for Jane. He knew that Coltrain had taken her marriage hard, and that he seemed sometimes to talk about her to the exclusion of everyone else. But things had changed in the past few weeks, since the hospital Christmas dance the first week of December.

"You see?" she muttered. "You can't deny it. He may have proposed to me, but it was..."

"Proposed?"

"Didn't you know?" She lifted her coffee cup to her lips and took a sip. "He wanted me to pretend to be engaged to him, just to get Nickie and Dana off his back. Then he decided that we might as well get married for real. He caught me at a weak moment," she added, without details, "and we went to buy an engagement ring. But Jane was there. She was rude to me," she said miserably, "and Jebediah didn't say a word to stop her. In fact, he acted as if I wasn't even there."

"And that was what hurt most, wasn't it?" he queried gently.

"I guess it was. I have no illusions about him, you know," she added with a rueful smile. "He likes kissing me, but he's not in love with me."

"Does he know how you feel?"

She nodded. "I don't hide things well. It would be hard to miss."

He caught her hand and held it gently. "Lou, isn't he worth taking a chance on?" he asked. "You could let Jane throw this party for you, because she badly wants to make amends. Then you could talk to Copper and get him to tell you exactly why he wants to marry you. You might be surprised."

"No, I wouldn't. I know why he wants to marry me," she replied. "But I don't want to get married. I'm crazy about him, that's the truth, but I've seen marriage. I don't want it."

"You haven't seen a good marriage," he emphasized. "Lou, I had one. I had twelve years of almost ethereal happiness. Marriage is what you make of it."

"My mother excused every brutal thing my father did," she said shortly.

"That sort of love isn't love," he said quietly. "It's a form of domination. Don't you know the difference? If she'd loved your father, she'd have stood up to him and tried to help him stop drinking, stop using drugs."

She felt as if her eyes had suddenly been opened. She'd never seen her parents' relationship like that. "But he was terrible to her..."

"Codependence," he said to her. "You must have studied basic psychology in college. Don't you remember any of it?"

"Yes, but they were my parents!"

"Your parents, anybody, can be part of a dysfunctional family." He smiled at her surprise. "Didn't you know? You grew up in a dysfunctional family, not a normal one. That's why you have such a hard time accepting the idea of marriage." He smoothed her hand with his fingers and smiled. "Lou, I had a normal upbringing. I had a mother and father who doted on me, who supported me and encouraged me. I was loved. When I married, it was a good, solid, happy marriage. They are possible, if you love someone and have things in common, and are willing to compromise."

She studied the wedding ring on Drew's left hand. He still wore it even after being widowed.

"It's possible to be happily married?" she asked, entertaining that possibility for the first time.

"Of course."

"Coltrain doesn't love me," she said.

"Make him."

She laughed. "That's a joke. He hated me from the

beginning. I never knew it was because of my father, until I overheard him talking to you. I was surprised later when he was so cool to Dana, because he'd been bitter about her betrayal. But when I found out how close he was to Jane Burke, I guess I gave up entirely. You can't fight a ghost, Drew." She looked up. "And you know it, because no woman will ever be able to come between you and your memories. How would you feel if you found out some woman was crazily in love with you right now?"

He was stunned by the question. "Well, I don't know. I guess I'd feel sorry for her," he admitted.

"Which is probably how Coltrain feels about me, and might even explain why he offered to be engaged to me," she added. "It makes sense, doesn't it?"

"Lou, you don't propose to people out of pity."

"Coltrain might. Or out of revenge, to get back at Jane for marrying someone else. Or to get even with Dana."

"Coltrain isn't that scatty."

"Men are unpredictable when they're in love, aren't they?" she mused. "I wish he loved me, Drew. I'd marry him, with all my doubts and misgivings, in a minute if I thought there was half a chance that he did. But he doesn't. I'd know if he did feel that way. Somehow, I'd know."

He dropped his gaze to their clasped hands. "I'm sorry."

"Me, too. I've been invited to join a practice in Houston. I'm going Monday to speak with them, but they've tentatively accepted me." She lifted her sad face. "I understand that Coltrain is meeting some prospects, too.

So I suppose he's finally taken me at my word that I want to leave."

"Don't you know?"

She shrugged. "We don't speak."

"I see." So it was that bad, he thought. Coltrain and Lou had both withdrawn, afraid to take that final step to commitment. She had good reasons, but what were Copper's? he wondered. Did he really feel pity for Lou and now he was sorry he'd proposed? Or was Lou right, and he was still carrying a torch for Jane?

"Jane is a nice woman," he said. "You don't know her, but she isn't the kind of person who enjoys hurting other people. She feels very unhappy about what she said. She wants to make it up to you. Let her. It will be a nice gesture on your part and on hers."

"Dr. Coltrain will come," she muttered.

"He'd better," he said, "or the gossips will say he's glad to be rid of you."

She shook her head. "You can't win for losing."

"That's what I've been trying to tell you. Let Jane give the party. Lou, you'd like her if you got to know her. She's had a hard time of it since the wreck that took her father's life. Just being able to walk again at all is a major milestone for her."

"I remember," she said. And she did, because Coltrain had been out at the ranch every waking minute looking after the woman.

"Will you do it?"

She took a long breath and let it out. "All right."

"Great! I'll call Jane the minute I get home and tell her. You won't regret it. Lou, I wish you'd hold off about that spot in Houston."

She shook her head. "No, I won't do that. I have to get away. A fresh start is what I need most. I'm sure I won't be missed. After all, Dr. Coltrain didn't want me in the first place."

He grimaced, because they both knew her present circumstances were Drew's fault. Saying again that he meant well wouldn't do a bit of good.

"Thanks for lunch," she said, remembering her manners.

"That was my pleasure. You know I'll be going to Maryland to have Christmas with my in-laws, as usual. So Merry Christmas, if I don't see you before I leave."

"You, too, Drew," she said with genuine affection.

It wasn't until the next Thursday afternoon that the office closed early for Christmas holidays—if Friday and Monday, added to the weekend, qualified as holidays—that Coltrain came into Lou's office. Lou had been to Houston and formally applied for a position in the family practitioner group. She'd also been accepted, but she hadn't been able to tell Coltrain until today, because he'd been so tied up with preholiday surgeries and emergencies.

He looked worn-out, she thought. There were new lines in his lean face, and his eyes were bloodshot from lack of sleep. He looked every year of his age.

"You couldn't just tell me, you had to put it in writing?" he asked, holding up the letter she'd written him.

"It's legal this way," she said politely. "I'm very grateful for the start you gave me."

He didn't say anything. He looked at the letter from

the Houston medical group. It was written on decal-edge bond, very expensive, and the lettering on the letterhead was embossed.

"I know this group," he said. "They're high-powered city physicians, and they practice supermarket medicine. Do you realize what that means? You'll be expected to spend five minutes or less with every patient. A buzzer will sound to alert you when that time is up. As the most junior partner, you'll get all the dirty jobs, all the odd jobs, and you'll be expected to stay on call on weekends and holidays for the first year. Or until they can get another partner, more junior than you are."

"I know. They told me that." They had. It had depressed her no end.

He folded his arms across his chest and leaned back against the wall, his stethoscope draped around his neck. "We haven't talked."

"There's nothing to say," she replied, and she smiled kindly. "I notice that Nickie and Dana have become very businesslike, even to me. I'd say you were over the hump."

"I asked you to marry me," he said. "I was under the impression that you'd agreed and that was why we were picking out a ring."

The memory of that afternoon hurt. She lowered her eyes to the clipboard she held against her breasts. "You said it was to get Nickie and Dana off your back."

"You didn't want to get married at all," he reminded her.

"I still don't."

He smiled coldly. "And you're not in love with me?"

She met his gaze levelly. This was no time to back down. "I was infatuated with you," she said bluntly. "Perhaps it was because you were out of reach."

"You wanted me. Explain that."

"I'm human," she told him, blushing a little. "You wanted me, too, so don't look so superior."

"I hear you're coming to Jane's party."

"Drew talked me into it." She smoothed her fingers over the cold clipboard. "You and Jane can't help it," she said. "I understand."

"Damn it! You sound just like her husband!"

She was shocked at the violent whip of his deep voice. He was furious, and it showed.

"Everyone knows you were in love with her," she faltered.

"Yes, I was," he admitted angrily, and for the first time. "But she's married now, Lou."

"I know. I'm sorry," she said gently. "I really am. It must be terrible for you…."

He threw up his hands. "My God!"

"It's not as if you could help it, either of you," she continued sadly.

He just shook his head. "I can't get through to you, can I?" he asked with a bite in his deep voice. "You won't listen."

"There's really nothing to say," she told him. "I hope you've found someone to replace me when I go."

"Yes, I have. He's a recent graduate of Johns Hopkins. He wanted to do some rural practice before he made up his mind where he wanted to settle." He gazed at her wan face. "He starts January 2."

She nodded. "That's when I start, in Houston." She tugged the clipboard closer.

"We could spend Christmas together," he suggested.

She shook her head. She didn't speak. She knew words would choke her.

His shoulders rose and fell. "As you wish," he said quietly. "Have a good Christmas, then."

"Thanks. You, too."

She knew that she sounded choked. She couldn't help herself. She'd burned her bridges. She hadn't meant to. Perhaps she had a death wish. She'd read and studied about people who were basically self-destructive, who destroyed relationships before they could begin, who found ways to sabotage their own success and turn it to failure. Perhaps she'd become such a person, due to her upbringing. Either way, it didn't matter now. She'd given up Coltrain and was leaving Jacobsville. Now all she had to do was survive Jane's little going-away party and get out of town.

Coltrain paused in the doorway, turning his head back toward her. His eyes were narrow, curious, assessing. She didn't look as if the decision she'd made had lifted her spirits any. And the expression on her face wasn't one of triumph or pleasure.

"If Jane hadn't turned up in the jewelry store, would you have gone through with it?" he asked abruptly.

Her hands tightened on the clipboard. "I'll never know."

He leaned against the doorjamb. "You don't want to hear this, but I'm going to say it. Jane and I were briefly more than friends. It was mostly on my side. She loves her husband and wants nothing to do with anyone else. Whatever I felt for her is in the past now."

"I'm glad, for your sake," she said politely.

"Not for yours?" he asked.

She bit her lower lip, worriedly.

He let his blue gaze fall to her mouth. It lingered there so long that her heart began to race, and she couldn't quite breathe properly. His gaze lifted then, to catch hers, and she couldn't break it. Her toes curled inside her sensible shoes, her heart ran wild. She had to fight the urge to go to him, to press close to his lean, fit body and beg him to kiss her blind.

"You think you're over me?" he drawled softly, so that his voice didn't carry. "In a pig's eye, Doctor!"

He pushed away from the door and went on his way, whistling to himself as he went down the corridor to his next patient.

Lou, having given herself away, muttered under her breath and went to read the file on her next patient. But she waited until her hands stopped shaking before she opened the examining room door and went in.

They closed up the office. Coltrain had been called away at the last minute to an emergency at the hospital, which made things easier for Lou. She'd be bound to run into him while she was making her rounds, but that was an occupational hazard, and there would be plenty of other people around. She wouldn't have to worry about being alone with him. Or so she thought.

When she finished her rounds late in the afternoon, she stopped by the nurses' station to make sure they'd been able to contact a new patient's husband, who had been out of town when she was admitted.

"Yes, we found him," the senior nurse said with a smile. "In fact, he's on his way over here right now."

"Thanks," she said.

"No need. It goes with the job," she was assured.

She started back down the hall to find Coltrain coming from the emergency room. He looked like a thundercloud, all bristling bad temper. His red hair flamed under the corridor lights, and his blue eyes were sparking.

He caught Lou's arm, turned and drew her along with him without saying a word. People along the corridor noticed and grinned amusedly.

"What in the world are you doing?" she asked breathlessly.

"I want you to tell a—" he bit off the word he wanted to say "—*gentleman* in the emergency room that I was in the office all morning."

She gaped at him, but he didn't stop or even slow down. He dragged her into a cubicle where a big, angrylooking blond man was sitting on the couch having his hand bandaged.

Coltrain let Lou go and nodded curtly toward the other man. "Well, tell him!" He shot the words at Lou.

She gave him a stunned glance, but after a minute, she turned back to the tall man and said, "Dr. Coltrain was in the office all morning. He couldn't have escaped if he'd wanted to, because we had twice our usual number of patients, anticipating that we'd be out of the office over the holidays."

The blond man relaxed a little, but he was still glaring

at Coltrain when there was a small commotion in the corridor and Jane Burke came in the door, harassed and frightened.

"Todd! Cherry said that you'd had an accident and she had to call an ambulance...!" She grabbed the blond man's hand and fought tears. "I thought you were killed!"

"Not hardly," he murmured. He drew her head to his shoulder and held her gently. "Silly woman." He chuckled. "I'm all right. I slammed the car door on my hand. It isn't even broken, just cut and bruised."

Jane looked at Coltrain. "Is that true?"

He nodded, still irritated at Burke.

Jane looked from him to Lou and back to her husband. "Now what's wrong?" she asked heavily.

Todd just glowered. He didn't say anything.

"You and I had been meeting secretly this morning at your house, while he and Cherry were away," Coltrain informed her. "Because the mailman saw a gray Jaguar sitting in your driveway."

"Yes, he did," Jane said shortly. "It belongs to the new divisional manager of the company that makes my signature line of leisure wear. *She* has a gray Jaguar exactly like Copper's."

Burke's hard cheekbones flushed a little.

"That's why you slammed the door on your hand, right?" she muttered. "Because the mailman is our wrangler's sister and he couldn't wait to tell you what your wife was doing behind your back! He'll be lucky if I don't have him for lunch!"

The flush got worse. "Well, I didn't know!" Todd snapped.

Coltrain slammed his clipboard down hard on the examination couch at Burke's hip. "That does it, by God," he began hotly.

He looked threatening and Burke stood up, equally angry.

"Now, Copper," Jane interrupted. "This isn't the place."

Burke didn't agree, but he'd already made a fool of himself once. He wasn't going to try for twice. He glanced at Lou, who looked as miserable as he felt. "They broke up your engagement, I understand," he added. "Pity they didn't just marry each other to begin with!"

Lou studied his glittery eyes for a moment, oblivious to the other two occupants of the cubicle. It was amazing how quickly things fell into place in her mind, and at once. She leaned against the examination couch. "Dr. Coltrain is the most decent man I know," she told Todd Burke. "He isn't the sort to do things in an underhanded way, and he doesn't sneak around. If you trusted your wife, Mr. Burke, you wouldn't listen to old gossip or invented tales. Small towns are hotbeds of rumor, that's normal. But only an idiot believes everything he hears."

Coltrain's eyebrows had arched at the unexpected defense.

"Thanks, Lou," Jane said quietly. "That's more than I deserve from you, but thank you." She turned back to her husband. "She's absolutely right," Jane told her husband. She was mad, too, and it showed. "I married you because I loved you. I still love you, God knows why!

You won't even listen when I tell you the truth. You'd rather cling to old gossip about Copper and me."

Lou blushed scarlet, because she could have been accused of the same thing.

She wouldn't look at Coltrain at all.

"Well, here's something to take your mind off your foul suspicions," Jane continued furiously. "I was going to wait to tell you, but you can hear it now. I'm pregnant! And, no, it isn't Copper's!"

Burke gasped. "Jane!" He exploded, his injured hand forgotten as he moved forward to pull her hungrily into his arms. "Jane, is it true?"

"Yes, it's true," she muttered. "Oh, you idiot! You idiot…!"

He was kissing her, so she had to stop talking. Lou, a little embarrassed, edged out of the cubicle and moved away, only to find Coltrain right beside her as she left the emergency room.

"Maybe that will satisfy him," he said impatiently. "Thank you for the fierce defense," he added. "Hell of a pity that you didn't believe a word you were saying!"

She stuck her hands into her slacks pockets. "I believe she loves her husband," she said quietly. "And I believe that there's nothing going on between the two of you."

"Thanks for nothing."

"Your private life is your own business, Dr. Coltrain, none of mine," she said carelessly. "I'm already a memory."

"By your own damn choice."

The sarcasm cut deep. They walked through the parking lot to the area reserved for physicians and surgeons, and she stopped beside her little Ford.

"Drew loved his wife very much," she said. "He never got over losing her. He still spends holidays with his in-laws because he feels close to her that way, even though she's dead. I asked him how he'd feel if he knew that a woman was in love with him. Know what he said? He said that he'd pity her."

"Do you have a point?" he asked.

"Yes." She turned and looked up at him. "You haven't really gotten over Jane Burke yet. You have nothing to offer anyone else until you do. That's why I wouldn't marry you."

His brows drew together while he searched her face. He didn't say a word. He couldn't.

"She's part of your life," she continued. "A big part of it. You can't let go of the past, even if she can. I understand. Maybe someday you'll come to terms with it. Until you do, it's no good trying to be serious about anyone else."

He jiggled the change in his pockets absently. His broad shoulders rose and fell. "She was just starting into rodeo when I came back here as an intern in the hospital. She fell and they brought her to me. We had an instant rapport. I started going to watch her ride, she went out with me when I was free. She was special. Her father and I became friends as well, and when I bought my ranch, he helped me learn the ropes and start my herd. Jane and I have known each other a long, long time."

"I know that." She studied a button on his dark jacket. "She's very pretty, and Drew says she has a kind nature."

"Yes."

Her shoulders rose and fell. "I have to go."

He put out a lean hand and caught her shoulder, preventing her from turning away. "I never told her about my father."

She was surprised. She didn't think he had any secrets from Jane. She lifted her eyes and found him staring at her intently, as if he were trying to work out a puzzle.

"Curious, isn't it?" he mused aloud. "There's another curious thing, but I'm not ready to share that just yet."

He moved closer and she wanted to move away, to stop him... No, she didn't. His head bent and his mouth closed on hers, brushing, lightly probing. She yielded without a protest, her arms sliding naturally around his waist, her mouth opening to the insistence of his lips. He kissed her, leaning his body heavily on hers, so that she could feel the metal of the car at her back and his instant, explosive response to her soft warmth.

She made a sound, and he smiled against her lips.

"What?" He bit off the words against her lips.

"It's...very...public," she breathed.

He lifted his head and looked around. The parking lot was dotted with curious onlookers. So was the emergency room ramp.

"Hell," he said irritably, drawing away from her. "Come home with me," he suggested, still breathing roughly.

She shook her head before her willpower gave out. "I can't."

"Coward," he drawled.

She flushed. "All right, I want to," she said fiercely. "But I won't, so there. Damn you! It isn't fair to play on people's weaknesses!"

"Sure it is," he said, correcting her. He grinned at

her maddeningly. "Come on, be daring. Take a chance! Risk everything on a draw of the cards. You live like a scientist, every move debated, planned. For once in your life, be reckless!"

"I'm not the reckless sort," she said as she fought to get her breath back. "And you shouldn't be, either." She glanced ruefully toward the emergency room exit, where a tall blond man and a pretty blond woman were standing, watching. "Was it for her benefit?" she added, nodding toward them.

He glanced over her shoulder. "I didn't know they were there," he said genuinely.

She laughed. "Sure." She pulled away from him, unlocked her car, got in and drove off. Her legs were wobbly, but they'd stop shaking eventually. Maybe the rest of her would, too. Coltrain was driving her crazy. She was very glad that she'd be leaving town soon.

Chapter 10

It didn't help that the telephone rang a few minutes after Lou got home.

"Still shaky, are we?" Coltrain drawled.

She fumbled to keep from dropping the receiver. "What do you want?" she faltered.

"An invitation to Christmas dinner, of course," he said. "I don't want to sit in front of the TV all day eating TV dinners."

She was still angry at him for making a public spectacle of them for the second time. The hospital would buzz with the latest bit of gossip for weeks. At least she wouldn't have long to put up with it.

"TV dinners are good for you," she said pointedly.

"Home cooking is better. I'll make the dressing and a fruit salad if you'll do turkey and rolls."

She hesitated. She wanted badly to spend that day

with him, but in the long run, it would make things harder.

"Come on," he coaxed in a silky tone. "You know you want to. If you're leaving town after the first, it will be one of the last times we spend together. What have you got to lose?"

My self-respect, my honor, my virtue, my pride, she thought. But aloud, she said, "I suppose it wouldn't hurt."

He chuckled. "No, it wouldn't. I'll see you at eleven on Christmas morning."

He hung up before she could change her mind. "I don't want to," she told the telephone. "This is a terrible mistake, and I'm sure that I'll regret it for the rest of my life."

After a minute, she realized that she was talking to a piece of equipment. She shook her head sadly. Coltrain was driving her out of her mind.

She went to the store early on Christmas Eve and bought a turkey. The girl at the check-out stand was one of her patients. She grinned as she totaled the price of the turkey, the bottle of wine and the other groceries Lou had bought to cook Christmas dinner.

"Expecting company, Doctor?" she teased.

Lou flushed, aware that the woman behind her was one of Coltrain's patients. "No. No. I'm going to cook the turkey and freeze what I don't eat."

"Oh." The girl sounded disappointed.

"Going to drink all that wine alone, too?" the woman behind her asked wickedly. "And you a doctor!"

Lou handed over the amount the cashier asked for.

"I'm not on duty on Christmas Day," she said irritably. "Besides, I cook with wine!"

"You won't cook with that," the cashier noted. She held up the bottle and pointed to the bottom of the label. It stated, quite clearly, Nonalcoholic Wine.

Lou had grabbed the bottle from the wrong aisle. But it worked to her advantage. She grinned at the woman behind her, who looked embarrassed.

The clerk packaged up her purchases and Lou pushed them out to her car. At least she'd gotten around that ticky little episode.

Back home, she put the turkey on to bake and made rolls from scratch. Nonalcoholic wine wasn't necessarily a bad thing, she told herself. She could serve it at dinner without having to worry about losing her wits with Coltrain.

The weather was sunny and nice, and the same was predicted for the following day. A white Christmas was out of the question, of course, but she wondered what it would be like to have snow on the ground.

She turned on the television that night, when the cooking was done and everything was put into the refrigerator for the next day. Curled up in her favorite armchair in old jeans, a sweatshirt and in her sock feet, she was relaxing after her housecleaning and cooking when she heard a car drive up.

It was eight o'clock and she wasn't on call. She frowned as she went to the front door. A gray Jaguar was sitting in the driveway and as she looked, a tall, redheaded man in jeans and a sweatshirt and boots got out of the car carrying a big box.

"Open the door," he called as he mounted the steps.

"What's that?" she asked curiously.

"Food and presents."

She was surprised. She hadn't expected him tonight and she fumbled and faltered as she let him in and closed the door again.

He unloaded the box in the kitchen. "Salad." He indicated a covered plastic bowl. "Dressing." He indicated a foil-covered pan. "And a chocolate pound cake. No, I didn't make it," he added when she opened her mouth. "I bought it. I can't bake a cake. Is there room in the fridge for this?"

"You could have called to ask before you brought it," she reminded him.

He grinned. "If I'd phoned, you'd have listened to the answering machine and when you knew it was me, you'd have pretended not to be home."

She flushed. He was right. It was disconcerting to have someone so perceptive second-guessing her every move. "Yes, there's room."

She opened the refrigerator door and helped him fit his food in.

He went back to the big box and pulled out two packages. "One for me to give you—" he held up one "—and one for you to give me."

She glared at him. "I got you a present," she muttered.

His eyebrows shot up. "You did?"

Her lower lip pulled down. "Just because I didn't plan to spend Christmas with you didn't mean I was low enough not to get you something."

"You didn't give it to me at the office party," he recalled.

She flushed. "You didn't give me anything at the office party, either."

He smiled. "I was saving it for tomorrow."

"So was I," she returned.

"Can I put these under the tree?"

She shrugged. "Sure."

Curious, she followed him into the living room. The tree was live and huge; it covered the whole corner and reached almost to the nine-foot ceiling. It was full of lights and decorations and under it a big metal electric train sat on its wide tracks waiting for power to move it.

"I didn't notice that when I was here before," he said, delighted by the train. He stooped to look at it more closely. "This is an American Flyer by Lionel!" he exclaimed. "You've had this for a while, haven't you?"

"It's an antique," she recalled. "My mother got it for me." She smiled. "I love trains. I have two more sets and about a mile of track in a box in the closet, but it seemed sort of pointless to set all those trains up with just me to run them."

He looked up at her with sparkling eyes. "Which closet are they in?" he asked in a conspiratorial tone.

"The hall closet." Her eyes brightened. "You like trains?"

"Do I like trains? I have HO scale, N scale, G scale and three sets of new Lionel O scale trains at home."

She gasped. "Oh, my goodness!"

"That's what I say. Come on!"

He led her to the hall closet, opened it, found the boxes and started handing them out to her.

Like two children, they sat on the floor putting tracks together with switches and accessories for the next two hours. Lou made coffee and they had it on the floor while they made connections and set up the low wooden scale buildings that Lou had bought to go with the sets.

When they finished, she turned on the power. The wooden buildings were lit. So were the engines and the cabooses and several passenger cars.

"I love to sit and watch them run in the dark," she said breathlessly as he turned on the switch box and the trains began to move. "It's like watching over a small village with the people all snug in their houses."

"I know what you mean." He sprawled, chest down, on the floor beside her to watch the trains chug and whistle and run around the various tracks. "God, this is great! I had no idea you liked trains!"

"Same here," she said, chuckling. "I always felt guilty about having them, in a way. Somewhere out there, there must be dozens of little kids who would do anything for just one train and a small track to run it on. And here I've got all this and I never play with it."

"I know how it is. I don't even have a niece or nephew to share mine with."

"When did you get your first train?"

"When I was eight. My granddad bought it for me so he could play with it," he added with a grin. "He couldn't afford a big set, of course, but I didn't care. I never had so much fun." His face hardened at the memories. "When Dad took me to Houston, I missed the train almost as much as I missed my granddad and grandmother. It was a long time before I got back there." He shrugged. "The train still worked by then, though, and it was more fun when the threat of my father was gone."

She rolled onto her side, peering at him in the dim light from the tree and the small village. "You said that you never told Jane about your father."

"I didn't," he replied. "It was something I was deeply ashamed of for a long time."

"Children do what they're told, whether it's right or wrong," she reminded him. "You can't be held responsible for everything."

"I knew it was wrong," he agreed. "But my father was a brutal man, and when I was a young boy, I was afraid of him." His head turned. He smiled at her. "You'd understand that."

"Yes."

He rested his chin on his hands and watched the trains wistfully. "I took my medicine—juvenile hall and years of probation. But people helped me to change. I wanted to pass that on, to give back some of the care that had been given to me. That's why I went into medicine. I saw it as an opportunity to help people."

"And you have," she said. Her eyes traced the length of his fit, hard-muscled body lovingly. He was so different away from the office. She'd never known him like this, and so soon, it would all be over. She'd go away. She wouldn't see him again. Her sad eyes went back to the trains. The sound of them was like a lullaby, comforting, delightful to the ears.

"We need railroad caps and those wooden whistles that sound like old steam engines," he remarked.

She smiled. "And railroad gloves and crossing guards and flashing guard lights."

"If there was a hobby shop nearby, we could go and get them. But everything would be closed up on Christmas Eve, anyway."

"I guess so."

He pursed his lips, without looking at her. "If you stayed, after the New Year, we could pool our layouts and have one big one. We could custom-design our own buildings and bridges, and we could go in together and buy one of those big transformer outfits that runs dozens of accessories."

She was thinking more of spending that kind of time with Coltrain than running model engines, but it sounded delightful all the same. She sighed wistfully. "I would have enjoyed that," she murmured. "But I've signed a new contract. I have to go."

"Contracts can be broken," he said. "There's always an escape clause if you look hard enough."

Her hips shifted on the rug they were lying on. "Too many people are gossiping about us already," she said. "Even at the grocery store, the clerk noticed that I bought a turkey and wine and the lady behind me said I couldn't possibly be going to drink it alone."

"You bought wine?" he mused.

"Nonalcoholic wine," she said, correcting him.

He chuckled. "On purpose?"

"Not really. I picked up the wrong bottle. But it was just as well. The lady behind me was making snide comments about it." She sighed. "It rubbed me the wrong way. She wouldn't have known that my father was an alcoholic."

"How did he manage to keep his job?"

"He had willing young assistants who covered for him. And finally, the hospital board forced him into early retirement. He *had* been a brilliant surgeon," she reminded him. "It isn't easy to destroy a career like that."

"It would have been better than letting him risk other people's lives."

"But he didn't," she replied. "Someone was always there to bail him out."

"Lucky, wasn't he, not to have been hit with a multimillion-dollar malpractice suit."

He reached out and threw the automatic switches to change the trains to another set of tracks. "Nice," he commented.

"Yes, isn't it? I love trains. If I had more leisure time, I'd do this every day. I'm glad we're not on call this weekend. How did you manage it?"

"Threats and bribery," he drawled. "We both worked last Christmas holidays, remember?"

"I guess we did. At each other's throats," she recalled demurely.

"Oh, that was necessary," he returned, rolling lazily onto his side and propping on an elbow. "If I hadn't snapped at you constantly, I'd have been laying you down on examination couches every other day."

"Wh...what?" she stammered.

He reached out and brushed back a long strand of blond hair from her face. "You backed away every time I came close to you," he said quietly. "It was all that saved you. I've wanted you for a long, long time, Dr. Blakely, and I've fought it like a madman."

"You were in love with Jane Parker," she said.

"Not for a long time," he said. He traced her cheek lightly. "The way I felt about her was a habit. It was one I broke when she married Todd Burke. Although, like you, he seems to think Jane and I were an item even after they married. He's taken a lot of convincing. So have you."

She moved uncomfortably. "Everyone talked about you and Jane, not just me."

"I know. Small communities have their good points and their bad points." His finger had reached her mouth. He was exploring it blatantly.

"Could you...not do that, please?" she asked unsteadily.

"Why? You like it. So do I." He moved closer, easing one long, hard-muscled leg over hers to stay her as he shifted so that she lay on her back, looking up at him in the dim light.

"I can feel your heart beating right through your rib cage," he remarked with his mouth poised just above hers. "I can hear your breath fluttering." His hand slid blatantly right down over her breast, pausing there to tease its tip into a hard rise. "Feel that?" he murmured, bending. "Your body likes me."

She opened her mouth, but no words escaped the sudden hard, warm pressure of his lips. She stiffened, but only for a few seconds. It was Christmas Eve and she loved him. There was no defense; none at all.

He seemed to know that, because he wasn't insistent or demanding. He lay, just kissing her, his lips tender as they moved against hers, his hand still gently caressing her body.

"We both know," he whispered, "why your body makes every response it does to the stimuli of my touch. But what no one really understands is why we both enjoy it so much."

"Cause…and effect?" she suggested, gasping when his hand found its way under the sweatshirt and the lacy bra she was wearing to her soft flesh.

He shook his head. "I don't think so. Reach behind you and unfasten this," he added gently, tugging on the elastic band.

She did as he asked, feeling brazen.

"That's better." He traced over her slowly, his eyes on her face while he explored every inch of her above the waist. "Can you give this up?" he asked seriously.

"Wh…what?"

"Can you give it up?" he replied. "You aren't responsive to other men, or you wouldn't still be in your present pristine state. You allow me liberties that I'm certain you've never permitted any other man." He cupped her blatantly and caressed her. She arched, shivering. "You see?" he asked quietly. "You love my touch. I can give you something that you've apparently never experienced. Do you think you can find it with someone else, Lou?"

She felt his mouth cover hers. She didn't have enough breath to answer him, although the answer was certainly in the negative. She couldn't bear the thought of letting someone else be this intimate with her. She looped her arms around his neck and only sighed jerkily when he moved, easing his length against her, his legs between both of hers, so that when his hips pressed down again, she could feel every hardening line of his body.

"Jebediah," she moaned, and she wasn't certain if she was protesting or pleading.

His mouth found her closed eyelids and tasted the helpless tears of pleasure that rained from them. His hips shifted and she jerked at the surge of pleasure.

He felt it, too, like a throbbing ache. "We're good together," he whispered. "Even like this. Can you imagine how it would feel to lie naked under me like this?"

She cried out, burying her face in his neck.

His lips traced her eyelashes, his tongue tasted them. But his body lay very still over hers, not moving, not insisting. Her nails dug into his shoulders as she felt her control slipping away.

But he still had his own control. He soothed her, every soft kiss undemanding and tender. But he didn't move away.

"A year," he whispered. "And we knew nothing about each other, nothing at all." He nibbled her lips, smiling when they trembled. "Trains and old movies, opera and cooking and horseback riding. We have more in common than I ever dreamed."

She had to force her body to lie still. She wanted to wrap her legs tight around him and kiss him until she stopped aching.

He seemed to know it, because his hips moved in a sensual caress that made her hands clench at his shoulders. "No fear of the unknown?" he whispered wickedly. "No virginal terror?"

"I'm a doctor." She choked out the words.

"So am I."

"I mean, I know…what to expect."

He chuckled. "No, you don't. You only know the mechanics of it. You don't know that you're going to crave almost more than I can give you, or that at the last minute you're going to sob like a hurt child."

She was too far gone to be embarrassed. "I don't have anything," she said miserably.

"Anything…?" He probed gently.

"To use."

"Oh. That." He chuckled and kissed her again, so tenderly that she felt cherished. "You won't need it tonight. I don't think babies should be born out of wedlock. Do you?"

She wasn't thinking. "Well, no. What does that have to do…with this?"

"Lou!"

She felt her cheeks burn. "Oh! You mean…!"

He laughed outrageously. "You've really gone off the deep end, haven't you?" he teased. "When people make love, the woman might get pregnant," he explained in a whisper. "Didn't you listen to the biology lectures?"

She hit him. "Of course I did! I wasn't thinking… Jeb!"

He was closer than he'd ever been and she was shivering, lost, helpless as she felt him in a burning, aching intimacy that only made it all worse.

He pressed her close and then rolled away, while he could. "God, we're explosive!" he said huskily, lying very still on his belly. "You're going to have to marry me soon, Lou. Very soon."

She was sitting up, holding her knees to her chest,

trying to breathe. It had never been that bad. She said so, without realizing that she'd spoken aloud.

"It will get worse, too," he said heavily. "I want you. I've never wanted you so much."

"But, Jane..."

He was laughing, very softly. He wasn't angry anymore. He rolled over and sat up beside her. He turned her face up to his. "I broke it off with Jane," he said gently. "Do you want to know why, now?"

"You...you did?"

He nodded.

"You never said that you ended it."

"There was no reason to. You wouldn't let me close enough to find out if we had anything going for us, and it didn't seem to matter what I said, you wanted to believe that I was out of my mind over Jane."

"Everyone said you were," she muttered.

He lifted an eyebrow. "I'm not everyone."

"I know." She reached out hesitantly and touched him. It was earthshaking, that simple act. She touched his hair and his face and then his lean, hard mouth. A funny smile drew up her lips.

"Don't stop there," he murmured, drawing her free hand down to his sweatshirt.

Her heart jumped. She looked at him uncertainly.

"I won't let you seduce me," he mused. "Does that make you feel more confident?"

"It was pretty bad a few minutes ago," she said seriously. "I don't want... Well, to hurt you."

"This won't," he said. "Trust me."

"I suppose I must," she admitted. "Or I'd have left months ago for another job."

"That makes sense."

He guided her hand under the thick, white fabric and drew it up until her fingers settled in the thick, curling hair that covered his chest. But it wasn't enough. She wanted to look...

There was just enough light so that he could see what she wanted in her expression. With a faint smile, he pulled the sweatshirt off and tossed it to one side.

She stared. He was beautiful like that, she thought dizzily, with broad shoulders and muscular arms. His chest was covered by a thick, wide wedge of reddish-gold hair that ran down to the buckle of his belt.

He reached for her, lifting her over him so that they were sitting face-to-face, joined where their bodies forked. She shivered at the stark intimacy, because she could feel every muscle, almost every cell of him.

"It gets better," he said softly. He reached down and found the hem of her own sweatshirt. Seconds later, that and her bra joined his sweatshirt on the floor. He looked down at her, savoring the hard peaks that rose like rubies from the whiteness of her breasts. Then he drew her to him and enveloped her against him, so that they were skin against skin. And he shivered, too, this time.

Her hands smoothed over his back, savoring his warm muscles. She searched for his mouth and for the first time, she kissed him. But even though it was sensual, and she could feel him wanting her, there was tenderness between them, not lust.

He groaned as his body surged against her, and then he laughed at the sudden heat of it.

"Jeb?" she whispered at his lips.

"It's all right," he said. "We won't go all the way. Kiss me again."

She did, clinging, and the world rocked around them.

"I love you," she murmured brokenly. "So much!"

His mouth bit into hers hungrily, his arms contracted. For a few seconds, it was as if electricity fused them together. Finally he was able to lift his lips, and his hands caught her hips to keep them still.

"Sorry," she said demurely.

"Oh, I like it," he replied ruefully. "But we're getting in a bit over our heads."

He lifted her away and stood up, pulling her with him. They looked at each other for a long moment before he handed her things to her and pulled his sweatshirt back on.

He watched the trains go around while she replaced her disheveled clothing. Then, with his hands in his pockets, he glanced down at her.

"That's why I broke up with Jane," he said matter-of-factly.

She was jealous, angry. "Because she wouldn't go all the way with you?"

He chuckled. "No. Because I didn't want her sexually."

She watched the trains and counted the times they crossed the joined tracks. Her mind must not be working. "What did you say?" she asked politely, turning to him.

"I said I was never able to want Jane sexually," he said simply. "To put it simply, she couldn't arouse me."

Chapter 11

"A woman can arouse any man if she tries hard enough," she said pointedly.

"Maybe so," he said, smiling, "but Jane just never interested me like that. It was too big a part of marriage to take a chance on, so I gradually stopped seeing her. Burke came along, and before any of us knew it, she was married. But I was her security blanket after the accident, and it was hard for her to let go. You remember how she depended on me."

She nodded. Even at the time, it had hurt.

"But apparently she and her husband have more than a platonic relationship, if their forthcoming happy event is any indication," he said, chuckling. "And I'm delighted for them."

"I never dreamed that it was like that for you, with her," she said, dazed. "I mean, you and I...!"

"Yes, indeed, you and I," he agreed, nodding. "I touch

you and it's like a shot of lightning in my veins. I get drunk on you."

"So do I, on you," she confessed. "But there's a difference, isn't there? I mean, you just want me."

"Do I?" he asked gently. "Do I really just want you? Could lust be as tender as this? Could simple desire explain the way we are together?"

"I love you," she said slowly.

"Yes," he said, his eyes glittering at her. "And I love you, Lou," he added quietly.

Dreams came true. She hadn't known. Her eyes were full of wonder as she looked at him and saw them in his own eyes. It was Christmas, a time of miracles, and here was one.

He didn't speak. He just looked at her. After a minute, he picked up the two parcels he'd put under the tree and handed them to her.

"But it's not Christmas," she protested.

"Yes, it is. Open them."

She only hesitated for a minute, because the curiosity was too great. She opened the smallest one and inside was a gray jeweler's box. With a quick glance at him, she opened it, to find half a key chain inside. She felt her heart race like a watch. It was half of a heart, in pure gold.

"Now the other one," he said, taking the key chain while she fumbled the paper off the second present.

Inside that box was the other half of the heart.

"Now put them together," he instructed.

She did, her eyes magnetized to the inscription. It was in French: *plus que hier, moins que demain.*

"Can you read it?" he asked softly.

"It says—" she had to stop and clear her throat "—more than yesterday, less than tomorrow."

"Which is how much I love you," he said. "I meant to ask you again tomorrow morning to marry me," he said. "But this is as good a time as any for you to say yes. I know you're afraid of marriage. But I love you and you love me. We've got enough in common to keep us together even after all the passion burns out, if it ever does. We'll work out something about your job and children. I'm not your father and you're not your mother. Take a chance, Lou. Believe me, there's very little risk that we won't make it together."

She hadn't spoken. She had both halves of the key chain in her hands and she was looking at them, amazed that he would have picked something so sentimental and romantic for a Christmas gift. He hadn't known if he could get her to stay or not, but he would have shown her his heart all the same. It touched her as a more expensive present wouldn't have.

"When did you get them?" she asked through a dry throat.

"After you left the jeweler's," he said surprisingly. "I believe in miracles," he added gently. "I see incredible things every day. I'm hoping for another one, right now."

She raised her eyes. Even in the dim light, he could see the sparkle of tears, the hope, the pleasure, the disbelief in her face.

"Yes?" he asked softly.

She couldn't manage the word. She nodded, and the next instant, she was in his arms, against him, close and safe and warm while his mouth ravished her lips.

It was a long time before he had enough to satisfy him, even momentarily. He wrapped her up tightly and rocked her in his arms, barely aware of the train chugging along at their feet. His arms were faintly unsteady and his voice, when he laughed, was husky and deep.

"My God, I thought I was going to lose you." He ground out the words. "I didn't know what to do, what to say, to keep you here."

"All you ever had to say was that you loved me," she whispered. "I would have taken any risk for it."

His arms tightened. "Didn't you know, you blind bat?"

"No, I didn't! I don't read minds, and you never said—!"

His mouth covered hers again, stopping the words. He laughed against her breath, anticipating arguments over the years that would be dealt with in exactly this way, as she gave in to him generously, headlong in her response, clinging as if she might die without his mouth on hers.

"No long engagement," he groaned against her mouth. "I can't stand it!"

"Neither can I," she admitted. "Next week?"

"Next week!" He kissed her again. "And I'm not going home tonight."

She laid her cheek against his chest, worried.

He smoothed her hair. "We won't make love," he assured her. "But you'll sleep in my arms. I can't bear to be parted from you again."

"Oh, Jeb," she whispered huskily. "That's the sweetest thing to say!"

"Don't you feel it, too?" he asked knowingly.

"Yes. I don't want to leave you, either."

He chuckled with the newness of belonging to someone. It was going to be, he decided, the best marriage of all time. He looked down into her eyes and saw years and years of happiness ahead of them. He said so. She didn't answer him. She reached up, and her lips said it for her.

The going-away party that Jane Burke threw for Lou became a congratulatory party, because it fell on the day after Coltrain and Lou were married.

They almost stayed at home, so wrapped up in the ecstasy of their first lovemaking that they wouldn't even get out of bed the next morning.

That morning, he lay looking at his new bride with wonder and unbounded delight. There were tears in her eyes, because it had been painful for her at first. But the love in them made him smile.

"It won't be like that again," he assured her.

"I know." She looked at him blatantly, with pride in his fit, muscular body, in his manhood. She lifted her eyes back up. "I was afraid…"

He traced her mouth, his eyes solemn. "It will be easier the next time," he said tenderly. "It will get better every time we love each other."

"I know. I'm not afraid anymore." She touched his hard mouth and smiled. "You were apprehensive, too, weren't you?"

"At first," he had to admit.

"I thought you were never going to start," she said on a sigh. "I know why you took so long, so that I'd be ready when it happened, but I wondered if you were planning on a night of torture."

He chuckled. "You weren't the only one who suffered." He kissed her tenderly. "It hurt me, to have to hurt you, did you know? I wanted to stop, but it was too late. I was in over my head before I knew it. I couldn't even slow down."

"Oh, I never noticed," she told him, delighted. "You made me crazy."

"That goes double for me."

"I thought I knew everything," she mused. "I'm a doctor, after all. But theory and practice are very different."

"Yes. Later, when you're in fine form again, I'll show you some more ways to put theory into practice," he drawled.

She laughed and pummeled him.

They were early for Jane's get-together, and the way they clung to each other would have been more than enough to prove that they were in love, without the matching Victorian wedding bands they'd chosen.

"You look like two halves of a whole," Jane said, looking from Lou's radiant face to Copper's.

"We know," he said ruefully. "They rode us high at the hospital when we made rounds earlier."

"Rounds!" Todd exclaimed. "On your honeymoon?"

"We're doctors," Lou reminded him, grinning. "It goes with the job description. I'll probably be trying to examine patients on the way into the delivery room eventually."

Jane clung to her husband's hand and sighed. "I can't

wait for that to happen. Cherry's over the moon, too. She'll be such a good older sister. She works so hard at school. She's studying to be a surgeon, you know," she added.

"I wouldn't know," Copper muttered, "having already had four letters from her begging for an hour of my time to go over what she needs to study most during her last few years in school."

Jane chuckled. "That's my fault. I encouraged her to talk to you."

"It's all right," he said, cuddling Lou closer. "I'll make time for her."

"I see that everything finally worked out for you two," Todd said a little sheepishly. "Sorry about the last time we met."

"Oh, you weren't the only wild-eyed lunatic around, Mr. Burke," Lou said reminiscently. "I did my share of conclusion jumping and very nearly ruined my life because of it." She looked up at Coltrain adoringly. "I'm glad doctors are persistent."

"Yes." Coltrain chuckled. "So am I. There were times when I despaired. But Lionel saved us."

They frowned. "What?"

"Electric trains," Coltrain replied. "Don't you people know anything?"

"Not about trains. Those are kids' toys, for God's sake," Burke said.

"No, they are not," Lou said. "They're adult toys. People buy them for their children so they'll have an excuse to play with them. Not having children, we have no excuses."

"That's why we want to start a family right away,"

Coltrain said with a wicked glance at Lou. "So that we have excuses. You should see her layout," he added admiringly. "My God, it's bigger than mine!"

Todd and Jane tried not to look at each other, failed and burst into outrageous laughter.

Coltrain glared at them. "Obviously," he told his new wife, "some people have no class, no breeding and no respect for the institution of marriage."

"What are you two laughing at?" Drew asked curiously, having returned to town just in time for the party, if not the wedding.

Jane bit her lower lip before she spoke. "Hers is bigger than his." She choked.

"Oh, for God's sake, come and dance!" Coltrain told Lou, shaking his head as he dragged her away. The others, behind them, were still howling.

Coltrain pulled Lou close and smiled against her hair as they moved to the slow beat of the music. There was a live band. Jane had pulled out all the stops, even if it wasn't going to be a goodbye party.

"Nice band," Dana remarked from beside them. "Congratulations, by the way," she added.

"Thanks," they echoed.

"Nickie didn't come," she added, tongue-in-cheek. "I believe she's just accepted a job in a Victoria hospital as a nurse trainee."

"Good for her," Coltrain said.

Dana chuckled. "Sure. See you."

She wandered away toward one of the hospital staff.

"She's a good loser, at least," Lou said drowsily.

"I wouldn't have been," he mused.

"You've got a new partner coming," she remembered suddenly, having overlooked it in the frantic pace of the past few days.

"Actually," he replied, "I don't know any doctors from Johns Hopkins who would want to come to Jacobsville to practice in a small partnership. The minute I do, of course, I'll hire him on the...oof!"

She'd stepped on his toe, hard.

"Well, I had to say something," he replied, wincing as he stood on his foot. "You were holding all the aces. A man has his pride."

"You could have said you loved me," she said pointedly.

"I did. I do." He smiled slowly. "In a few hours, I'll take you home and prove it and prove it and prove it."

She flushed and pressed closer into his arms. "What a delicious idea."

"I thought so, too. Dance. At least while we're dancing I can hold you in public."

"So you can!"

Drew waltzed by with a partner. "Why don't you two go home?" he asked.

They laughed. "Time enough for private celebrations."

"I hope you have enough champagne," Drew said dryly, and danced on.

As it happened, they had a magnum of champagne between them before Coltrain coaxed his wife back into bed and made up for her first time in ways that left her gasping and trembling in the aftermath.

"That," she gasped, "wasn't in any medical book I ever read!"

"Darlin', you've been reading the wrong books," he whispered, biting her lower lip softly. "And don't go to sleep. I haven't finished yet."

"What?"

He laughed at her expression. "Did you think that was *all?*"

Her eyes widened as he moved over her and slid between her long legs. "But, it hasn't been five minutes, you can't, you *can't...!*"

He not only could. He did.

Two months later, on Valentine Day, Copper Coltrain gave his bride of six weeks a ruby necklace in the shape of a heart. She gave him the results of the test she'd had the day before. He told her later that the "valentine" she'd given him was the best one he'd ever had.

Nine months later, Lou's little valentine was delivered in Jacobsville's hospital; and he was christened Joshua Jebediah Coltrain.

* * * * *

THE *Essential* COLLECTION

by Diana Palmer

YES! Please send me *The Essential Collection* by Diana Palmer. This collection will begin with 3 FREE BOOKS and 2 FREE GIFTS in my very first shipment—and more valuable free gifts will follow! My books will arrive in 8 monthly shipments until I have the entire 51-book *Essential Collection* by Diana Palmer. I will receive 2 free books in each shipment and I will pay just $4.49 U.S./$5.39 CDN for each of the other 4 books in each shipment, plus $2.99 for shipping and handling.* If I decide to keep the entire collection, I'll only have paid for 32 books because 19 books are free. I understand that accepting the 3 free books and gifts places me under no obligation to buy anything. I can always return a shipment and cancel at any time. My free books and gifts are mine to keep no matter what I decide.

279 HDK 9860   479 HDK 9860

Name	(PLEASE PRINT)	

Address		Apt. #

City	State/Prov.	Zip/Postal Code

Signature (if under 18, a parent or guardian must sign)

Mail to the **Reader Service:**

IN U.S.A.: P.O. Box 1867, Buffalo, NY 14240-1867
IN CANADA: P.O. Box 609, Fort Erie, Ontario L2A 5X3

* Terms and prices subject to change without notice. Prices do not include applicable taxes. Sales tax applicable in N.Y. Canadian residents will be charged applicable taxes. This offer is limited to one order per household. All orders subject to credit approval. Credit or debit balances in a customer's account(s) may be offset by any other outstanding balance owed by or to the customer. Please allow 4–6 weeks for delivery. Offer available while quantities last. Offer not available to Quebec residents.

Your Privacy—The Reader Service is committed to protecting your privacy. Our Privacy Policy is available online at www.ReaderService.com or upon request from the Reader Service.

We make a portion of our mailing list available to reputable third parties that offer products we believe may interest you. If you prefer that we not exchange your name with third parties, or if you wish to clarify or modify your communication preferences, please visit us at www.ReaderService.com/consumerschoice or write to us at Reader Service Preference Service, P.O. Box 9062, Buffalo, NY 14269. Include your complete name and address.

ECDPBPA11